The Nature of Consciousness

In *The Nature of Consciousness*, Mark Rowlands develops an innovative and radical account of the nature of phenomenal consciousness, one that has significant consequences for attempts to find a place for it in the natural order. The most significant feature of consciousness is its dual nature: consciousness can be both the directing of awareness and that upon which awareness is directed. Rowlands offers a clear and philosophically insightful discussion of the main positions in this fast-moving debate, and argues that the phenomenal aspects of conscious experience are aspects that exist only in the directing of experience towards non-phenomenal objects, a theory that undermines reductive attempts to explain consciousness in terms of what is not conscious. His book will be of interest to a wide range of readers in the philosophy of mind and language, psychology, and cognitive science.

MARK ROWLANDS is Lecturer in Philosophy at University College, Cork. His publications include *Supervenience and Materialism* (1995), *Animal Rights* (1998), *The Body in Mind* (1999), *The Environmental Crisis* (2000) and numerous journal articles.

The Nature of Consciousness

Mark Rowlands

University College, Cork

CAMBRIDGE
UNIVERSITY PRESS

PUBLISHED BY THE PRESS SYNDICATE OF THE UNIVERSITY OF CAMBRIDGE
The Pitt Building, Trumpington Street, Cambridge, United Kingdom

CAMBRIDGE UNIVERSITY PRESS
The Edinburgh Building, Cambridge CB2 2RU, UK
40 West 20th Street, New York, NY 10011-4211, USA
10 Stamford Road, Oakleigh, VIC 3166, Australia
Ruiz de Alarcón 13, 28014 Madrid, Spain
Dock House, The Waterfront, Cape Town 8001, South Africa

http://www.cambridge.org

First published 2001

Printed in the United Kingdom at the University Press, Cambridge

Typeface Plantin 10/12 pt.   *System* LATEX 2_ε [TB]

A catalogue record for this book is available from the British Library.

Library of Congress Cataloguing in Publication Data
Rowlands, Mark.
The Nature of Consciousness / Mark Rowlands.
   p.   cm.
Includes bibliographical references and index.
ISBN 0 521 80858 8
1. Consciousness.   I. Title.
B808.9 .R69   2001
126 – dc21   2001035253

ISBN 0 521 80858 8

Contents

Preface

Colin McGinn first got me thinking about consciousness. I was finishing up a D.Phil. at Oxford, where Colin was my supervisor. He had just thought up the basic line of argument behind 'Can we solve the mind–body problem?', and I *may* have been one of the first people he explained it to. I thought he was mad! A decade or so later, when I returned to look at his work, I was struck by how sane the old man had become in the intervening years. Also, much to my chagrin, I was struck by how much my own developing position owed to his. Somewhat in this spirit of chagrin, then, I did my best to distinguish my view from his, and this resulted in chapter 3.

My thinking on the nature of supervenience, and, in particular, on the distinction between ontological and epistemological interpretations, has been profoundly influenced by the work of John Post, as anyone who has read his *Faces of Existence* – a work of the highest quality – will know. The influence of Sydney Shoemaker will also be evident in many of the pages that follow.

An earlier version of chapter 5 appeared in *Mind and Language*, as 'Consciousness and higher-order thoughts'. I am grateful to Sam Guttenplan, Editor of the journal, and to Blackwell publishers for permission to use this work.

Thanks to Hilary Gaskin at Cambridge University Press. Colin Allen, in his capacity as reader for Cambridge University Press, made several helpful suggestions. My thanks to him. And thanks to Joanne Hill for some outstanding copy-editing.

This work was supported by a grant from the Faculty of Arts Research Grants Committee at University College, Cork. My thanks. Thanks also to my colleagues in the Department of Philosophy at University College, Cork who have helped foster a very pleasant working environment, and to Des Clarke, whose creative approach towards my current leave of absence greatly facilitated the completion of this work.

1 The problem of phenomenal consciousness

Consciousness is perceived by many to provide the principal threat to materialist accounts of the mind. This threat has been developed, in somewhat different ways, by a lineage of writers from Nagel (1974) through Jackson (1982, 1986), Levine (1983, 1993) to McGinn (1989, 1991) and Chalmers (1996). While the precise nature of the threat posed by consciousness has tended to vary, the concept of consciousness perceived to underlie this threat has held relatively constant. It is *phenomenal* consciousness that is considered problematic. There are serious problems, if the authors of the above lineage are correct, involved in finding a place for phenomenal consciousness in the natural order. This book is concerned with these problems, with why they are problems, and with whether these problems admit of a solution.

1   What is phenomenal consciousness?

Any study of phenomenal consciousness faces an immediate problem. There is no perspicuous way of defining the associated concept. That is, there is no non-circular way of specifying the content of the concept of phenomenal consciousness that does not rely on concepts that are equally obscure. Attempts to explain its content, accordingly, tend to rely on a number of devices, linguistic and otherwise.

Examples

Attempts to explain what phenomenal consciousness is often proceed by way of examples: the way things look or sound, the way pain feels, and, more generally, the experiential properties of sensations, feelings and experiences. Sensations and feelings will include things such as pain, itches, tickles, orgasms, the feeling one gets just before one sneezes, the feeling one gets just after one has sneezed, the feeling of cold feet, and so on. When experiences are enlisted to provide an explanation of the concept of phenomenal consciousness, it is typically perceptual (and, to

1

a lesser extent, proprioceptive) experiences that are to the fore. These will include visual (colour, shape, size, brightness, darkness, depth, etc.), auditory (sounds of various degrees of complexity, decomposable into quantities such as pitch, timbre and the like), olfactory (newly mown grass, rotting fish, freshly baked bread, a paper mill, the sea, etc.), tactile (the feel of fur, velvet, cold steel, newly sanded wood, greasy hair, sand beneath one's toes) and gustatory (habanero sauce, ripe versus unripe apples, Hermitage La Chapelle 1988 versus my father's home-made wine, etc.) experiences.

The list could, obviously, be expanded indefinitely, both within each category and by the adding of new categories (emotions, imagery, conscious thought, etc.). But this is not necessary. One point is, perhaps, worth noting. There is often a tendency, particularly in the case of visual examples, to place undue emphasis on perceptually basic, or near basic, experiences: experiences of a patch of redness, and the like. But this, as Wittgenstein would put it, might provide a diet of philosophically one-sided examples. Often, the phenomenal character of an experience can depend on its *significance* for the experiencer, and this, at least ostensibly, cannot be reduced to the significance of a conglomeration of perceptually basic, or near basic, properties. I once saw Muhammad Ali at Nashville airport, and, believe me, this was an experience which very definitely had a phenomenal character, one which could not be reduced to the aggregation of significances of patches of colour, shape, contours, and the like. Nor is it clear that we *must* think of this as a combination of perceptual experience plus emotional response, with the richer phenomenal character lurking in the latter rather than the former. Or, if this strategy is available here, then it is not clear why it would not be available in the case of our experience of perceptually basic properties; and this would undermine the idea that visual experiences, as opposed to the emotional response they evoke, have a phenomenal character.

In any event, the idea that motivates these sorts of examples is simply that anyone who has had any of the above experiences will know that they *feel* or *seem* a certain way, that there is *something that it is like* to undergo them. This brings us to device no. 2.

Rough synonyms

The concept of phenomenal consciousness is sometimes explained, and I use the term loosely, by way of terms that are roughly synonymous with the original expression. Thus, phenomenally conscious states are ones which have, or are defined by, a *phenomenology*, which have a certain *qualitative feel* or *qualitative character*. Such states are *experiential* ones, *subjective* ones. They are states that essentially possess *qualia*. Most importantly, perhaps, for any phenomenally conscious state, there is *something that it is like* to be, or to undergo, that state. 'Fundamentally', writes Thomas Nagel, 'an organism has conscious mental states if and only if there is something that it is like to be that organism – something it is like *for* the organism' (1974: 166).

Just do it

The third device embodies what we might call the *Nike*^{TM} approach. Just do it. More precisely, one is invited to construct the circumstances that will produce in one states with a particular form of phenomenal consciousness. Sometimes, for example, one is invited to inflict mild bodily trauma on one's person to reacquaint oneself with the content of talk of phenomenal consciousness (Searle 1997: 97–9). The possibilities here are, of course, endless.

I think we would be advised to treat these devices with some suspicion, and some of the grounds for this will be examined more closely later on. Fundamentally, however, what seems to unite all three types of device is that they are, essentially, devices of *ostension*; they are means of *pointing*, or attempting to point, at phenomenal consciousness. And we are all familiar with the problematic status of attempts to point at private, inner, qualities, such as phenomenal consciousness purports, or is commonly taken, to be. So, the assumption that these devices are collectively sufficient to fix the meaning, or delineate the content, of the concept of phenomenal consciousness is far from certain. Indeed, this is precisely one of the assumptions that those who are sceptical of phenomenal consciousness will reject (see, for example, Dennett 1997: 117–18).

If the devices, even collectively, do not show that we know what we are talking about when we talk about phenomenal consciousness, they do show something much weaker, but something perhaps robust enough to provide a stepping-off point for further investigation. What the devices, or more importantly, the widespread presumed efficacy of the devices, do show is that a large number of people *think* they know what they are talking about when they talk about phenomenal consciousness. Indeed, I am one of those people. In fact, the people who explicitly deny that they know what they are talking about when they talk about phenomenal consciousness (and most of them do still talk about phenomenal consciousness, if only to deny the coherence of the concept) are, in all probability, limited to those antecedently *in the grip* of some quite specific theory of mind. A completely unscientific survey of some of my drinking acquaintances, for example – who, I think they will not mind me saying, are very definitely *not* in the grip of some quite specific theory of the mind – indicates that they at least *seem* to have no difficulty in understanding what I am talking about when I talk about the what it is like of experience. Or perhaps they are just being polite. Or trying to shut me up.

In any event, that we, or most of us, *think* we know what we are talking about when we talk about phenomenal consciousness, even if we are mistaken in this thought, is the place where this book begins. This, then, is a book for all those who *think* they know what they are talking about when they talk about phenomenal consciousness. If the collection of devices outlined above is not sufficient to convince you that you at least think you know what you are talking about when you, or someone else, talks about phenomenal consciousness, then there is probably nothing in this book for you.

In fact, I labour our inability to define phenomenal consciousness, or to specify in any standard and perspicuous way the content of this concept, for a quite specific reason. *This is an essential datum that any account of consciousness should explain.* Our inability on this score is not something to be treated with embarrassment, swept under the carpet, lip-serviced, or mentioned at the outset and then forgotten. Rather, it is a feature of our understanding of the concept that any adequate account of consciousness should address and, hopefully, explain. Approaches that are, broadly speaking, eliminativist about phenomenal consciousness will explain this by saying that there is no coherent concept there to specify, or that what is there is a jumbled mish-mash of conceptually variegated strands that cannot be rendered into any coherent whole. While I am not convinced that such an explanation would work, even on its own terms, this book is, in any event, realist, not eliminativist, about phenomenal consciousness, and, as such, has no recourse to such strategy. The seeming ineffability of the concept of phenomenal consciousness imposes a fairly pressing requirement on realist accounts. If phenomenal consciousness is real, and if the corresponding concept is coherent, or reasonably so, then we should be able to *eff* it. And, if we cannot do this, then we have to come up with some explanation of why the concept of phenomenal consciousness cannot be *effed*.

2   The scope of 'There is . . . '

To say that an organism is conscious is, Nagel claims in his seminal (1974) paper 'What is it like to be a bat?', to say that 'there is something that it is like to be that organism – something it is like *for* the organism' (166).

And the claim that *there is something that it is like* to undergo a conscious experience is now one of the most common ways of explaining the idea that experiences, and the organisms that undergo them, are phenomenally conscious. The claim, however, is open to a variety of interpretation, some of which can, I think, be reduced to questions of the scope of the existential quantifier.

One obvious construal of Nagel's claim is that there is some object of conscious acquaintance and that all bats are acquainted with this object, while there is a distinct object of acquaintance such that all humans are acquainted with it. More generally, there is a certain form of consciousness that associates with being human, a distinct one that associates with being a bat, and so on. Indeed, it is possible to adopt an even broader conception of the what it is like of conscious experience. Flanagan (1992: 87), for example, claims that there is something that it is like to be conscious. And, again, one way of understanding this is as the claim that there is some object of conscious acquaintance and that all conscious creatures are acquainted with this object.

It is possible, however, to narrow considerably the scope of this claim. Thus, one might claim that what it is like is associated not with being conscious in general, nor with being a particular species of conscious organism, but, rather, with types of experience. One construal of this claim would entail that for every type of conscious experience there is some object of conscious acquaintance such that a creature which undergoes this type of experience is acquainted with that object. One might narrow the scope even further and claim that what it is like associates only with particular tokens of types of experience. On this view, for example, while there is no one thing that it is like to be in pain, there is something that it is like to suffer a particular token of pain. In an important, but strangely neglected, passage, Wittgenstein gestures towards the latter construal:

Let us consider the experience of being guided, and ask ourselves: what does this experience consist in when for instance our *course* is guided? Imagine the following cases:

You are in a playing field with your eyes bandaged, and someone leads you by the hand, sometimes left, sometimes right; you have to be constantly ready for the tug of his hand, and must also take care not to stumble when he gives an unexpected tug.

Or again: someone leads you by the hand where you are unwilling to go, by force.

Or: you are guided by a partner in a dance; you make yourself as receptive as possible, in order to guess his intention and obey the slightest pressure.

Or: someone takes you for a walk; you are having a conversation; you go wherever he does.

Or: you walk along a field track, simply following it . . .

'But being guided is surely a particular experience!' – The answer to this is: you are now *thinking* of a particular experience of being guided. (1953: #172–3)

There is no one thing that it is like to undergo the experience of being guided, but, rather, this what it is like fragments into the what it is like of particular (i.e. token) experiences of being guided.

There is, in fact, no straightforward inconsistency between the view that the what it is like attaches, in the first instance, to experiential tokens, and Nagel's claim that there is something that it is like to be a bat (or human). There are at least two ways of rendering these claims consistent, one in terms of the idea of set membership, the other which appeals to higher-order properties of what it is like. According to the first strategy, to say that what it is like to be a bat is different from what it is like to be a human is to say (i) that for each (actual or possible) bat experience-token there is an associated what it is like, and for each (actual or possible) human experience-token there is an associated what it is like, but either (ii) the set of bat what it is likes does not overlap with the set of human what it is likes or (iii) the overlap between the two sets falls below a certain threshold. According to the second strategy, the what it is likes of bat experience-tokens instantiate a certain essential higher-order property B, while the what it is likes of human experience-tokens instantiate a certain higher-order property H, and B is distinct from H. That is, what it is like instantiates various higher-order properties, properties which vary from human to bat. On this view, what it is like attaches primarily to mental tokens and derivatively (in virtue of its higher-order properties) to organisms.

The claim that the what it is like of conscious experience attaches primarily either to experience-tokens (or to experience-types), however, does give rise to the following, more radical, possibility. The claim that there is something that it is like to undergo a token of one experience-type, say pain, might mean something distinct from the claim that there is something that it is like to undergo a token of a different type of mental state, for example, to token-instantiate (occurrently) the belief that Ouagadougou is the capital of Burkina Faso. That is, it cannot be assumed at the outset that consciousness is a unitary property that attaches uniformly across all mental states.

The suspicion that it is not such a property can, in fact, be independently motivated by the following, well-known, considerations. Consider, first, the distinction between sensations and propositional attitudes. Propositional attitudes can certainly be associated with a phenomenology. There can be, in a given instance, something that it is like to have, say, a certain belief. However, propositional attitudes, it is commonly thought, are not *defined* by a phenomenology, and their possession by a subject does not entail that this subject is presented with any phenomenology at all, let alone a particular phenomenology. However, this does not seem to be the case with at least some sensations. While, if Wittgenstein is correct, the phenomenology associated with an experience E may vary from one token of E to another, it seems that having some phenomenology or other, and indeed having a phenomenology constrained within certain reasonably definite limits, is essential to the tokening of at least some, and perhaps all, sensations. Even within the category of sensations there appear to be important differences. It is not only common, but also seemingly perfectly appropriate, to characterise the phenomenology of bodily sensations – pains, itches, orgasms, and so on – in terms of the notion of *feel*. With items such as perceptual experiences, however, the characterisation of their phenomenology in terms of the notion of feel sits a lot less comfortably. This is why the epithet 'feels' is, in the case of perceptual experiences, typically replaced by 'seems'. If we do want to say that it *feels* a certain way to see a green wall, or Muhammad Ali, then it is far from clear that *feel* means the same thing in this context as it does in the case of sensations. But, of course, *feel* is often used as an alternative appellation for the what it is like of conscious experience, sensational, perceptual or otherwise. To say that there is something that it is like to undergo a conscious experience is often taken as equivalent to saying that having that experience feels a certain way. And if this is correct, then we cannot assume, *a priori*, that the existential quantifier in the claim 'There is something that it is like to undergo X' ranges across the same quantity for all Xs.

Therefore, we should be alive to the possibility that what it means for a mental state to be phenomenally conscious can vary from one category of mental state to another, perhaps from one type of mental state to another, perhaps even from one token mental state to another. Perhaps the concept of phenomenal consciousness is a fundamentally hybrid concept.[1] And, if this is so, we would look in vain for a unified account of in what phenomenal consciousness consists. At the very least, this is not something to be ruled out *a priori*.

In later chapters, when the real argument starts, I propose to avoid these potential difficulties by focusing on, and working with, certain very general features that any instances of phenomenal consciousness must,

---

[1] Of course, many have claimed that the concept of consciousness is a hybrid one. What they typically have in mind, roughly, is the idea that consciousness comes in many forms: phenomenal, introspective, self, monitoring, reportability, etc., etc. The present point, however, concerns only the category of phenomenal consciousness, and the possibility being mooted is that this is itself a hybrid category.

I shall argue, possess. Whether or not phenomenal consciousness turns out to be a conceptually or theoretically unified item, I shall try to show that anything that could possibly count as an instance of a phenomenally conscious state must have certain features, and it is upon these features that the arguments will be built.

3   What is the problem of phenomenal consciousness?

The above problems, unclarities, and cautionary notes notwithstanding, we perhaps (hopefully) have enough in the way of a preliminary characterisation of the concept of phenomenal consciousness to proceed to a preliminary (again) characterisation of the problem or problems it raises. Phenomenal consciousness is widely, though far from universally, accepted to create at least the appearance of a problem for materialism. Agreement on precisely what this problem is, or appears to be, however, is far less widespread. The intuition that there is at least the semblance of a problem, here, is commonly supported by the way of various intuition pumps.

1   Abused scientists

Mary has been forced to live her entire life in a black and white room and has never seen any colours before, except for black, white, and shades of grey (Jackson 1982, 1986). Filling in the details would be a rather fatuous exercise, but presumably her skin has also been treated with some pigment that makes it appear a shade of grey, which pigment has also transformed her irises appropriately, her hair has been dyed black, etc., etc. Despite her dysfunctional upbringing, Mary has become the world's leading neuroscientist, specialising in the neurophysiology of colour vision. She knows everything there is to know about the neural processes involved in the processing of visual information, about the psychophysics of optical processes, about the physics of environmental objects, and so on. However, despite this extensive knowledge, when she is let out of her black and white room for the first time, it seems plausible to suppose, she learns something new; she learns what it is like to experience colour. And, if this is correct, then this knowledge is neither something she possessed before nor something that could be constructed from the knowledge she possessed before.

2   Zombies

A zombie, in the philosophical as opposed to the Hollywood sense, is an individual that is physically and functionally human, but which lacks conscious experience (Chalmers 1996; Kirk 1974, 1994). Thus, my zombie twin is physically identical to me and, we can suppose, is embedded in an identical environment. Moreover, he is functionally identical to me in that he is processing information in the same way, reacting in the same way as me to the same inputs, and so on. Nevertheless, he lacks phenomenal experience; he has no phenomenal consciousness. My zombie twin is not, it is generally accepted, a natural possibility (that is, he is incompatible with the laws of nature) but he is, it has been argued, a logical possibility.

3   Deviants

It is logically possible for there to be a world where qualia are inverted relative to the actual world (Shoemaker 1982; Chalmers 1996). My inverted twin is physically identical to me but has inverted conscious experiences. Thus, for example, where I have a red experience (i.e. an experience *as* of red) my inverted twin has a green experience (i.e. an experience *as* of green). That is, when he looks at a fire engine, he has an experience of the same qualitative colour character as I do when I look at grass. Again, my inverted twin may not be a natural possibility, but he is, it has been argued, a logical possibility.

4   Demons

Laplace's Demon is able to read off all non-basic facts from basic ones (Chalmers 1996). That is, the Demon knows every detail about the physics of the universe, the configuration and evolution of all the basic fields and particles that make up the spatiotemporal manifold. And from this knowledge, the Demon can read off, or infer, every other fact about the universe. Or, rather, *almost* every other fact. For, it has been argued, the Demon would not be able to read off facts about conscious experience (Chalmers 1996). Indeed, the Demon could not even work out, from its knowledge of the basic facts alone, that there is any conscious experience at all, let alone what it is.

A motley crew. Surely, it is only in recent discussions of consciousness – and perhaps some fairly questionable B-movies – that one could possibly find such a collection of characters. But the question is: what does all this mean? And this is a good question, one that subsequent chapters will spend some time trying to work out, and one that as yet has nothing even close to an accepted answer.

However, it is possible to broadly identify two axes along which potential answers may be developed. On the one hand, one can understand the examples as establishing, or suggesting, an ontological or *metaphysical* conclusion that is, essentially, dualistic in character. Phenomenal experiences are distinct from, and not reducible to, any physical event, state or process. This conclusion is (or has at one time been) endorsed, on the basis of one or more of the above scenarios, by Jackson (1982, 1986) and Chalmers (1996). On the other hand, one can understand the examples as establishing, or suggesting, an *epistemological* conclusion. Roughly speaking, our knowledge of physical facts does not, in some way, add up to knowledge of conscious experience, and, consequently (perhaps) physical explanations do not, in some way, add up to explanations of consciousness. There is, as it is often put, an *explanatory gap* between consciousness and the physical. This conclusion has been endorsed by Levine (1983, 1993) and McGinn (1989, 1991, 1993) among others. Of course, those who endorse the metaphysical conclusion are also going to endorse the epistemological claim, and this is the case with Jackson and Chalmers. However, it is possible to endorse the epistemological claim alone.

In fact, there are, in my view, good reasons for endorsing the epistemological claim alone. All the above examples turn, ultimately, on a difference between phenomenal and physical *concepts*, and it is difficult to turn this into any substantive difference between phenomenal and physical *properties*. But it is the latter difference that is required to underwrite the metaphysical conclusion.

To see this, consider the knowledge argument. There are, in fact, various strategies available to the materialist should she want to resist the metaphysical interpretation of the significance of the knowledge argument. The one I favour is due to Brian Loar (1990). According to Loar, the materialist can allow that Mary acquires new information when she leaves the room, but she does so only under an *opaque* reading. Transparent construals of the information acquired by Mary would, in effect, beg the question against materialism. Drawing (legitimate) metaphysical conclusions from opaque contexts is never easy. And, given the opaque construal of what Mary learns, we can construct *prima facie* analogous cases, where a metaphysical conclusion manifestly does not follow from the premises. Thus, to borrow from Loar, Kate learns that the bottle before her contains CH_3CH_2OH. But, on an opaque reading, she does not know that the bottle contains alcohol. That is, she does not know that the bottle contains stuff called alcohol, or that the bottle contains the intoxicating component of wine and beer, the component that makes people drunk. Indeed, we can suppose that innocent Kate even lacks the ordinary concept of alcohol. Then, when she inadvisedly consumes the bottle's contents, she acquires new information: that the bottle contains alcohol. If the knowledge argument, on the metaphysical construal, had a generally valid form, we could then infer from Kate's epistemic situation that alcohol is not identical with CH_3CH_2OH. And this, evidently, does not follow.

What seems to be going on here is that we have two distinct concepts associated with the same substance; one a theoretical-physical concept, the other what Loar calls a *recognitional* concept. The substance alcohol can be picked out both by way of theoretical description, and in terms of the properties by which one typically recognises it. However, the two types of concept are conceptually independent of each other, and this explains both why the above opaque reading of what Kate learns is possible and why this opaque reading does not yield a substantive metaphysical conclusion.

A recognitional concept has the form 'x is one of that kind'; i.e. they are type-demonstratives grounded in dispositions to classify, by way of perceptual discriminations, certain objects, events, and situations. Recognitional concepts, crucially, are typically conceptually independent of, and irreducible to, theoretical-physical concepts, even where both concepts, as in the above case, pick out the same property.

Loar argues that phenomenal concepts are essentially recognitional in character. Thus, materialism at the metaphysical level is underwritten by the claim that phenomenal and physical-functional concepts can pick out the same property, while the conceptual independence of these concepts is explained by the fact that recognitional and theoretical concepts are, in general, conceptually independent, and that the former cannot be reduced to the latter. Thus the epistemological reading of the knowledge argument is safeguarded and explained, and the metaphysical reading shown to be invalid.

This, of course, takes us only part of the way. It is not difficult to find a difference between the case of Kate and the case of Mary. Kate lacks knowledge of the contents of the bottle under a contingent description of it: stuff that gets you drunk. However, Mary's acquired information of what it is like to experience colour does not conceive it under a contingent mode of presentation. It is not as if she is conceiving of a property that presents itself *contingently* thus: it is like such and such to experience P. Being experienced in this way is essential to the property Mary conceives. Thus, when Mary later acquires new information (construed opaquely) the novelty of this information cannot be explained – as in the case of Kate – as her acquiring a new contingent mode of presentation of something she has known all along. This is why, according to its proponents, the knowledge argument can be valid on an opaque reading. There is no contingency in Mary's conception of the new phenomenal information that explains it as a novel take on old facts. Therefore, we must suppose that she learns new facts *simpliciter*, and not new conceptions of old facts.

As Loar points out, however, there is an implicit assumption in this argument: a statement of property identity that links conceptually independent properties is true only if at least one concept picks out its associated property by way of a contingent mode of presentation of that property. Conversely, the underlying idea is that if two concepts both pick out the same property by way of its essential properties, neither mediated by contingent modes of presentation, then one ought to be able to see *a priori* – at least after optimal reflection – that they pick out the same property. If the two concepts pick out the same property by way of essential modes of presentation, then those concepts themselves must be logically connected.

However, Loar argues, convincingly in my view, that this assumption should be rejected. It rests on the idea that (i) if a concept picks out a property by way of an essential mode of presentation, then that concept must capture the *essence* of the property picked out, and (ii) if two concepts capture the essence of the same property, then there must exist constitutive conceptual connections between those concepts, such that one concept is derivable from the other *a priori*. However, when expressed in this way, it is fairly clear that these are equivocating uses of 'capture the essence of'. On one use, it expresses a referential notion that comes to no more than 'directly rigidly designate'. On the other, it means something like 'be conceptually interderivable with some theoretical predicate that reveals the internal structure of' the designated property. But the former does not imply the latter. Claims about rigid designation do not, in general, imply the conceptual interderivability of the designating concepts.

Once we allow that phenomenal and physical concepts can both (i) pick out a property by way of an essential mode of presentation, but (ii) still be conceptually independent of each other, then essentially the same deflationary strategy can be adopted with respect to the rest of the assorted cast listed above. The logical possibility of zombies, that is, need only be taken as indicative of the conceptual independence of phenomenal and physical-functional concepts, and not of any deeper metaphysical division. A similar account will be applicable to the case of the qualia-inverted deviants; their logical, as opposed to natural, possibility, need be indicative only of the logical independence of phenomenal from physico-functional concepts. And the failure of Laplace's Demon to read off phenomenal facts from non-phenomenal ones, again, need only indicate the conceptual independence of phenomenal concepts from physical or functional ones.

Loar's account, of course, will not satisfy everyone. Indeed, despite my general sympathy to this line of reasoning, I think that Loar's claim that phenomenal concepts are recognitional ones needs to be severely qualified (see chapter 7). Nevertheless, I suspect that a story substantially similar to the one Loar tells can be made to work. And, for this reason, I am going to treat the problem of phenomenal consciousness as a primarily epistemological one. This may be incorrect. Perhaps consciousness provides a metaphysical problem also. If so, then so be it. If there is a genuine metaphysical problem, then it is outside the scope of this book. The book's subject is the epistemological problem posed for materialism by phenomenal consciousness: the existence, or apparent existence, of an explanatory gap between the phenomenal and the material. One thing is clear: if consciousness is not an epistemological problem, then it is not a metaphysical problem either.

4   Explaining consciousness

The problem of explaining phenomenal consciousness is the problem of explaining how consciousness can come from what is not conscious. And one can understand the idea of consciousness coming from what is not conscious either *causally* or *constitutively*. For various reasons I prefer the constitutive construal. Suppose, for example, we say that phenomenal consciousness is causally produced by brain activity (McGinn 1989, 1991; Searle 1992). Causal relations, as Hume taught us, involve distinct existences. So, if we talk of consciousness being causally produced by neural activity then there is a danger that we have already implicitly bought in to a metaphysical understanding of the problem: we have already implicitly assumed that consciousness is distinct from this neural activity. We can avoid this metaphysical temptation by regarding the causal relations by which consciousness is produced as diachronic, rather than synchronic. But then the production of consciousness by the brain has to be understood in terms of the idea that a phenomenal property instantiated at time t is produced by brain activity occurring at $t-1$. But this does not seem to be the correct model for understanding the production of consciousness by neural activity. What neural activity occurring at time $t-1$ actually causally produces is neural activity occurring at t. And then we still have the problem of explaining how consciousness is produced by this neural activity of time t. If we want to insist that this relation of production is a causal relation, then we fall right back into the metaphysical construal of the problem.

Intuitively, the relation of production we require seems to be more like the relation between the observable properties of water and its underlying structure, and this (*pace* Searle 1992) is not a causal relation. Rather, the observable properties of water are, in some sense, *constituted* by the under-lying molecular properties. Phenomenal consciousness, on this construal, is somehow constituted by neural activity, and the problem of conscious-ness is the problem of explaining how this could (possibly) be so. More generally, how can consciousness be constituted by what is not conscious?

While, for these and other reasons, I favour the constitutive rather than causal construal of the claim that consciousness is produced by what is not conscious, nothing much turns on this assumption. The arguments to be developed in the following chapters have, I think, an application broad enough to cover both constitutive and causal senses, and, accordingly, I shall usually employ the more general term *production* to subsume both constitutive and causal senses of the relation between consciousness and the material.

The focus of this book, then, is whether it is possible to provide an explanation of how phenomenal consciousness is produced by what is not conscious. We know, I shall suppose, that it is, in fact, produced by what is not conscious, that is why we are not concerned with the metaphysical construal of the problem. What we want is an explanation of how it is so produced.

In attempting to provide an explanation of phenomenal consciousness, it is possible to adopt two quite distinct strategies; one, as I shall put it, *vertical*, the other *horizontal*. Vertical strategies, roughly speaking, attempt to *build consciousness up* from what is not conscious. Horizontal strategies, again roughly, attempt the explanatory task by attempting to *pull con-sciousness out* into what is not conscious, i.e. the world. The next two sections deal with the former type of explanatory strategy, the one after that deals with the latter.

5   Vertical strategies I: the mind–body problem

To build consciousness up from what is not conscious is to show how various non-conscious processes can, collectively, constitute conscious activity. This strategy of, as we might call it, *phenomenal tectonics*, of con-structing the phenomenal from the non-phenomenal, divides into two distinct approaches. On the one hand, we can try to build consciousness up from processes that are neither conscious nor mental. Our appeal, here, is likely to be to the brain, to neural activity broadly construed. On the other, we can try to construct consciousness from processes that are non-conscious but which are mental. The explanation here is likely to involve, quite centrally, higher-order mental states of some sort, states which are identified as not being essentially conscious, or, at the very least, as not being phenomenally conscious. The former strategy requires solving the *mind–body* problem, the latter requires, in effect, solving the *mind–mind* problem.

As an example of the former strategy, consider the much-trumpeted hypothesis of Francis Crick and Christof Koch (1990) that 40 Hertz oscillations in the visual cortex and elsewhere may be the fundamental neural feature responsible for conscious experience. According to Crick and Koch, 40Hz oscillations play a crucial role in the *binding* of various sorts of information into a unified and coherent whole. Two different kinds of information about a visual scene – the shape and distance of an object, for example – may be represented quite separately, but Crick and Koch suggest that these separate neural representations may have a common oscillatory frequency and phase-cycle, allowing the information to be bound together by later processes and stored in working memory.

This provides a neurobiological model of how disparate information might be integrated in working memory. And it might, with suitable elaboration, be developed into an account of how information is integrated and brought to bear in the global control of behaviour. However, what it is not, or does not seem to be, is an explanation of phenomenal consciousness. Crick and Koch have, in fact, presented only an account of how a certain functional capacity – the capacity for integration of disparate information – is implemented in the brain. But this would be an explanation of phenomenal consciousness only if it could be shown, I think it is fair to say counterintuitively, that such consciousness could be reduced to a feature of, or function of, the capacity for binding. Much further argument is required; Crick and Koch have not presented such argument; and it is, indeed, difficult to see what such further argument might look like.

Similar limitations seem to affect Gerald Edelman's neurobiological theory of consciousness (Edelman 1989, 1992). The core of his theory is provided by the idea of re-entrant neural circuits which afford the conceptual categorisation of perceptual signals before they contribute to memory. On the basis of this, perceptual information interacts with internal states in various ways and give rise to 'primary consciousness'. The introduction of a new memory element of 'semantic bootstrapping' explains the generation of 'higher-order consciousness', and the concepts of the self, past and future. And this is linked to language production through Broca's and Wernicke's areas. Once again, and as Edelman in effect acknowledges, this is not an explanation of phenomenal consciousness. Rather, insofar as Edelman's theory is devoted to consciousness at all (as opposed to what appear to be its primary concerns with perception, memory and language), what it seems it might explain are certain aspects of perceptual aspect-consciousness – the effects of perceptual processing on later processing operations and on the global control of behaviour – and aspects of self-consciousness, in particular, the origin of the concept of the self. Edelman's theory, then, is an account of certain forms of access-consciousness, not an account of phenomenal consciousness.

The limitations, or perceived limitations, of these approaches are indicative of a general problem with attempts to build consciousness up out of neural processes. It seems that no matter how much we know about the neural processes implicated in the production of consciousness – about oscillatory frequencies and phase-cycles in the visual cortex, the structure and function of re-entrant neural circuits, and so on – this goes no further than providing an explanation of certain *functional* capacities of the brain. Such knowledge might enable us to see how the brain binds disparate information into a unitary whole, how it underwrites the ability to categorise perceived events, and so on. But, glaringly, what it does not seem to provide is an explanation of phenomenal consciousness. In particular, such information does not enable us to see *how* the brain produces phenomenal consciousness.

Therefore, the standard objection to neural models of consciousness, and at present this is an objection I simply note not advocate, is that they do not bridge the perceived explanatory gap between the phenomenal and the physical. On the contrary, they merely reinforce that gap. This objection has been developed, in important and sophisticated forms, by Colin McGinn and David Chalmers. Both Chalmers and McGinn argue that phenomenal consciousness cannot be reductively explained in physical terms. Chalmers' argument is examined in chapter 2, McGinn's in chapter 3.

6   Vertical strategies II: the mind–mind problem

The second type of vertical strategy attempts to build phenomenal consciousness up out of states that are not conscious, or not essentially so, but which are, nonetheless, mental. The most influential recent forms of this strategy consist in the attempt to explain phenomenal consciousness in terms of *monitoring* or *introspective* consciousness.

Introspective consciousness, very broadly speaking, is the process either by which we can become aware *of* our internal states or, on some accounts (e.g. Shoemaker 1994; Dretske 1995), by which we become aware *that* we instantiate certain internal states. Reflecting the distinction between being aware *of* and being aware *that*, there are several, quite

different, models of in what such awareness consists. On a simple object perception model, for example, introspection will have essentially
the same dyadic structure as perception, a structure constituted by a
content bearing state whose directedness towards its intentional object is
typically regarded as being effected by way of some sort of causal relation. On such a model, introspective abilities afford us access to mental
events, states, processes, or objects. On other models, however, introspection affords us access to mental facts, where such access is commonly
thought to be grounded in displaced perception of non-mental (typically,
but not necessarily, environmental) events, states, processes, or objects.
We learn *that* we instantiate certain mental properties (where a mental
fact is conceived of as the instantiation of a mental property in a person
at a time) in virtue of our displaced perception of non-mental objects
(Shoemaker 1994; Dretske 1995). The principle is very much like dis-
covering how much petrol is in the tank of one's car by way of perception
of the fuel gauge.

Monitoring consciousness can, also, take at least two forms. According
to the *higher-order experience* model associated with Armstrong (1968,
1981) and Lycan (1987, 1996), the consciousness of any given mental
state M is to be explained in terms of the subject of that state having a
quasi-perceptual experience of M. Both Armstrong and Lycan flesh out
this general idea in terms of the notion of *internal scanning*. A subject's
access to her mental states takes the form of an internal scanning, or
monitoring, of those states by higher-order neural structures (that is,
neural structures whose function is to register the activity occurring in
other neural structures). And when a subject has such access to a given
mental state, that mental state is a conscious one.

A related, but importantly distinct, account of monitoring consciousness is provided by the *higher-order thought* model associated with
Rosenthal (1986, 1993) and also with Carruthers (1996). According
to this account, access to one's mental states takes the form of higher-
order thoughts about those mental states. On this view, very roughly,
the consciousness of any given mental state M consists in the subject of
M possessing a higher-order thought to the effect that he possesses, or
instantiates, M.

Monitoring and introspective consciousness are often run together.
This need not be a conflation, still less a confusion. It is possible to draw
a distinction here, but it is far from clear that the distinction will correspond, in any salient way, to the use of the terms 'monitoring' and
'introspective' in the relevant literature: for this use varies. Nonetheless,
if we do want to preserve a distinction between introspective and monitoring consciousness, and given the variability of the use of the terms in

the literature such a distinction is by no means obligatory, we can do so by regarding introspective consciousness as related to monitoring consciousness as genus is to species. Internal scanning, for example, is one way of understanding how an object perception model of introspection might be *implemented*. And an appeal to higher-order thoughts might be one way of understanding how introspection affords us access to mental facts, if we assume that in being aware of a thought we are thereby aware of its content. Thus, it is possible (though certainly not necessary) to view accounts of monitoring consciousness as causal or (probably more accurately) quasi-causal models of how the conceptual analyses proffered by accounts of introspection might be implemented.

Usually, however, monitoring models are presented not just as relatively determinate models of introspective consciousness, but as models of consciousness in general. Armstrong, for example, promotes his monitoring model as an account of 'consciousness in the most interesting sense of the word'. This is because Armstrong thinks that introspective consciousness has a peculiar centrality relative to other forms. And similar claims for the comprehensive scope of the monitoring model, claims resting on a similar faith in the centrality of introspection, can be found, to a greater or lesser extent, in most of the model's principal defenders. Such claims are often accompanied by a paring down (unacceptable to many) of what a model of consciousness can be expected to explain, or of what features can legitimately be thought of as essential to consciousness. Lycan (1996), for example, presents his version of the internal monitoring model as an account of consciousness. However, he also claims that there are certain aspects of consciousness – specifically its phenomenal character – that cannot be explained in terms of internal monitoring, He is unperturbed by this since he thinks that 'qualia problems and the nature of conscious awareness are mutually independent and indeed have little to do with each other' (1990: 756). Rosenthal (1990), on the other hand, is more equivocal. On the one hand, he explicitly separates consciousness from 'sensory quality', and says he is giving only a theory of the first. This suggests that phenomenal consciousness lies outside the scope of his account. On the other hand, he also says that a state is conscious when there is something that it is like to be in that state, which suggests that his subject is phenomenal consciousness after all. Carruthers (1996, 1998) asserts, reasonably explicitly, that his higher-order thought model is intended as an account of phenomenal consciousness also.

What unites introspective and monitoring consciousness, in all their forms, is that the corresponding concepts are all *functional* concepts. Indeed, not only are these concepts of consciousness all functional concepts, they all seem to be assimilable to a particular type of functional concept, broadly understood. That is, they all seem understandable in terms of the notion of *access*. Introspective and monitoring consciousness, in whatever specific form they take, consist in access to one's mental states.

In an important paper, Block (1995) has distinguished between phenomenal consciousness and access-consciousness (*P-consciousness* and *A-consciousness* in his terminology). And Chalmers (1996) draws the essentially equivalent distinction between what he calls *consciousness* and *awareness*. In the spirit of Block, but the letter of Chalmers, we can characterise *access-consciousness* in the following way.

Access-consciousness: a subject, S, is access-conscious of some information, I, if and only if I is directly available for the global control of S's behaviour.

To talk of information being used in the *global* control of behaviour is just to say that this information is available to be brought to bear in a wide range of behavioural processes: verbal, motor, attentive, and the like (Chalmers 1996: 225). The motivation for the inclusion of *directness* in the above definition lies in the intuitive idea that states of consciousness, of whatever stripe, must be *occurrent* rather than *dispositional* in character.

The claims that phenomenal consciousness can be explained in terms of higher-order experiences or higher-order thoughts, then, are specific versions of a more general thesis: phenomenal consciousness can be explained in terms of access-consciousness. Both Block and Chalmers have provided reasons, in my view compelling reasons, for thinking that this thesis cannot be true. However, I shall focus on the specific versions of the thesis: the idea that phenomenal consciousness can be explained in terms of monitoring consciousness. Thus, chapter 4 examines higher-order experience accounts of consciousness; chapter 5 is concerned with the higher-order thought alternative.

However, it is well known that there are serious *prima facie* problems with the attempt to assimilate phenomenal consciousness to the possession of either higher-order experiences or higher-order thoughts. If the notion of a higher-order experience is (as in Armstrong 1981) explained in terms of the concept of internal scanning, then the problem seems to be that such scanning is not sufficient for phenomenal consciousness. As Rey (1983) has pointed out, ordinary laptop computers are capable of internal scanning, and it is not clear who would want to claim that they are conscious.[2] If, on the other hand, it is asserted that, unlike the case of

---

[2] Rey, in fact, advocates that we accept that internal scanning is sufficient for consciousness, if there is such a thing, and so he concludes that consciousness is a concept that includes and precludes laptop computers, and hence that the concept of consciousness is incoherent. Far more plausible, I think, is simply to reject the claim that internal scanning is sufficient for phenomenal consciousness, If so, we get no incoherence.

the laptop, the higher-order experiences must be conscious ones, then the account immediately runs into a problem of regress. On the other hand, interpreting the monitoring account in terms of higher-order thoughts seems *prima facie* equally problematic. Most obviously, the identification of phenomenal consciousness with the possession of higher-order thoughts shares the apparent over-intellectualism of the identification of phenomenal consciousness with self-consciousness. Dogs and human infants, it seems overwhelmingly likely, have phenomenally conscious states without thoughts to the effect that they have those states.

Of course, none of these considerations can, as yet, be taken as compelling. But they do raise a certain problem of *procedure*. The *prima facie* implausibilities associated with the idea that phenomenal consciousness can be explained in terms of either higher-order experience or higher-order thought models often leads to a certain type of fall-back strategy being embraced by defenders of such models. The strategy involves, essentially, a *paring down* of the explanandum: consciousness is often divested of those properties that are most problematic for higher-order representation models. Thus, as was mentioned earlier, Lycan (1990, 1996) seeks to divest at least the core notion of consciousness of its traditional association with qualia and phenomenal character. The core concept of consciousness, for Lycan, is awareness, and this can be accounted for in terms of the internal monitoring model associated with Armstrong. Consciousness, according to Lycan, is 'the functioning of internal attention mechanisms directed upon lower-order psychological states and events', and these attention mechanisms are devices that 'have the job of relaying and/or co-ordinating information about ongoing psychological events and processes' (1990: 755). Qualia, and the phenomenal character of experience in general, are to be explained by other means (according to Lycan, a functionalist-representationist account will do the trick).

The paring down of reduced properties is, of course, a standard part of the process of reduction and, in itself, is unobjectionable. However, in the case of phenomenal consciousness, this practice seems peculiarly problematic. In particular, it is necessary, but difficult, to steer a middle ground between twin dangers. The one danger is that of triviality, and this seems to threaten Lycan's account in particular. The danger is that one pares down the concept of consciousness so much that what one is left with is simply the claim that internal monitoring is internal monitoring. The problem then is that we have all these other properties – in particular, phenomenal character – whose nature we still have to explain. In this case, the access-consciousness model has not bought us very much. Much of the hard work is left to do. Thus, we find that much of Lycan's account of consciousness is provided not by his internal monitoring model, but by his functionalist-representationist account of qualia, which he needs because he acknowledges that his internal monitoring model will not yield an explanation of phenomenal character.

The other danger is that we are forced to introduce distinctions into our discussion of consciousness that opponents will not accept. Consider, for example, Dennett's (1991) position. One strand of Dennett's argument consists in the claim that the idea that experiences have a phenomenal character is the result of a quasi-cognitive illusion brought about by our being in the grip of various illicit assumptions about the nature of the mind. This position, however, seems to force on us the claim that consciousness does not really have phenomenal character, it just *seems* as if it does. However, this involves foisting on the discussion the very appearance/reality distinction that defenders of phenomenal consciousness will reject. Phenomenal properties are precisely properties of *seeming*. So, if consciousness *seems* to have phenomenal properties, it thereby *does* have phenomenal properties (Strawson 1994). And their nature is, therefore, something that still requires explanation.

Either way, it seems there is still explanatory work to do subsequent to the reduction, or alleged reduction. Either the reduction requires that we pare down the concept of phenomenal consciousness so much that there are properties left over that the reduction does not incorporate. Then, all the hard work is still to be done. Or, we implicitly reintroduce, by way of an appearance/reality distinction, phenomenal consciousness in an unreduced form. Either way, we have not succeeded in reducing phenomenal consciousness.

If these ruminations indicate anything at all, then it is that the dialectical situation is rather complex. I (i) might object to higher-order representation accounts on the grounds that they do not explain features which (ii) their proponents' claim they do not have to explain but (iii) where I claim that their proponents' claim that they do not have to explain such features is illegitimate on the grounds that it commits them to triviality or illegitimate distinctions, but where (iv) their proponents will claim that there is nothing illegitimate about these distinctions and the triviality is only apparent, and so on. Clearly what is needed is a way of cutting through the dialectical complexity.

So, here it is. In chapters 4 and 5, when I develop the case against higher-order representation accounts of consciousness, I shall not even suppose that such models are in the business of explaining phenomenal consciousness. Rather, I shall assume only that they are in the business of explaining our access to our own mental states or to mental facts that we instantiate. And, then I shall argue that they cannot even do this. We do not, in these chapters, even need to get into the issue of *phenomenal* consciousness; higher-order models cannot even explain *introspective* consciousness. And if there is one thing that remains clear amidst the dialectical cut and thrust, it is surely this: if higher-order models cannot even explain introspective consciousness – our access to mental states we possess or facts we instantiate – then they have no hope of explaining phenomenal consciousness.

7   Horizontal strategies

Horizontal strategies are characterised by the attempt to explain phenomenal consciousness not by building it up out of neural or functional components, but by, figuratively speaking, *pulling consciousness out* into the world. That is, very roughly, a horizontal strategy will try to show that the principal features of phenomenal consciousness are constituted not by features of neural or functional activity but, rather, by features of the world in which this activity is situated. The most common form of horizontal strategy is known as *representationism*. Very roughly, this is the view that the phenomenal character of an experience does not go beyond its representational content or, equivalently, that all phenomenal differences are representational differences. The phenomenal, that is, can, ultimately, be explained in terms of the representational.

Tye (1995) supplies a recent, sophisticated, version of representationism. According to Tye, the phenomenal *character* of an experience is identical with the phenomenal *content* of that experience, and phenomenal content is just a species of *intentional* or representational content. Specifically, phenomenal content is PANIC: poised, abstract, non-conceptual, intentional content.

The claim that the relevant contents are *poised* is the claim that they attach to the output representations of the relevant sensory modules and, thus, are in a position to make a direct impact on the belief/desire system. To say that the contents are in a position to impact the belief/desire system is not to claim that they actually do make such impact. Rather, it is to say that they supply the inputs for certain cognitive processes, ones which have the job of producing beliefs, or desires, directly from the appropriate perceptual representations if attention is properly focused (and the relevant concepts are possessed).

The claim that the relevant contents are *abstract* is the claim, roughly, that no particular concrete objects enter into these contents. This is required by the fact that different concrete objects can, phenomenally, look or feel exactly the same. The identity of the object presented to the subject of an experience, then, does not matter for the phenomenal content of that experience. Rather, the content depends on the general, phenomenal, features presented to the experience's subject.

The claim that phenomenal content be *non-conceptual* is the claim that these general features entering into the content of an experience need not be ones for which the experience's subject possesses matching concepts. It is possible to recognise, for example, far more different shades of colour than for which we possess stored representations. Perceptual discriminability outstrips our conceptual resources. Hence, phenomenal content is non-conceptual.

Tye's account provides one of the most sophisticated, and influential, forms of representationism. But what unites all forms of representationism is the idea that the phenomenal character – the what it is like – of a conscious experience is determined, indeed constituted, by the representational features of that experience. Since representational properties are not determined purely by what is occurring inside the head of an experiencing subject, representationism is committed to the view that phenomenal character is not constituted by processes occurring inside the head of experiencing subjects. The phenomenal character of an experience is constituted not just by what is going on inside the head of an experiencing subject, but also by what exists in the world in which that experiencing subject is situated.

There is no reason, of course, to regard vertical and horizontal strategies as mutually exclusive. They can be combined in a variety of ways. Lycan, for example, advocates a vertical approach to explaining (what he calls) awareness, and a horizontal, representationist, approach to explaining phenomenal character. More generally, it may turn out that a vertical approach is able to handle some features of phenomenal consciousness while a horizontal strategy is able to handle the rest. Or it may not so turn out. In any event, the horizontal, representationist, account of phenomenal character will be examined in chapter 9.

8   The shape of things to come

The book to follow can, nominally, be thought of as divided into two parts. Part 1, which consists of chapters 2–5, is concerned with vertical attempts to explain consciousness. Of these chapters, the first two examine the prospects of attempts to explain consciousness in physical terms. Or, more precisely, they examine two recent and (deservedly) influential attempts to show that these prospects are minimal or non-existent. Chapter 2 focuses on Chalmers' attempt to show that consciousness cannot be reductively explained in physical terms. Chapter 3 examines McGinn's case for the claim that there exists an unbridgeable explanatory gap between consciousness and the physical world.

My attitude to both positions is somewhat equivocal. I believe that both McGinn and Chalmers *might* be right, but I am not *convinced* that they are.

More specifically, I shall try to show that the arguments of both McGinn and Chalmers are far from conclusive. In so far as anything concrete emerges from chapters 2 and 3, then, it is simply that consciousness might be reductively explainable in physical terms.

Chapters 4 and 5, the remaining chapters of part 1, are concerned with attempts to explain phenomenal consciousness in terms of access- , specifically monitoring, consciousness. Chapter 4 examines the higher-order experience account of consciousness. In chapter 5, the focus is on higher-order thought models. I shall argue that both types of model fail as explanations of consciousness. They are not even adequate as models of introspective consciousness; and have no chance whatsoever of explaining phenomenal consciousness.

The nominal part 2 of this book comprises chapters 6–10. In these chapters, I shall develop a case against the possibility of explaining phenomenal consciousness in terms of what is not conscious, a case that applies equally against both vertical and horizontal explanatory strategies. In particular, I shall argue that the real reason why phenomenal consciousness is so problematic, from an explanatory point of view, has not been understood. The real reason, I shall argue, is this. The phenomenal aspects – the what it is like – of experience are not themselves objects of conscious awareness. They are not items *of* which we are aware in the having of an experience. Rather, they are items that constitute the taking of distinct, and non-phenomenal, items as the objects of experience. That is, the phenomenal aspects of experience are not items *of* which we are aware in the having of an experience, but (in a sense to be made clear) items *in virtue of* which, or *with* which, we are aware in the having of that experience. Alternatively, in a sense again to be made clear, phenomenal features are not *empirical* but *transcendental* features of experience. The bulk of the argument for these claims is to be found in chapters 6, 7 and 8.

This view of the phenomenal, it will be shown, has certain clear affinities with the representationist account of phenomenal character, in particular, the rejection of the view that phenomenal features are constituted purely by what is going on inside the head of an experiencing subject. However, in chapter 9, I shall draw attention to some of the important differences between this view and the representationist one. There, I shall argue that the transcendental status of phenomenal features of experience rules out the representationist attempt to explain the phenomenal in terms of the representational.

In chapter 10, the final chapter, I shall argue that the transcendental status of phenomenal properties or features is incompatible with any attempt to reductively explain the phenomenal in terms of the non-phenomenal.

The problem of phenomenal consciousness, the problem of *explaining* how phenomenal consciousness can come from what is not conscious, has no solution. We know consciousness is produced by what is not conscious, but we can never understand how. Chapter 10 also explores the wider question of the place of phenomenal consciousness in the natural order. It will be argued that the prospects for finding a place for consciousness in the natural order are not as bleak as the failure of reductive explanation might lead us to think.

2   Consciousness and supervenience

In his deservedly influential book, *The Conscious Mind* (1996), David Chalmers develops a sophisticated case against what, in the previous chapter, were identified as vertical strategies of type 1. Phenomenal consciousness, Chalmers argues, cannot be explained in physical terms. In particular, he develops the following general argument against the possibility of a reductive physical explanation of phenomenal consciousness.

1. Consciousness is reductively explainable in physical terms only if it is logically supervenient on the physical.
2. Consciousness is not logically supervenient on the physical.
3. Therefore, consciousness is not reductively explainable.

This chapter tries to show that the argument fails and why this is so. The failure of the argument is, I think, important not simply because it reopens the possibility that consciousness is reductively explainable but also because it is indicative of a significant and pervasive misunderstanding of the relation of supervenience, and what this relation does and does not entail.

In more detail, it will be argued that Chalmers operates with a crucially ambiguous interpretation of the concept of supervenience. One interpretation turns around the idea of supervenience as an ontological relation of determination; the other is primarily epistemological in character and is based on the idea that logical supervenience allows us to 'read off' facts about consciousness from knowledge of the physical facts. These interpretations Chalmers treats as equivalent, but, as I shall try to show, they are far from this. Once we clearly distinguish these interpretations, and understand the basis for this distinction, Chalmers' argument is seen to face a dilemma. On the ontological interpretation of supervenience, premise 2 is simply false. On the epistemological interpretation, premise 2 is arguably true, but is so in a way that undermines premise 1.

1 Logical supervenience: ontological and epistemological interpretations

Central to Chalmers' argument is the distinction between what he calls *logical* and *natural* supervenience (1996: 38). This section deals with the logical version of supervenience, the next section deals with the natural.

According to Chalmers, F-properties supervene *logically* on G-properties if no two logically possible situations are identical with respect to their G-properties but distinct with respect to their F-properties (1996: 35). Logical possibility, here, should be understood as what is often referred to as *broad* logical possibility, as opposed to the *strict* logical possibility that depends on formal systems. That is, in determining what counts as logically possible in this broad sense, the constraints are largely *conceptual*. A logically possible situation is one that contains no internal inconsistency or contradiction. A logically possible world is one that it would have been in God's power to create had He so chosen. God could not have created a world with married bachelors, but could have created one where the cow did, in fact, jump over the moon. If the term 'situations' in Chalmers' definition is taken to refer to individuals, this yields a characterisation of *local* supervenience; if it is taken to refer to worlds, the definition yields a characterisation of *global* supervenience. The difference, for Chalmers' purposes (and for ours), is not important.

Within this general framework, however, Chalmers has three distinct ways of developing the notion of logical supervenience. He seems to think of these as equivalent. The first way of characterising logical supervenience is in terms of what God would hypothetically have to do in order to create a world containing certain facts. According to Chalmers, what is characteristic of logical supervenience is that once God creates the subvenient facts, the supervenient facts come for free. For example, at the global level, biological properties supervene on physical properties, where the latter are understood as the fundamental properties that are invoked by a completed physics. God could not have created a world that was physically identical to ours but biologically distinct, for there is simply no logical space for the biological facts to vary independently of physical ones. The biological facts are, in an important sense, constituted by the physical facts (1996: 35). Let us call this the *ontological* interpretation of logical supervenience.

Chalmers also characterises the idea of logical supervenience in terms that are clearly epistemological. He claims that if logical supervenience is true, then a hypothetical superbeing such as Laplace's Demon, who knows the location of every particle in the universe, would be able to straightforwardly 'read off' all the biological facts, once given all the microphysical facts. The microphysical facts are enough for such a being to construct a model of the microscopic structure and dynamics of the world throughout space and time, from which it can straightforwardly deduce the macroscopic structure and dynamics (1996: 35). We can call this the *epistemological* interpretation of logical supervenience.

Chalmers also sometimes develops the idea of supervenience in yet a third way. In a case of logical supervenience, subvenient facts *entail* the supervenient facts. In general, Chalmers claims, when F-properties supervene logically on G-properties, we can say that the G-facts *entail* the F-facts (1996: 36). We can call this the *deducibility* construal of logical supervenience. This may seem like another formulation of the epistemological interpretation. However, Chalmers defines entailment in terms of the idea of broad logical possibility: one fact entails another if it is logically impossible for the first to hold without the second. Given this is so, it is probably more accurate to regard the deducibility construal as closer to the ontological interpretation. At the very least, it contains elements of both interpretations. But, in any event, there is no reason for thinking that the deducibility construal introduces anything not already contained in the first two interpretations, and it proves unimportant for our purposes.

Chalmers continually slides between ontological and epistemological interpretations of logical supervenience in a manner that strongly suggests he regards them as equivalent. I shall argue, however, that these interpretations are not equivalent and that much of the apparent plausibility of Chalmers' case rests on their illegitimate conflation. In particular, if we adopt the ontological interpretation, premise 2 is false (or, at the very least, Chalmers has done nothing to suggest it is true). If we adopt the epistemological interpretation, premise 1 is without foundation. In other words, Chalmers' argument gains its plausibility through understanding logical supervenience in the ontological sense in premise 1, but in the epistemological sense in premise 2. The fallacy is, thus, one of equivocation.

Even worse, however, is that there is a very real sense in which Chalmers' arguments do not even get as far as a fallacy of equivocation. The fallacy would be one of equivocation if his ontological and epistemological interpretations of supervenience were both (i) legitimate, but (ii) non-equivalent. However, as I shall also try to show, both interpretations are, in fact, almost certainly spurious.

2   (Merely) natural supervenience

In whichever of the above ways logical supervenience is understood, it should, according to Chalmers, be firmly distinguished from natural, or *merely* natural, supervenience. According to Chalmers, F-properties supervene naturally on G-properties if any two *naturally possible* situations with the same G-properties have the same F-properties. A naturally possible situation is understood as one that could actually occur in nature without violating any natural laws (1996: 36). Natural possibility, thus, corresponds to what some have called *nomological* possibility (Kim 1984).

Chalmers reinforces the distinction between logical and natural supervenience by way of the following metaphor, deriving from Kripke (1972). If F-properties supervene logically on G-properties, then once God creates a world with certain G-facts, the F-facts come along for free as an automatic consequence. In cases of logical supervenience, supervenient facts are, as Chalmers puts it, a *free lunch*. However, this is not so in cases of natural supervenience. If F-properties merely supervene naturally on G-properties, then after fixing the G-facts God still has something else to do in order to fix the F-facts: He has to make sure there is a law relating the G-facts and the F-facts. Once the law is in place in a given world, the relevant G-facts will, in that world, automatically necessitate the F-facts, but one could, in principle, have a world in which they did not.

There is, I shall argue, a serious problem in developing the idea of natural, or nomological, supervenience in this manner: it makes the concept of natural supervenience incoherent. This is, no doubt, a problem for Chalmers because not only is the distinction between natural and logical supervenience essential to his argument (1996: 38), he also endorses the positive claim that consciousness is naturally supervenient on the physical, and this provides the basis for his positive theory of consciousness developed in part III of his book. Even worse, as I shall try to show, given one further assumption, which Chalmers also endorses (1996: 108), the incoherence with which this model imbues the idea of natural supervenience threatens to spill over and infect the concept of logical supervenience also.

3   The incoherence of (Chalmers' versions of) supervenience

Chalmers, as we have seen, distinguishes logical and natural supervenience. In addition, I have argued that Chalmers adopts two distinct conceptions of supervenience: as an ontological relation of determination, and as an epistemological relation which allows us to 'read off' supervenient facts from knowledge of subvenient facts. Thus, there are four possible positions to be considered: logical and natural versions of ontological supervenience, and logical and natural versions of epistemological supervenience. This section, and the one to follow it, will be concerned with supervenience understood as an ontological relation of determination. I shall argue that, if understood in this way, Chalmers' versions of both natural and logical supervenience are incoherent.

Chalmers, as we have seen, claims that the distinction between logical and natural supervenience amounts to this. In a case of logical supervenience, supervenient facts come for free; in a case of natural supervenience, they do not. Rather, in the latter case, supervenient facts are determined, partly but essentially, by connecting bridge principles. In a case of natural supervenience, but not in a case of logical supervenience, God must fix not only the distribution of subvenient facts, but also the distribution of connecting bridge principles, in order to fix the distribution of supervenient facts. Thus, suppose F-facts supervene naturally on G-facts. Then, what, in a given world W, determines the distribution of F-facts in W? The primary reason for introducing supervenience – whether logical or natural – is, of course, to express the claim that the distribution of G-facts in W determines the distribution of F-facts in W. But, on Chalmers' understanding of the notion of natural supervenience, this claim must, in fact, be rejected. For, on Chalmers' construal of natural supervenience, it is possible for God to create a world W^* in which the distribution of G-facts is identical to that in W but where the supervenience relations instantiated in W^* are distinct from those instantiated in W. Where we have natural supervenience, according to Chalmers, it is not enough that God creates the G-facts. After God has done this, He still has more work to do. In order to create the F-facts, God must create bridge principles linking G- and F-facts. Thus, because of the difference in supervenience relations instantiated in W and W^*, the distribution of F-facts in the two worlds will also differ. And this means that what determines the distribution of F-facts in each world will not be the distribution of G-facts alone, but, also, the supervenience relations instantiated in each world.

This, I think, is an excellent illustration of how *not* to think about the supervenience relation. The problem, in a nutshell, is that this way of thinking about the relation of supervenience makes the concept of supervenience incoherent. Let us call the supervenience relations obtaining between G- and F-facts SR1 relations. SR1 relations are not, of course, purely G-facts; they are composed partly, but essentially, of F-facts. So, to adopt Chalmers' construal of natural supervenience is to abandon the idea that the distribution of G-facts alone determines the distribution of F-facts. What determines the distribution of F-facts is both the distribution of G-facts and the distribution of SR1 relations. And SR1 relations are not purely G-facts (they are, it seems, G-F facts). If F-facts naturally supervene on G-facts, *as Chalmers understands natural supervenience*, then F-facts don't seem to supervene on G-facts at all.

However, this is only the beginning of the problem. The problem will, given one further assumption, go on and infect Chalmers' account of logical supervenience also. Unfortunately for Chalmers, this is an assumption he endorses (1996: 108). The assumption is this. In a case of logical supervenience, supervenience bridge principles are not further facts about the world, but, rather, are themselves logically supervenient on the low-level or subvenient facts. Thus, in a case of logical supervenience, but not in a case of natural supervenience, given the way G-facts are distributed in W there can be one and only one distribution of supervenience relations in W. Therefore, in the case of logical supervenience, the possibility of worlds identical in their distribution of G-facts but distinct with regard to their instantiation of supervenience relations is not, in fact, a genuine possibility.

This assumption allows the incoherence of Chalmers' construal of natural supervenience to pass over to and similarly infect his account of logical supervenience. Given the assumption, we now have the supervenience of supervenience relations upon G-facts. We have called the original supervenience relations (i.e. those obtaining between G- and F-facts) SR1 relations. SR1 relations are, thus, G-F facts. The new supervenience relations will obtain between G-facts and SR1 relations. Call these SR2 relations. SR2 relations are, thus G-SR1 facts. Then, it is clear that if SR1 relations are not purely G-facts, then SR2 relations cannot be purely G-facts either. If SR1 relations are essentially composed of F-facts (and hence are not purely G-facts), then G-SR1 relations (i.e. SR2 relations) must also be essentially composed of F-facts. Thus, if the distribution of F-facts is determined by G-SR1 relations, then the distribution of F-facts is not determined purely by the G-facts. So, whether the type of supervenience is understood as natural or logical in character, we must give up the idea that the F-facts are determined by the G-facts. But the idea of the supervenience of F-facts on G-facts is surely just the idea that the F-facts are determined by the G-facts. Thus, to adopt Chalmers' construal of supervenience – and we see now that this applies to his account of both natural *and* logical supervenience – is to abandon the idea of supervenience. Chalmers' understanding of both logical and natural supervenience is, thus, internally inconsistent.

What has gone wrong? I suggest that it is a conflation of two different interpretations of natural supervenience, a conflation that is underwritten by an illegitimate understanding of the nature of supervenience relations. Consider, first, the conflation. The concept of natural supervenience is, in itself, a perfectly legitimate concept, one that is introduced to give expression to the idea that within a given set of worlds – naturally possible worlds – G-facts determine F-facts. That is:

(1) Within class of worlds W_1, where set $S = \{ s_1 \ldots s_n \}$ of supervenience relations obtain, G-facts determine F-facts.

To reiterate, there is absolutely nothing wrong with (1). However, it should not be confused with a quite different claim:

(2) Within class of worlds W_1, where set $S = \{ s_1 \ldots s_n \}$ of supervenience relations obtain, G-facts plus $s_1 \ldots s_n$ determine F-facts.

The legitimate content of the concept of natural supervenience is, I think, exhausted by (1), whereas Chalmers understands this concept in terms of (2). The problem with (2) is that it commits one to abandoning what is surely the core concept of supervenience: that in any case of supervenience, the distribution of subvenient facts determines the distribution of supervenient ones. For, according to (2), what determines the distribution of supervenient facts is, in essence, a combination of subvenient *and* supervenient facts.

This conflation is underwritten, I think, by a mistaken understanding of the nature of supervenience relations. The mistake is to suppose that supervenience relations form the *basis* of the dependency between subvenient and supervenient facts when, in fact, they are simply *reflections* of a dependency that is fixed by other means.

One way of explaining the mistake is in terms of a distinction between what we can call a *reified* and a *non-reified* interpretation of the language of supervenience relations. According to a *non-reified* construal of supervenience language, talk of the supervenience relation is simply a way of adverting to the fact that two families of properties or facts are related in the way specified by one's preferred formulation of supervenience. A non-reified construal can allow that there is something about the subvenient G-facts that makes for, and thus potentially explains, the instantiation of supervenient F-facts. However, the commitments of the non-reified construal include nothing more than G- and F-facts. Most importantly, supervenience relations obtaining between G- and F-facts play no role in fixing the distribution of F-facts. The distribution of F-facts is determined or fixed by the nature of G-facts, and the way these facts are distributed, and talk of supervenience relations obtaining between G- and F-facts is simply a way of talking about the relations that obtain – in virtue of the nature and distribution of G-facts – between these two families. Our talk of supervenience relations, then, is simply a reflection or an expression of a dependency that is fixed by other means.

On the other hand, according to what we can call a *reified* interpretation of supervenience, the relatedness of G- and F-facts is to be explained in terms of a relation – the supervenience relation – that holds between the two sets of properties. The distribution of F-facts in a given world is to be explained not just in terms of the nature and distribution of G-facts in that world, but also in terms of the supervenience relations instantiated in that world. Our talk of supervenience relations, according to the reified construal, is talk not just of the ways in which G- and F-facts are related, it is, in addition, talk of the way in which this relatedness comes to be determined. Reference to supervenience relations, on the reified interpretation, is reference to a factor that, in part, fixes the relation between G- and F-facts.

This sort of distinction is quite familiar for other types of determination relations. In the area of causal determination, for example, we are quite comfortable with the distinction between dispositional properties and the underlying structural bases of those properties. Dispositional properties do not determine or fix the behaviour of items that possess them. Rather, to talk of the dispositional properties of an object is to talk of its propensities to behave in ways that are determined by that object's underlying structural properties. To talk of an object's dispositional properties is not to talk of the *basis* of that object's behaviour. Rather, such talk is a reflection or *expression* of a basis that is fixed by other means, namely by the underlying structural properties.

Although I would not want to claim (*pace*, for example, Searle 1992) that supervenience relations are a species of causal relation, I think there is a parallel distinction to be made between what fixes the relation between G- and F-facts, and the relation itself. This distinction I have attempted to capture by way of the distinction between reified and non-reified interpretations of supervenience language. To adopt a non-reified construal is to think of supervenience relations as the analogues, in the domain of supervenience, of dispositional properties in the domain of causation. That is, neither supervenience relations, nor dispositions, can be thought of as the basis of a dependency. Rather, talk of these features is talk of a dependency that is fixed by other means.

Chalmers, as we have seen, presupposes a reified construal of the supervenience language. This is particularly evident in his account of natural supervenience, but, as we have seen, tends to sneak into his account of logical supervenience also. However, the price he has to pay for this presupposition is the rendering inconsistent of his concept of supervenience, both natural and, ultimately, logical. The reified construal forces us to think of supervenience relations as the basis, or part of the basis, of the dependency between subvenient and supervenient properties. Thus, it is not, in any given world, the distribution of G-facts alone which determines the distribution of F-facts; it is the distribution of G-facts *plus* the supervenience relations that obtain in that world, that determines the distribution of F-facts. Once we think of the supervenience relation as the partial basis of the dependency in this sort of way, we are forced, in effect, to abandon the claim that F-facts supervene on G-facts. To assert the supervenience of F-facts on G-facts, and to then adopt a reified gloss of the truth-conditions of that assertion, is to abandon the supervenience of F-facts on G-facts.

We can avoid rendering the concept of supervenience internally inconsistent by adopting a non-reified construal. Supervenience relations do not form the basis, whole or partial, of the dependency between subvenient and supervenient facts. Rather, reference to supervenience relations is an *expression* or *reflection* of a dependency that is fixed by other means (by the nature and distribution of the G-facts). Supervenience bridge principles do not, in a metaphysical sense, fix anything at all, they cannot do so. Rather, when we assert, in any given case, that a relation of supervenience obtains between a fact G and a fact F, we are simply claiming that there is a certain type of correlation – roughly asymmetrical dependence – between G and F, a correlation that is properly expressed by our preferred formulation of supervenience, *and* a correlation that is presumably explained by the nature of G. What we are precisely *not* claiming is that there is some relation, S, obtaining between G and F which provides the basis of the asymmetrical dependence of F on G.

To avoid misunderstanding here, it is perhaps worth reiterating that there is nothing incoherent about the concept of natural supervenience as such. What introduces the inconsistency into Chalmers' account of natural supervenience is his reified gloss of this concept, a gloss surreptitiously introduced via his use of the 'what God has to do' metaphor. Although the distinction between natural and logical supervenience, properly understood, is a legitimate one, it is not possible to capture the distinction in terms of this metaphor, and the associated idea that in a case of logical supervenience the supervenient facts come for free. For this is true of both forms of supervenience. When we understand logical supervenience in the way Chalmers suggests, that is, in terms of the idea that supervenient facts come for free, then *all supervenience is logical supervenience*. In any genuine case of supervenience, once we fix the subvenient facts, the supervenient facts are a free lunch. Always. They must be if the concept of supervenience is to have any coherent content. God, therefore, does not have to do anything other than create the G-facts in order to fix the distribution of F-facts.

Thus, *if* we insist on understanding the concept of logical supervenience as Chalmers tells us to, and which forms the basis for premise 2 of his argument, *then* there is no distinction between logical and natural supervenience. Consequently, when understood in the way that forms the basis of Chalmers' argument, all (ontological) supervenience is logical supervenience. And, therefore, if we adopt Chalmers' understanding of supervenience, premise 2 must be rejected.

4   Natural supervenience and weak supervenience

Further light can be thrown on this issue by way of a comparison between natural supervenience, as understood by Chalmers, and what, following Kim (1984), is usually referred to as *weak* supervenience. Let A and B be two non-empty families of properties closed under the usual Boolean property-forming operations. Then, Kim defines weak supervenience as follows:

A weakly supervenes on B just in case necessarily for any x and y, if x and y share all properties in B then x and y share all properties in A – that is, indiscernibility with respect to B entails indiscernibility with respect to A (1984: 158)

The weakness of weak supervenience lies in this: as defined it prohibits the possibility of two things agreeing in base properties but differing in supervenient properties only *within* any possible world. Transworld B-indiscernibility permits transworld A-discernibility. This leaves us with a puzzle developed by Blackburn (1985) as follows. In any possible world, once there is an object which is F and whose F-ness supervenes on G, then, in that world, anything else which is G is F also. Call these G/F worlds. However, weak supervenience allows that there are other worlds in which things are G but not F. Call these G/O worlds. The problem is: why are there no mixed worlds where some things are G and F and some things are G but not F? That is, why are there no worlds of the form G/FvO? These worlds are ruled out by weak supervenience, but it is difficult to see the justification for this. After all, weak supervenience allows both G/F and G/O worlds.

The difficulty is that once we have imagined a G/F world and a G/O world, we have done enough to imagine a G/FvO world, and have implicitly denied ourselves a right to forbid its existence. So, the ban on mixed worlds seems to have no authority. In other words, we are to suppose that G determines F in one world, a G/F world, but not in another, G/O world. But then it becomes unclear in what sense G determines F in the G/F world. For the existence of the G/O world seems to indicate that it cannot be G *simpliciter* determining F but, rather, that it is something about the world in which G occurs that is also a partial determinant of

F, something such as, for example, a bridge law. And then it becomes unclear just in what sense the relation expressed by weak supervenience is a relation of determination at all.

Given one further assumption, this lack of clarity develops into a serious problem. As with natural supervenience, it is important to distinguish two very different claims.

(1*) Within world W_1, where set $S = \{s_1 \ldots s_n\}$ of supervenience relations obtain, G-facts determine F-facts.

As with the corresponding formulation of natural supervenience, there is nothing wrong with (1*). It expresses a genuine relation of determination, albeit a rather weak one. However, (1*) should not be confused with a quite different claim:

(2*) Within world W_1, where set $S = \{s_1 \ldots s_n\}$ of supervenience relations obtain, G-facts plus $s_1 \ldots s_n$ determine F-facts.

The legitimate content of the concept of weak supervenience is, I think, exhausted by (1*). If we adopt (2*), then weak supervenience becomes not just a weak relation, but an incoherent one. It is not G-facts that determine F-facts, not even within W_1. But weak supervenience, surely, *purports* to be an expression of the idea that, in a given world, G-facts determine F-facts. The concept of weak supervenience, therefore, cannot deliver what it is supposed to deliver if we understand it in terms of (2*). Happily, we do not have to understand it in this way.

At root, Chalmers' interpretation of natural supervenience – by which I shall mean his formulation of the relation *plus* his reified gloss of that formulation – faces precisely the same difficulties as the version of weak supervenience understood in terms of (2*). Indeed, at root, the only difference between Chalmers' interpretation of natural supervenience and the understanding of weak supervenience expressed in (2*) is this. With weak supervenience there is only *one* G/F world, with Chalmers' construal of natural supervenience, there are several – the naturally possible worlds. But since we also have G/O worlds, the problem of mixed worlds still applies. And Chalmers' account of natural supervenience, expressed in terms of (2), is no more coherent than the understanding of weak supervenience expressed in (2*).

In conclusion, whenever we imagine supervenience in terms of a tripartite structure of subvenient facts, supervenient facts, and a reified connecting relation that in part determines the relation between subvenient and supervenient facts, then what we have in fact imagined is an incoherent relation. To adopt this construal is, effectively, to abandon the claim of supervenience that it purports to explain.

If this is correct, then Chalmers' attempt to distinguish between natural and logical supervenience will not work. The dependency between subvenient and supervenient facts can never have, as part of its basis, a supervenience relation. If it did, the concept of supervenience would be incoherent. However, Chalmers proposes to understand the difference between logical and natural supervenience in terms of the idea that, with the latter relation but not the former, supervenient facts do not come for free but must be, in part, determined by the connecting bridge principles. Hence, Chalmers' way of drawing the distinction should be rejected.

5   Natural supervenience as an epistemological concept

The above remarks (especially if the disclaimer at the end of section 3 is ignored) might make it appear that I am denying the legitimacy of the notion of natural supervenience. But this is not, in fact, the case. Firstly, as we have seen, the concept of natural supervenience has a perfectly coherent content if this content is divorced from the reified gloss that the 'what God has to do' metaphor tends to covertly introduce. Secondly, there is another sense in which the concept of natural supervenience has a perfectly legitimate content: it has a content that is *epistemological*, rather than ontological, in character. Another way of understanding the distinction between logical and natural supervenience is as an epistemological distinction; one pertaining to different kinds of knowledge we might have of one and the same ontological relation. This section is concerned with the epistemological understanding of natural supervenience.

As we have seen, Chalmers also adopts an epistemological construal of supervenience in terms of the ability to 'read off' supervenient facts from subvenient ones. (As will become clear, I think the idea of 'reading off' one set of facts from another is so potentially dangerous that I shall continue to employ the expression within scare quotes.) We encountered Chalmers' epistemological construal in section 1. The idea is that, in cases of logical supervenience, Laplace's Demon, who is in possession of all subvenient facts, would, thereby, be able to 'read off' all supervenient facts. Natural supervenience is, then, distinguished from logical supervenience precisely by way of its failure to underwrite the Demon's capacity to 'read off' supervenient from subvenient facts.

However, it is important to realise that Chalmers' epistemological understanding of the distinction between logical and natural supervenience is quite distinct from a more common, and, I think, preferable, epistemological reading. The more common reading runs, roughly, as follows. Suppose we are presented with two objects indiscernible with regard to properties of a subvenient family G, and are asked to consider their possession of properties from a supervenient family F. Sometimes we realise that to deny their indiscernibility with respect to F-properties would be simply conceptually confused; we would, in, of course, a broadly logical sense, be contradicting ourselves were we to deny this indiscernibility. Sometimes, however, we think that we would be wrong to deny such indiscernibility, but not conceptually confused. To deny such indiscernibility would commit us to denying a relevant natural law, and this might be a manifestation of ignorance, perhaps extreme ignorance, on our part. But this is an entirely different matter, so we *might* think, from exhibiting conceptual confusion.

There is nothing in this account that requires any firm distinction between conceptual and empirical truths. The account sketched here is compatible with the broadly naturalistic view that the relation between conceptual and empirical truth should be conceived of along the lines of a spectrum rather than a dichotomy. The absence of a firm distinction is not the absence of a distinction. One can allow that empirical truths shade by degree into conceptual ones, and consequently that empirical ignorance shades by degree into conceptual confusion, while allowing that we understand some truths as conceptual and others as empirical; consequently, that we regard some assertions as empirical errors and others as conceptual confusions.

This is a purely epistemological way of distinguishing logical from natural supervenience. The distinction does not, at least not directly, correspond to a difference in the way the F-facts are determined in each case, nor to a distinction in the force or necessity with which they are determined. In all genuine cases of supervenience, the supervenient facts come for free, they are nothing over and above the subvenient facts. Rather, the distinction corresponds simply to a difference in our knowledge of the way in which supervenient facts are determined and (our knowledge of) the strength with which they are determined. And this, epistemologically speaking, is all the difference between logical and natural supervenience can come to.

As an example of this general idea, and also of some of the confusions to which one can easily fall victim, consider Chalmers' treatment of moral supervenience, the supervenience of moral facts on natural ones (1996: 83). Interestingly, Chalmers is willing to consider moral supervenience as at least a candidate for the failure of logical supervenience, whereas it is more commonly thought of precisely as an instance of such supervenience (e.g., Blackburn 1971, 1985). Why is this? Because in this instance, he is operating with an epistemological interpretation of logical supervenience according to which it entails the possibility of 'reading off' supervenient facts from their subvenient bases. Thus, he thinks that the claim, advanced by Moore (1922) and others, that there is no conceptual connection between natural and moral facts is relevant to the question of whether moral facts logically supervene on natural ones (1996: 83). If there is nothing about the meaning of terms such as 'goodness' that allows that facts about goodness should be entailed by natural facts, then goodness cannot be logically supervenient on natural facts.

In fact, however, the question of whether natural facts entail moral ones, or whether moral facts can be 'read off' from natural ones, is simply irrelevant to the question of whether moral facts supervene logically on natural ones. Actually, moral facts are more commonly thought to supervene logically on natural ones, but this has nothing to do with the possibility of 'reading off' the former from the latter, and nothing to do with the latter somehow entailing the former. Rather, when it is claimed that moral facts supervene logically on natural ones, what is usually meant by this claim is something like this. Suppose we have two objects of moral evaluation. Suppose, for example, we have two persons, Hitler and his twin earth counterpart, Twitler. Hitler and Twitler, we will suppose, share any natural properties that might conceivably be relevant to their moral evaluation. Both perform the same actions: starting a world war, sending six million people to the gas chambers, etc. And both perform these actions with precisely the same intentions or motives. In short, whatever natural qualities you think are relevant to the moral evaluation of Hitler, assume that these qualities are shared also by Twitler. In this sort of situation, it would simply *make no sense* to assign different moral evaluations to Hitler and Twitler. If Hitler is bad, then Twitler must be also. It would be logically incoherent (in the broad sense), or conceptually confused, to assign a different moral evaluation to each person. Now, moral realists might explain this confusion in terms of objective relations between moral and natural properties, while moral anti-realists might regard this as a constraint on the use of moral language. But whatever the source of the supervenience claim, the idea is that moral facts supervene logically on natural ones in that one is logically or conceptually confused if one assigns different moral properties to objects indiscernible with respect to their natural properties. Now I am not saying that moral facts do logically supervene on natural ones. Rather, my point is that when people claim that moral facts supervene on natural ones, this is what they have in mind.

Now, it does not follow from this that it is possible to 'read off' moral facts from natural ones. Being presented with Hitler's natural qualities does not automatically enable you to tell whether Hitler was a bad or good person. It simply tells you that, *on pain of contradicting yourself* (in a broadly logical sense), you cannot assign Hitler a certain moral evaluation while assigning another person, indiscernible in all relevant natural respects, a distinct one. And, even on a global level, it does not follow from logical supervenience alone that acquaintance with all the micro-physical facts alone will thereby yield acquaintance with the distribution of moral facts in that world (or even that there are any moral facts in that world). All logical supervenience tells you is that if there is another world indiscernible (in a non-epistemic sense) from the world under consideration, then this other world will possess the same distribution of moral facts. To claim that the distribution of moral facts is different in each world would involve a *conceptual confusion*.

Similarly, when it is claimed that a family of properties, F, supervenes naturally (or, more commonly, 'nomologically'), rather than logically, on another family of properties, G, then what is usually meant by this is simply that while the distribution of the latter determines the distribution of the former, one can, in any particular case, assert that objects x and y, while indiscernible with respect to G-properties, are discernible with respect to F-properties without, necessarily, exhibiting any conceptual confusion. Such an assertion might commit one to denying a given *law of nature*, therefore might be revelatory of gross ignorance on one's part, nonetheless, it does not commit one to denying a so-called *law of thought*.

To see this, consider one of Chalmers' favourite examples of logical supervenience on the physical: the supervenience of biological on physical facts. We can imagine, Chalmers tells us, that a hypothetical superbeing such as Laplace's Demon, who knows the location of every particle in the universe, would be able to straightforwardly 'read off' all the biological facts once given all the physical facts. But, as we have seen, this is simply irrelevant to the issue of whether biological facts logically supervene on physical ones. That issue turns simply on this: whether it is possible to assert that two objects indiscernible with regard to their instantiation of physical facts are distinct with regard to their instantiation of biological facts. And I think that someone who made such an assertion as this may be empirically very ignorant indeed, but they would not necessarily be conceptually confused or logically inconsistent. (Alternatively, perhaps they may be. I need take no stand on this issue. All that is required for present purposes is the above way of drawing the distinction between natural and logical supervenience. Which examples of supervenience fall on which side of the division is another issue.)

Similarly, and more generally, it is plausible to suppose that macrophysical facts fail to supervene logically on microphysical facts when logical supervenience is understood in an epistemological sense. Thus, *if* one can (i) assert that two objects have the same microphysical properties, and (ii) deny that they share the same macrophysical properties, and, in so doing, (iii) exhibit only gross empirical ignorance rather than conceptual confusion, then this is sufficient to show that macrophysical properties do not logically supervene on microphysical ones, where, to reiterate, this supervenience is understood epistemologically.

To repeat: what logical supervenience gives you is this. Any two objects which instantiate the same G-facts also, necessarily, instantiate the same F-facts, where the modal operator denotes logical necessity. So, from this, if you know that object x instantiates certain relevant G-facts, and x is F, then you know that any other object which instantiates the same G-facts must, logically, also be F. You know that you must believe this on pain of being conceptually confused, or logically incoherent. But logical supervenience does not, by itself, allow one to 'read off' the fact that x is F from knowledge of which G-facts it instantiates.

6   More on 'reading off'

Nothing in the above account entails that the idea of 'reading off' one type of fact from knowledge of other facts is without foundation. The above account claims merely that the concept of logical supervenience *is* not typically understood in this way, not that it *cannot* be so understood. In fact, however, there is a very good reason why the concept of logical supervenience should not be understood in terms of the idea of the ability to 'read off' one set of facts from another. The reason is that this idea is an ambiguous, thus potentially confusing, one, and almost certainly cannot be understood in the way Chalmers requires it to be understood.

Kim (1984) has argued, plausibly, that the (strong) supervenience of F-properties on G-properties entails the existence of (i) modal bi-conditionals connecting F-properties with disjunctive G-properties, and (ii) modal conditionals running from G-properties to F-properties. This, then, is an entailment of logical supervenience. And given this is so, it might be thought that logical supervenience does entail the possibility of 'reading off' the F-facts from the G-facts. Logical supervenience, that is, entails the existence of bridge principles, and perhaps even laws, connecting G- and F-properties, and these principles entail the possibility of 'reading off' F-properties or facts from G-properties or facts. However, care must be taken here. The conclusion of Kim's argument is an ontological one, pertaining to the sorts of relations that exist in the world, relations entailed by the strong supervenience of one set of properties on another. As Kim himself has pointed out (1984: 172–3), it does not, in any straightforward way, license any epistemological claim. The question then is whether the sort of epistemological construal of supervenience in terms of 'reading off' one set of facts from another, the construal Chalmers requires, is obtainable from the relation of logical supervenience.

The 'reading off' of one set of facts from another, of course, is one construal of what Laplace's Demon (henceforth LD) is supposed to do. LD, who possesses knowledge of all the basic facts, is, on this construal, able to 'read off' all facts logically supervenient on the basic ones. That is, according to Chalmers, the ability of LD to 'read off' a given set, S, of facts is dependent on the obtaining of two conditions: (i) LD knows all the (relevant) *basic* facts, and (ii) all facts that are members of S are logically supervenient on these basic facts. I shall argue that this is a bad idea.

Consider, first, what Chalmers means by basic facts. A basic fact, for Chalmers, is the instantiation of a basic property. And he is quite clear that by 'basic property' he means 'the fundamental properties that are invoked by a completed theory of physics' (1996: 33) Similarly, when he talks about the supervenience of properties or facts on the physical, then he means 'physical' in this sense also. Physical properties in this sense might include items such as mass, charge, spatiotemporal position, and so on. But they will not include such high-level properties as juiciness, lumpiness, giraffehood, and the like (1996: 33). Therefore, when other facts supervene on the physical, they supervene, ultimately, on the fundamental properties invoked by a completed physics, and not physical properties in this broader sense. Therefore, the basic facts of which LD has exhaustive knowledge are the physical facts in this restricted sense.

Suppose LD inhabits a world where a set S of non-basic facts logically supervene on basic facts; physical facts in Chalmers' restricted sense. If LD is to be able to 'read off' the members of S armed only with exhaustive knowledge of the basic, physical, facts, then, it must be able to somehow construct knowledge of the non-basic facts from its knowledge of the basic ones. The question is: how can it do this?

One thing is clear. We cannot give LD free knowledge of the relations licensed by strong supervenience; the modal conditionals and biconditionals that Kim argues are consequences of (strong) supervenience. If we did, then the idea of LD 'reading off' non-basic facts from basic ones would be vacuous. For these relations are, in effect, composite facts: combinations of basic and non-basic facts and, as such, non-basic. If LD is to have knowledge of these composite facts, it must be able to construct such knowledge from its knowledge of the basic facts. So, once again, we have the question: how can it do this?

The reason Chalmers thinks LD could construct such knowledge is that he thinks all logically supervenient facts are, essentially, instantiations of *causal* or *functional* properties. And this entails that (i) supervenience relations connecting these facts are themselves logically supervenient on the basic facts, and, therefore, (ii) it is possible, in cases of logical supervenience, for LD to read off supervenience relations from basic facts. The ability of LD, that is, stems ultimately from the nature of logically supervenient facts.

In broad outline, Chalmers' idea can be explained as follows. Non-basic, or (logically) supervenient, facts are instantiations of functional properties. And a functional property can be analysed in terms of its place in a nexus of causal relations. If, then, a basic property, or, more likely, combination of such properties, fits into this place in the causal nexus then the basic facts, the instantiation of these basic properties, explain the non-basic ones. Let AP represent a generic basic property, and AF represent the instantiation of this property. AP and AF stand for 'atomic property' and 'atomic fact' respectively. And, similarly, let MP represent a non-basic property, and MF the instantiation of that property. MP and MF stand for 'molecular property' and 'molecular fact', respectively. (The denominations 'A' and 'M', here, merely denote relative level of complexity: M-properties and facts are, in a sense to be made clear, composed of A-properties and facts.) Then, according to the model endorsed by Chalmers, MP can be analysed in terms of a causal role, C. And when a basic property AP fills C, then AF, the instantiation of AP, explains MF, the instantiation of MP. For example, the property of being alive can be analysed in terms of a complex causal role involving such properties as growth, respiration, reproduction and the like. Therefore, anything that instantiates the conjunction of growth, reproduction and respiration will thereby instantiate the property of being alive, and the instantiation of the former thereby explains the instantiation of the latter.

Let us suppose Chalmers is correct about non-basic properties being analysable as causal roles. Does this mean that LD is able to 'read off' non-basic facts – instantiations of non-basic properties – from its exhaustive knowledge of the basic facts? Well, it seems LD will certainly be able to do so if it knows the causal analyses of non-basic properties. However, there is no way that causal analyses of non-basic properties can be regarded as basic facts. Therefore, if Chalmers is serious about the idea that logical supervenience entails that LD should be able to read off the non-basic facts from its exhaustive knowledge of basic ones, it seems that LD will have to be able to construct the causal analyses of non-basic properties from its knowledge of the basic facts. So, once again, we return to essentially the same question: how can it do this?

The answer is: LD cannot do this. And its failure is related to the failure of a cousin of its, *Watson's Demon* (henceforth WD). According to legend, WD was able to read off all mental facts from its exhaustive knowledge of the behavioural facts. However, legend was unreliable on this score: there never was, and could not be, a demon who could accomplish this. This is because of the *holism of the mental*. The problem the holism of the mental provides for WD is that any attempt to specify in behavioural terms what a given mental state is, eventually but inevitably, will make reference to some other mental state. This is because any given mental state will have consequences for behaviour only in combination with other mental states. So, WD cannot read off mental facts purely from its knowledge of behavioural ones; in order to read off any given mental fact, it requires knowledge of both behavioural facts and (further) mental facts. And the reason for this, ultimately, seems to be that mental states form a complex, holistic, network, and the identity conditions of any given mental state depend, at least in part, on its position in this network.

The problem for LD is closely related to the predicament of its cousin for the simple reason that once we buy into the causal-functional analysis of supervenient properties that is supposedly necessary for LD to construct supervenient facts from basic ones, we have thereby bought into the sort of holistic view of supervenient properties that undermined the demonic purposes of WD. LD, in other words, faces a problem of the *holism of the physical*. Logically supervenient facts are the instantiation of logically supervenient properties, and if we adopt the sort of causal-functional analysis of such properties endorsed by Chalmers (and, I think, independently plausible anyway), then we are led, pretty straightforwardly, into a holistic account of their identity conditions. The instantiation of logically supervenient property P consists in the filling of causal role C. But, then, the properties referred to in the specification of C will themselves be logically supervenient on more basic properties, and so their instantiation will, in turn, consist in the filling of further causal roles, and so on.

The problem that the holism of the mental provided for WD derived, ultimately, from the view of mental facts (the instantiation of mental properties) as individuated by their place in a network of systematic relations. However, the causal-functional account of supervenient properties entails an almost precisely analogous view of supervenient facts and their identity conditions. Indeed, the holism of the physical implicit in the causal account of supervenient properties endorsed by Chalmers seems, if anything, even more extreme than the holism of the mental. This is because whatever reasons there are for thinking that mental properties are not individuated purely holistically, not simply in terms of their place in a functional network, derive from the view that mental properties are representational as well as causal, and, consequently, that there are aspects of the content of such states that are not captured by way of their causal role. To the extent that mental properties are individuated in terms of their representational features, then, such individuation is not, or need not be, holistic. But this option is, of course, not available for the individuation of non-representational properties.

LD's attempt to read off supervenient facts from subvenient ones is, it seems, going to be stymied by the holism of the physical in precisely the same way that WD's attempt to read off mental facts was thwarted by the holism of the mental. In other words, given the causal-functional analysis, non-basic facts, like mental facts, form a tight circle; and even LD cannot read them off from knowledge of basic facts alone, not even in a world where all non-basic facts logically supervene on basic ones.

We can, I think, generalise this conclusion in the following way. Suppose we have a non-basic property MP, whose instantiation in a particular case is MF. Along with Chalmers, we can suppose that MP, being non-basic, is analysable in terms of a (perhaps complex) causal role C_1. Suppose also that there is a basic property AP which, when instantiated as the basic fact AF, fills causal role C_1. The instantiation of MP, therefore, consists in the instantiation of AP, and the latter explains the former. Would LD be able to infer MF from AF? How could it, unless it knew what MF was taken to be; that is, unless it knew that MF was the instantiation of a property MP that is defined by causal role C_1? However, that MP is defined by causal role C_1 is not knowledge of an A-fact, it is knowledge of an M-fact. Therefore, if LD is to 'read off' MF armed only with knowledge of A-facts, it must be able to construct the knowledge that MP is defined by causal role C_1 from its knowledge of A-facts. However, its attempt to do this will fail for the same reasons as WD's forlorn attempt to 'read off' mental facts from behavioural ones. The properties that will be referred to in the specification of C_1 are M-properties, hence defined by further causal roles $C_2 \ldots C_n$. Thus, in order to 'read off' MF from AF, LD must know that MP is that property which, when instantiated in conjunction with property MP_n, causes the instantiation of $MP_{n+x} \ldots$ etc., etc. At each point, the properties will themselves be defined in terms of further causal roles. The result is that LD's attempt to read off M-facts from A-facts will entail LD becoming caught up in a circle of M-concepts in precisely the same way that afflicted WD's attempt to read off mental facts from behavioural ones.

If this is correct, the idea that LD can 'read off' the non-basic facts from knowledge of the basic facts alone is a mistaken one, even in a world where all non-basic facts are logically supervenient on basic ones. LD can no more 'read off' supervenient facts from basic ones alone than WD could 'read off' mental facts from behavioural ones alone. The holism of the physical will preclude the former capacity just as the holism of the mental is known to preclude the latter. In a world where all non-basic facts are logically supervenient on basic ones, then what knowledge of all basic facts bestows on LD is not the deductive or quasi-deductive ability to 'read off' all the non-basic facts. Rather, it is the, for want of a better word, *hermeneutic* ability to combine knowledge of the basic facts, with the *non-basic* causal analyses of non-basic properties, to work out what instantiation of basic properties the instantiation of a given non-basic property consists in. Or, if one would prefer not to throw words like 'hermeneutic' around, what logical supervenience gives LD is, *in conjunction with Ramsey-sentence analyses of logically supervenient properties*, the ability to work out what basic properties satisfy these sentences. The difference between this and a simple 'reading off' of one set of facts from another is, I think, clear enough.

Worse still for Chalmers, he implicitly, but effectively, concedes that LD is not going to be able to 'read off' logically supervenient facts from exhaustive knowledge of their underlying bases. In explaining the idea of logical supervenience, he writes:

In general, when B-properties supervene logically on A-properties, we can say that A-facts entail the B-facts ... In such cases, Laplace's demon could read off the B-facts from a specification of the A-facts, *as long as it possesses the B-concepts in question*. (1996: 36, emphasis mine)

In effect, I think, this passage concedes that LD could not read off logically supervenient B-facts from their underlying A-facts. In order to do so, Chalmers acknowledges, it requires the relevant B-concepts. The problem with this suggestion emerges when we consider what a B-concept is. The concept of giraffehood, for example, is, according to Chalmers, an example of a B-concept. What knowledge would LD need, in order to possess this B-concept? Well, presumably knowledge of the following sort: something is a giraffe if ... Where the dots are presumably filled in by specification of the relevant details of genetic structure (or of population interbreeding capacities, depending on which concept of species one is working with). But then LD will have to know certain facts. For example, he will have to know that, be aware of the fact that, something counts as a giraffe only if it fits a certain genetic profile. But this is clearly not an A-fact. Generally, the problem is that possession of B-concepts will almost certainly require possession of B-facts for the simple reason that the content of B-concepts is specified in terms of B-facts. And so to give LD free knowledge of B-concepts is, in effect, to render vacuous the idea that LD can read off all facts that are logically supervenient on A-facts simply from possession of A-facts alone.

The straightforward manner in which this qualification undermines his own position might, perhaps, indicate that Chalmers has something else in mind? Perhaps, according to Chalmers, the difference between logical and natural supervenience amounts to this. In a case of logical supervenience, once we possess knowledge of all subvenient A-facts, and once we possess Ramsey-style analyses of all B-properties, then we can 'read off' the B-facts. However, in a case of natural supervenience, we cannot do this. That is, in the latter case, but not the former, exhaustive knowledge of A-facts and of the Ramsey-style analyses of B-properties still leaves a conceptual gap that prevents us 'reading off' the B-facts.

The problem with this suggestion, however, is that it seems pretty clearly false. To see this, consider one of the few (non-consciousness based) examples of natural supervenience offered by Chalmers. He writes:

In the actual world, whenever there is a mole of gas at a given temperature and volume, its pressure will be determined: it is empirically impossible that two distinct moles of gas could have the same temperature and volume, but different pressure. It follows that the pressure of a mole of gas supervenes on its temperature and volume in a certain sense. But this supervenience is weaker than logical supervenience. It is *logically* possible that a mole of gas with a given temperature and volume might have a different pressure; imagine a world where the gas constant K is larger or smaller, for example. (1996: 36)

This passage is, I think, puzzling in several respects. But let us take Chalmers at his word when he says that this is a case of natural, and not logical, supervenience. Then, it simply is not true that, *once we have the relevant analyses of temperature, pressure and volume*, we can imagine what Chalmers claims we can imagine. Thus, we analyse temperature, roughly, as the mean kinetic energy of molecules in a given volume, and we analyse pressure, again roughly, in terms of the momentum of particles impacting on the boundaries of a given volume; then, with subsequent filling in of the details, it is not possible to imagine two moles of gas occupying a given volume, that have the same temperature but different pressure. And Chalmers' claim that all we have to do is imagine a world where the gas constant has a different value simply misunderstands the status of the gas constant: the constant is not the basis of the dependency between temperature, pressure, and volume, but a reflection of this dependency that is fixed by other means (i.e. by the underlying nature, as expressed in the relevant analyses, of these quantities). As we saw earlier, the tendency to confuse the basis of a relation with the reflection of a relation that is fixed by other means similarly infects Chalmers' account of supervenience as an ontological, rather than epistemic, relation.

Once you have an analysis of a given B-property, you have an account of in what the instantiation of that property consists, of what counts as the instantiation of that property. Once you know what A-facts fill the role specified in the analysis, then you are also able, from these, to 'read off' the relevant B-facts. And this is true whether the supervenience in question is logical *or* natural. The distinction between logical and natural supervenience is irrelevant to this ability. Indeed, it seems that it could only be relevant if we were willing to allow that logical and natural supervenience denoted two quite different, two ontologically distinct, kinds of relation. For this would allow us the sort of claim, often made by Chalmers, that in a case of logical supervenience the supervenient facts *consist in* the subvenient ones, whereas in a case of natural supervenience they do not. But this would require repeating the sort of mistakes identified in sections 3 and 4.

To summarise, I think we should conclude that the idea of 'reading off' logically supervenient facts from their underlying bases is a misguided idea. Even LD is not able to do this. Any attempt to 'read off' supervenient facts from subvenient bases will, eventually but inevitably, involve reference to further supervenient facts. Therefore, the idea of 'reading off' cannot be used to characterise the concept of logical supervenience, nor can it be used to distinguish logical from natural supervenience.

7   Logical supervenience and reductive explanation

Consciousness, according to Chalmers, is not logically supervenient on the physical. And in this, he claims, it stands alone, apart from, possibly, indexical facts, negative facts, facts about causation, and moral facts, most of which, in any case, may be consciousness-dependent. However, his claim that consciousness is not logically supervenient on the physical seems to rest on his epistemological interpretation of logical supervenience as consisting in, or entailing, the claim that it is possible to read off from the basic, physical, facts, all those facts that logically supervene upon them. Since it is not possible to 'read off' facts about consciousness from physical facts, Chalmers concludes that consciousness does not logically supervene on physical properties, hence cannot be reductively explained in terms of physical properties.

I have tried to undermine Chalmers' epistemological interpretation of logical supervenience in two ways. Firstly, I argued that, as the concept of logical supervenience is usually understood, to say that F facts supervene on G facts is to say that it is not possible to assert that two objects are identical with regard to their G properties while distinct with regard to their F properties *without exhibiting a form of conceptual confusion*, without contradicting oneself in the broadly logical sense. And there is nothing in this understanding of logical supervenience which entails that it is possible to 'read off' supervenient facts from subvenient ones.

Secondly, I have argued that the idea of being able to 'read off' logically supervenient facts armed *only* with knowledge of the subvenient facts is a deeply misguided ideal. In order to 'read off' the supervenient facts from the subvenient ones, even where the supervenience in question is logical, one must know in what the instantiation of a supervenient property consists, and this is knowledge that cannot be constructed from knowledge of subvenient facts alone.

The problem for Chalmers' argument now emerges. If we divorce the epistemological construal from the misguided idea that it is possible to 'read off' supervenient from subvenient facts alone, then consciousness most certainly does not stand on its own in failing to logically supervene on the physical. On the epistemological construal of logical supervenience, properly understood, many, and almost certainly most, facts will fail to supervene logically on the physical.

The reason is that what logical supervenience, understood epistemologically, means is that it is not possible to assert that two objects are identical with regard to their subvenient properties while distinct with regard to their supervenient properties *without exhibiting a form of conceptual confusion*. And, in this sense, most supervenience is *not* logical in character. It is possible, to use a favourite example of Chalmers, to assert that two objects are physically (in Chalmers' basic sense) identical but biologically distinct without exhibiting conceptual confusion, without contradicting oneself in the broadly logical sense. (Actually, to allow for the fact that not all biological properties are local, we should perhaps formulate this claim in terms of worlds. This qualification, however, is unimportant for present purposes.) Someone might believe, perhaps, that certain biological properties, life, for example, are not physical properties of individuals, but, say, non-physical gifts of God. Such a person may be grossly mistaken or misguided, she may be very confused, but it does not seem that her confusion here is conceptual in character. This form of biological dualism may be incorrect, but it does not seem that it is contradictory, even in the broadly logical sense.

So, if the epistemological construal of logical supervenience is understood in the way I have suggested it should be (and typically is) understood, then most supervenient properties fail to supervene logically on their bases. But this, surely, means that failure of logical supervenience in this epistemological sense does not entail failure of reductive explanation. The failure of consciousness to logically supervene, epistemologically speaking, on physical facts no more entails that consciousness cannot be reductively explained, than the corresponding failure of logical supervenience in the case of biological facts on (basic) physical facts entails that the former cannot be reductively explained in terms of the latter. Thus, again to use one of Chalmers' flagship examples, the logical possibility of a zombie that is microphysically identical to oneself can be taken to entail the failure of reductive explanation of consciousness only if the failure of biological properties to logically supervene on physical ones can be taken to entail the failure of reductive explanation of the former in terms of the latter. And it is not clear who would want to claim this. In short, if we understand logical supervenience in epistemological terms, then the failure of consciousness to logically supervene on the physical simply puts consciousness on a par with most other facts and properties, and can be taken to entail the failure of reductive explanation of consciousness only if we are willing to countenance an extremely widespread failure of such explanation generally. Therefore, if we understand logical supervenience in an epistemological sense, there is no reason for believing premise 1 of Chalmers' argument.

On the other hand, as we saw earlier, if we understand logical supervenience in an ontological sense, then there is no reason for thinking that consciousness fails to supervene logically on the physical. Understood ontologically, *all* supervenience is logical supervenience. Therefore, if we understand logical supervenience epistemologically, premise 1 should be rejected. If we understand it ontologically, premise 2 must go. If this is correct, then Chalmers' argument gains its apparent plausibility only through understanding supervenience ontologically in premise 1 and epistemologically in premise 2. The fallacy is, thus, one of equivocation.

Indeed, even to identify the mistake present in Chalmers' argument as one of equivocation is, perhaps, too generous. If the arguments developed in this chapter are correct, then Chalmers' ontological interpretation of supervenience is incoherent, and his epistemological interpretation is misguided. Thus, Chalmers does not even appear to have put the relevant concepts in place, ones with which it might be subsequently possible to equivocate. The argument, that is, does not even appear to get as far as a fallacy of equivocation.

3   The explanatory gap

It was Colin McGinn's important paper 'Can we solve the mind–body problem?' (McGinn 1989, 1991) which was, more than any single work, responsible for pitching consciousness back into the spotlight of philosophical preoccupation:

> How is it possible for conscious states to depend on brain states? How can Technicolor phenomenology arise from soggy grey matter? What makes the bodily organ we call the brain so radically different from other bodily organs, say the kidneys – the body parts without a trace of consciousness? How could the aggregation of millions of individually insentient neurones generate subjective awareness? We know that brains are the *de facto* causal basis of consciousness, but we have, it seems, no understanding whatever of how this can be so. It strikes us as miraculous, eerie, even faintly comic. Somehow, we feel, the water of the physical brain is turned into the wine of consciousness, but we draw a total blank on the nature of this conversion. (1991: 1)

Similar sentiments are echoed by Joseph Levine, David Chalmers, and others. The problem, here, is one of providing a physical explanation of phenomenal consciousness. The 'gap' between consciousness and the brain is essentially an explanatory gap rather than an ontological one. No matter how much we know about the brain, no matter how intricate, detailed and sophisticated our knowledge of the brain becomes, no matter how much headway we make in understanding the biology, chemistry, and even physics, of the brain, we shall still be at a loss to see *how* the brain produces consciousness. We know *that* the brain does it, hence no ontological gap, but we do not know *how*, hence the explanatory one.

At the outset, I suppose I should confess that, after resisting McGinn's position for ten years or so, I now strongly suspect that it, or something very like it, may well be correct. Nevertheless, in this chapter I shall present some arguments against McGinn's position. I understand that these arguments will not be found compelling by everyone, least of all by McGinn. My confidence in them, as one might gather, is less than absolute. Indeed, my faith in them is limited to the following: *if* there is a problem with McGinn's position, or hiatus in his argument, *then* I think that the objections developed in this chapter come pretty close to identifying it.

In this spirit, then, I shall argue that our failure to see how the brain produces consciousness is compatible with there being an explanation of how it produces consciousness, and, crucially, this explanation can be one that we are perfectly willing to recognise as adequate. Paradoxically, our failure to understand how the brain produces consciousness is compatible with our being in possession of, and understanding, what we accept is an adequate, indeed correct, explanation of how the brain produces consciousness. In other words, we should clearly distinguish, on the one hand, the idea of *seeing how the brain does it* from, on the other, the idea of an *adequate* neural explanation of consciousness. Conditions of adequacy for neural explanations of consciousness should not be cashed out in terms of our ability to see how the brain produces consciousness.

1   Intuitions and arguments

There are two strands of McGinn's position which must be kept separate on pain of misunderstanding its dialectical underpinning. McGinn's explanatory gap argument is not an argument in the usual sense of the word. It is not, that is, a deductively valid movement from premises to conclusion, and any attempt to evaluate it in these terms is to miss the point. Rather, the *argument* has two components (cf. Van Gulick 1993). Firstly, there is an *intuition*: no matter how much we know about the brain, this will never allow us to see *how* it produces consciousness. Secondly, there is the attempt to explain why the suspicion expressed in the intuition should in fact be true. That is, there is the attempt to give reasons for thinking that the intuition is a good one, one which may well turn out to be correct. So, it would be a mistake to object to McGinn's position on the grounds that he has not proved or demonstrated that consciousness cannot be explained in terms of brain processes: he has attempted to do no such thing. The strength of McGinn's argument lies in the plausibility of the intuition, plus the cogency of the reasons for thinking that the intuition might be true. And it is, of course, possible to accept the intuition without endorsing McGinn's reasons for thinking the intuition is, or is likely to be, true. This chapter is concerned largely with the intuition. This section, however, briefly considers the arguments McGinn uses to support the intuition, and the relation these supporting arguments bear to the intuition itself.

McGinn's argument in support of the intuition can be expressed (largely in his own words) as follows:

1. 'There exists some property P, instantiated in the brain, in virtue of which the brain is the basis of consciousness' (1991: 6).
2. 'There seem to be two possible avenues open to us in our aspiration to identify P . . . investigating consciousness directly . . . or . . . study of the brain' (1991: 7).
3. Direct investigation of consciousness cannot identify P.
4. Empirical study of the brain cannot identify P.

---

5. Therefore, we cannot identify P.

In this distillation of McGinn's argument (as presented in McGinn 1989, 1991 ch. 1), P is regarded as a property of the brain in virtue of which the brain produces consciousness. Elsewhere (McGinn 1991, chs 3 and 4), P is represented as a property of consciousness in virtue of which it is produced by the brain. The arguments may appear very different, but McGinn has argued, plausibly, that they are equivalent. And certainly, the supporting considerations McGinn provides in premises 3 and 4 are applicable, with small modifications, whichever way P is understood. Therefore, I shall accept McGinn's claim of equivalence and focus simply on this form of the argument.

Premise 1 is an expression of McGinn's naturalistic position, and is not controversial. Consciousness, whatever it should turn out to be, is not a supernatural feature of the world. Premise 2 simply reflects the fact that our access to consciousness, unlike our access to anything else, can be mediated by both first- and third-person perspectives. The controversial premises are 3 and 4.

Consider, first, McGinn's defence of premise 3. Direct investigation of consciousness, of course, takes the form of introspection. And, McGinn argues, it is fairly obvious that introspection alone cannot enable us to identify P. If it could, then we would be able to solve the problem of consciousness simply by introspecting. The problem is that introspection gives us access to only one term of the mind–body problem. It reveals our experience to us, but it does not reveal to us the way in which this experience depends on the brain. Introspection simply does not present conscious states *as* depending on the brain. Nor does it seem possible, McGinn argues, to extract P from the concepts of consciousness which introspection does bequeath us by some procedure of conceptual analysis. It seems no more plausible that we could, by conceptual analysis, identify the way in which consciousness depends on the brain than we could discover, by such analysis, how life depends on more basic physical processes. Therefore, McGinn claims, the faculty of introspection is *cognitively closed* with respect to P.

McGinn's defence of premise 4 comes in two parts. First, he argues that P is perceptually closed to us; P, that is, is not an observable feature of the brain. Secondly, he extends this claim from one of perceptual closure to one of conceptual closure by arguing that no form of inference from what is perceived in the brain can lead us to P (1991: 11).

The argument for perceptual closure begins with the thought that 'nothing we can imagine perceiving in the brain would ever convince us that we had located the intelligible nexus we seek' (1991: 11). No matter what property, no matter how complex and abstruse, we could see instantiated in the brain, we would always remain mystified as to how it could give rise to consciousness. The reason, McGinn thinks, for our befuddlement on this score lies in the fact that the senses are geared to representing a spatial world and, as such, essentially represent things as existing in space and with spatially defined properties. And it is precisely such properties that are incapable of solving the problem of consciousness. Consciousness cannot be linked to the brain by way of the spatial properties of the brain; it defies explanation in such terms. Therefore, P is not a perceptible property of the brain.

This claim is then extended to that of conceptual closure in the following way. Our introduction of theoretical (i.e. non-observational) concepts into a given domain obeys a certain principle of *homogeneity*. Thus, for example, we arrive at the concept of a molecule by taking our perceptual representations of macroscopic objects and conceiving of smaller objects of the same general kind. However, this will not work in the case of P, since analogical extensions of whatever properties it is that we observe in the brain are precisely as useless as the original properties were in explaining how the brain produces consciousness. If observable properties, being spatial, are inappropriate for explaining consciousness then, given this principle of homogeneity, so too will be any properties we postulate on the basis of observable properties.

On the face of it, the argument may seem puzzling in that it does not really yield the conclusion McGinn seems to require. The intuition McGinn is seeking to support is this:

(1) We cannot understand how the brain produces consciousness.

But the conclusion the argument seems to yield is this:

(2) We cannot identify the property of the brain in virtue of which it produces consciousness.

So the question is whether (2) entails (1). Does our failure to identify the property of the brain in virtue of which it produces consciousness entail that we cannot understand how the brain produces consciousness? And once we understand what is involved in McGinn's idea of identifying P, then it is in fact fairly clear that it does.

The crucial point is that whatever property P turns out to be, it will be some form of higher-order, theoretical, property, and not one that is perceptually basic. P is not (*pace* Garvey 1998) something that can be discovered by poking and slicing our way around a brain. Representational properties of objects, for example, are such higher-order properties. And no matter how much we slice up or poke around in a book, this is not going to tell us what the book is about, nor will it tell us which properties the book has in virtue of which it is about something. Similarly, no physical or chemical analysis of the water in a wave will tell us whether it is, as surfers say, 'workable'. Or consider Ryle's classic example, used to make a somewhat different point (1949: 18). No matter how much we poke around in various colleges, libraries, playing fields, museums, and administrative offices, we will not find the university. The university is a higher-order organisational (i.e., broadly speaking, 'theoretical') property, and to find it we cannot just look, we need to know *how* to look.

More generally, higher-order properties of objects are not, at least not typically, properties that one can just pick out by any means. In order to pick out such properties, one has to 'look' at objects which possess them in the right way. One cannot just 'see', such objects, one must 'see', them *as*. And what this means, very roughly, is that one must conceptualise the relevant object in the right way. And what *this* means, very roughly, is that one must carve up the object according to the joints provided by an appropriate theory. Chemical theory is not, for the surfer, the right theory for carving up a wave, at least not if he wants to see if it is a long, workable, break. And, in order to see the university *as* a university, we need to understand the organisational, social, economic and cultural (i.e., broadly speaking, the theoretical) setting in which the university, so to speak, emerges from the colleges, libraries, administrative offices, and the like. Theories provide us with categories, and categories provide us with a way of seeing an object *as*; seeing it, that is, in the right way. And McGinn's point, then, is that we do not have – indeed, if he is right we cannot develop – the right sort of theory for seeing the brain in such a way that P is revealed. It is as if we tried to see the university by staring more and more intently at the various buildings that constitute it.

Therefore, given McGinn's account of what is involved in the identification of P, understanding how the brain produces consciousness, and identifying P, are intrinsically connected, precisely because the former understanding requires an appropriate theoretical conceptualisation of the brain and this conceptualisation will automatically yield an identification of P. Thus, if we cannot identify P this is because we have not achieved the correct theoretical conceptualisation of the brain. And this means we will not be able to explain how the brain produces consciousness.

If there is a problem with McGinn's arguments in support of the intuition then, I think, it is this: the arguments supporting the intuition are not separable from the intuition itself. Indeed, the arguments appear to simply collapse back into the intuition they purport to underwrite. This collapse is most notable in McGinn's defence of premise 4.

In defending premise 4, McGinn first argues that P is perceptually closed to us, then goes on to extend this to conceptual closure. Consider, first, how he defends perceptual closure.

The argument for perceptual closure starts from the thought that nothing we can imagine perceiving in the brain would ever convince us we have located the intelligible nexus we seek . . . I hereby invite you to try to conceive of a perceptible property of the brain that might allay the feeling of mystery that attends our contemplation of the brain–mind link: I do not think you will be able to do it. (1991: 11)

However, it is pretty clear that this claim is simply another formulation of the intuition McGinn is trying to defend and, as such, cannot be employed as *support* for the intuition.

McGinn then goes on to offer an explanation of *why* we are incapable of conceiving of a perceptible property of the brain that provides the required intelligible nexus. He writes:

Basically, I think, it is because the senses are geared to representing a spatial world; they essentially present things in space with spatially defined properties. But it is precisely *such* properties that seem inherently incapable of resolving the mind–body problem: we cannot link consciousness to the brain in virtue of spatial properties of the brain . . . We simply do not understand the idea that conscious states might intelligibly arise from spatial configurations of the kind disclosed by perception of the world. (1991: 11–12)

However, this claim, again, seems little more than a restatement of the original intuition, this time in slightly modified form. Now, instead of the intuition that it is impossible (for us) to understand how consciousness might arise from physical processes, we have the intuition that it is impossible (for us) to understand how consciousness might arise from spatial processes, or from physical processes in virtue of their spatial character. But this claim can in no way be regarded as supporting the intuition; it is simply another version of that intuition.

Consider, now, McGinn's extension of perceptual closure to conceptual closure. If observable properties, being spatial, are inappropriate for explaining consciousness then, he argues, given the *homogeneity constraint* on concept introduction, so too will be any properties we postulate on the basis of observable properties. He writes:

Suppose we try out a relatively clear theory of how theoretical concepts are formed: we get them by a sort of analogical extension of what we observe. Thus, for example, we arrive at the concept of a molecule by taking our perceptual representations of macroscopic objects and conceiving of smaller scale objects of the same general kind ... but [this] will not help in arriving at P, since analogical extensions of the entities we observe in the brain are precisely as hopeless as the original entities were as solutions to the mind–body problem. (1991: 13)

Why are analogical extensions as 'hopeless as the original entities'? Presumably, because they are concepts of the 'same general kind' as the originals. In particular, if the original observational concepts are spatial, then so too will be the analogical extensions of those concepts. However, this means that McGinn's argument at this juncture is simply a restatement of the original intuition: we cannot imagine how anything spatial can produce consciousness. Even here, we are, essentially, no further along than restatement of intuition.

I think we should conclude that many (but perhaps not all) of McGinn's purported supporting arguments for the original intuition that consciousness cannot be physically explained cannot be accepted for the simple reason that they are not really supporting arguments at all but merely restatements, sometimes in slightly modified form, of that very intuition. However, this does not mean that the arguments are worthless. Far from it. Rather, it means that it is necessary to reassess their status. They are best understood, I think, not as attempts to support the original intuition, but, rather, as attempts to explicate and render more precise the content of that intuition. And nothing that has been said so far in any way undermines the intuition itself. Indeed, the intuition is, I think, a very profound one. And the plausibility of McGinn's position rests ultimately on this. Consequently, I think, McGinn's position can only seriously be damaged by an attack on the intuition itself. It is to an examination of this intuition that we now turn.

2   Analysing the intuition

The intuition to be explored, then, is this: no matter how much we know about the brain, this knowledge will never enable us to see *how* the brain produces consciousness. Upon further analysis, however, this intuition fragments into two logically separate claims, both of which are clearly evident in McGinn's argument. The first claim is this:

(1) A physical explanation of consciousness must proceed by way of identification of a *mechanism*. Mere correlation between brain states, properties, or processes and conscious states, properties, or processes is not enough.

Clearly, McGinn is committed to a claim of this sort. If a physical explanation of consciousness required only correlations between conscious and neural states, then not only would there *not* be any deep problem with providing an explanation of consciousness, we would, in fact, already be in possession of such an explanation. Correlations are not sufficient; a genuine (physical) explanation of consciousness must be based on the identification of underlying neural structures or mechanisms that are responsible for consciousness.

Moreover, if an underlying neural mechanism is to explain consciousness, then it must do so by eliciting in us a certain kind of insight:

(2) The neural mechanism that explains consciousness must allow us to see *how* consciousness is produced by the brain. The link between consciousness and the brain must be made intelligible (to us) by this mechanism.

This presupposition is clearly evident in just about everything McGinn has written about the problem of consciousness. Thus, the problem of consciousness, for McGinn, is a problem precisely because the production of consciousness by the brain 'strikes us as miraculous, eerie, even faintly comic' (1991: 1). Thus, no matter what property of the brain we imagine, there is a problem because 'we should always be baffled about how it could give rise to consciousness' (1991: 11). Accordingly, a genuine explanation of consciousness works to the extent, and only to the extent, that it allays 'the feeling of mystery that attends our contemplation of the brain–mind link' (1991: 11).

Both assumptions seem, *prima facie*, to be uncontroversially true. I shall argue, however, that both are, in fact, very questionable. The following sections examine claim (2).

3   Truth and adequacy

This section is concerned with assumption (2), the assumption that a reductive, mechanistic, explanation of consciousness must allow us to see *how* the brain produces it. In this section and the next, I shall argue that (2) is too simplistic. Future sections will examine ways of rehabilitating (2). However, I shall argue that such rehabilitations offer little support to McGinn's claim that there is an explanatory gap between consciousness and the brain.

This section is concerned with the concept of explanatory adequacy. It is important, at the outset, to distinguish this notion, at least as employed here, from the notion of explanatory truth. The adequacy of an explanation E does not consist in the truth of E. Rather, the adequacy of E, *as I shall use the term*, consists in its being taken, or accepted, as an explanation by us. This is an epistemic notion of adequacy, to be distinguished both from the notion of truth and from more familiar formal notions like simplicity, coherence, universality, etc. An explanation, on this usage, can be adequate even if it is not true, and even if it fails to meet familiar formal conditions of adequacy. The reason for this somewhat aberrant usage is simple. McGinn is quite willing to allow (indeed, insist) that there is a true explanation of how the brain produces consciousness. His claim, however, is that this explanation is not one that can be understood, therefore rationally accepted, by us. The crux of the issue, then, concerns not what is necessary for an explanation of consciousness to be true, but what is necessary for such an explanation to be understood, therefore accepted, by us.

Therefore, at present, I am concerned, primarily, with what is required for an explanation to be taken by us *as* an explanation. I am concerned, that is, with what is involved, and what is required, for us to accept an explanation as a potential explanation of a given phenomenon, as something capable, in principle, of doing the explanatory work required of it; in short, as an explanation that *might* be true, whether or not it in fact turns out to be so.

Failure to keep the distinction between explanatory truth and explanatory adequacy (in this sense) clearly in view will make the arguments to be developed in the following section appear rather trivial. For, I shall argue that the concept of explanatory adequacy, even as understood here, is not to be confused with certain types of inner processes occurring in would-be explainers. Conflating explanatory adequacy with explanatory truth would make this seem as if I am merely rehearsing the familiar point that the truth of a claim is independent of the inner states or processes of the subject who makes it. This, however, is not my point. Rather, I shall argue that what makes a subject understand an explanation as an explanation cannot be explained in terms of the sorts of inner processes that are commonly understood to constitute it. In particular, what makes a subject understand an explanation as an explanation cannot be explained in terms of the sort of inner processes McGinn appears to think are required for an explanation of consciousness.

4   Explanatory adequacy and epistemic satisfaction

Some explanations produce in us a feeling of what I shall call *epistemic satisfaction*. This is a feeling whose content we might characterise in terms of expressions such as 'Now I understand!', or 'Now I've got it!' An archetypal example of epistemic satisfaction is provided by the presumably fictitious account of Archimedes leaping from his bath and crying 'Eureka!', having been struck by the force of his revelation concerning displaced volume. And, perhaps no less fictitiously, Kekule is reported to have woken from dreams of snakes with their tails in their mouths, to realise for the first time that benzene has the structure of a ring. Epistemic satisfaction is the 'Eureka!' feeling; the feeling that 'Now I've got it', 'Now I understand' (or, following Wittgenstein, 'Now I can go on!'). The question to be explored in this section is whether the concept of explanatory adequacy can be explained in terms of epistemic satisfaction.

Consider, first, a good example of a mechanistic explanation which does seem to produce epistemic satisfaction. Graphite is an allotrope of carbon that has certain well-known macro-properties: ability to mark paper, to act as a lubricant, and so on. The explanation of these is that graphite consists in layers of carbon arranged in hexagonal rings. The atoms in each layer are covalently bonded to three neighbouring atoms at an angle of 120 degrees to each other. Within each layer, the covalent forces binding each atom to its neighbours are relatively strong. However, the layers themselves are bound together only by the very weak van der Waals forces. As a result, adjacent layers can slide over one another – resulting in the soft, flaky nature of graphite, its ability to mark paper, and its utility as a lubricant, etc.

This explanation produces, in me at least, and I suspect in most others, a feeling of *epistemic satisfaction*. If we assimilate all explanation to this stereotype, we will be tempted to suppose that our taking an explanation to be an explanation consists in, or is at least necessarily connected with, its producing epistemic satisfaction. That is, we will be tempted into thinking that the adequacy of an explanation consists in the epistemic satisfaction that it provokes. However, I think that such an account of explanatory adequacy rests, as Wittgenstein put it, on a one-sided diet of examples. Epistemic satisfaction, I shall try to show, is not a necessary condition of explanatory adequacy.

I shall remain neutral on the question of whether epistemic satisfaction is *sufficient* for explanatory adequacy. It is, of course, readily apparent that epistemic satisfaction is not a sufficient condition for explanatory correctness or truth: how often have we had the feeling 'Now I understand' ('Now I can go on') only for subsequent events to show us that we did not really understand at all. Explanatory adequacy, however, is not the same thing as explanatory truth. To say that an explanation is adequate is, according to present usage, to say that it is the sort of account that we recognise might be true, whether or not it in fact is. Epistemic satisfaction, at least *prima facie*, certainly seems sufficient for this. However, that it is is something I shall neither assume nor deny. My focus is on the question of whether epistemic satisfaction is necessary for explanatory adequacy, since establishing a negative answer to this question would be enough to show that an explanation of consciousness would not have to elicit epistemic satisfaction in order to be recognised by us as a (potential) explanation of consciousness.

Consider, now, another molecular explanation: that of solidity. This explanation is based on the idea that what makes a substance solid is the fact that its atoms combine together to form a rigid lattice structure. This is usually the result of ionic bonding, bonding that results from the transfer of an electron or electrons from the outer orbit of one electron to those of another. The resulting ions are, thus, held together strongly by electrostatic attraction. Covalent compounds, where the bonding is much weaker, generally occur as solids only at very low temperatures (except macromolecular compounds such as diamond and its allotropes; these are essentially giant molecules).

Michael Tye (1999) is one, among many others, who thinks that the molecular explanation of solidity is epistemically satisfying in the same sort of way as (I have claimed) is the explanation of (some of) the macro-properties of graphite: 'Once one understands that in solid things, the molecules are not free to move around as they are in liquids, one immediately grasps that solid things do not pour easily, that they tend to retain their shape and volume ... What it is for something to be solid is for it to be disposed to retain its shape and volume (roughly)' (1999). Very roughly. In fact, I think so roughly that this tends to undermine, to a considerable extent, Tye's claim.

A model of a molecule, made of balls fastened together by wire, can, if the wire is sufficiently rigid, retain its shape. It also does not pour easily, or, in fact, at all. It, of course, does not retain its volume. But the reaction of many children, upon being first presented with the molecular explanation of solidity, is to ask how solids can possibly retain their volume if they are, indeed, structured in this way (this is particularly true if they have already been presented with solar system analogies of atomic structure). Or, as they are more likely to put it, how can a solid object be made up of mostly empty space? And it is not as if the explanation has some latent property of epistemic satisfiability which manifests itself only after one has reached puberty. One comes to accept this as an adequate explanation for various reasons, some of which will be examined in the next section, but not, I think, because it is a natural conveyer of epistemic satisfaction.

The most natural response to this sort of objection is to accept that the epistemic satisfaction the explanation occasions is not what one might hope for under ideal conditions, but then explain away the less than ideal character of the conditions in terms of our empirical ignorance. According to this response, our failure to feel epistemically satisfied by the molecular explanation of solidity has to do not with the explanation as such but, rather, with our only partial acquaintance with it. That is, our failure to find the explanation epistemically satisfying is the result of our ignorance of the atomic level or quantum level facts and laws that underlie the specifics of molecular formation.

For example, we might explain the disposition of solids to retain their volume in terms of characteristics of the specifically ionic bonding that seems to be responsible for the solidity of (most of) those substances that can be solids at room temperature. Ionic bonding involves transfer of electrons between atoms, resulting in ions held together by electrostatic attraction. Covalent bonding, on the other hand, involves the sharing of electrons. Covalent bonds are not as powerful as ionic ones, hence most covalent substances tend to be liquids or gases at room temperature. So, we might try to explain the disposition of solids to retain volume as a specific feature of electrostatic attraction.

This strategy, however, merely pushes the problem back a stage. Why should an explanation of the disposition to retain volume couched in terms of features of ionic bonding be any more epistemically satisfying than the original explanation cast in terms of molecular structure? We know, for example, that ionic bonds, being electrostatic in character, are stronger than covalent ones. But what explains this? Something, of course, does. But, crucially, what reasons are there for supposing that *this* explanation will be any more epistemically satisfying than the original?

We might, then, try to explain the specific features of ionic bonding that lend solids the disposition to retain volume in lower level terms: by uncovering the relevant underlying quantum level mechanisms. For example, the disposition to retain its volume, possessed by a solid, might be explained in terms of electron orbits and exclusion, and the behaviour of electrons in this regard might be explainable in terms of the dynamics of wave interaction, superposition, and the like. And it might be thought that once we acquaint ourselves with the relevant laws of wave dynamics then all the rest will slip into place. Once we understand, for example, that waves behave in certain ways, that they can interfere with each other in ways that can both enhance and nullify their amplitudes, and so on, then everything else will fall into place. The relevant features of ionic bonding emerge quickly and easily from this account, and we use this to provide an epistemically satisfying account of the disposition of solids to retain volume.

However, once again, this merely pushes the problem back a stage (or two). In particular, why suppose that the explanation of the relevant features of ionic bonding in terms of wave dynamics is any more epistemically satisfying than the original explanation of the disposition to retain volume in terms of molecular structure? While it may be *true* that we can explain the relevant features of ionic bonding in terms of wave dynamics, is there any *a priori* reason to suppose that this explanation will be any more epistemically satisfying than the molecular explanation it underwrites? Why, for example, should waves behave in the manner specified by the laws of wave dynamics? The problem is that whenever we ground one explanation in a further one, and regard the epistemic satisfiability of the former as deriving from that of the latter, there is no *a priori* reason why the correlations appealed to in the latter explanation (wave dynamical property P – relevant feature Q of ionic bonds) should be any more epistemically satisfying than the correlations involved in the former (rigid lattice structure – solidity).

We can express this point in quite general terms. The idea under consideration is that we can, in principle, render a particular explanation more epistemically satisfying than it is, or seems to be, by appeal to the various physical laws that underwrite the explanation. The problem is, however, that there is no *a priori* reason why physical laws should be any more epistemically satisfying than the explanations they underwrite. Why *should* an object of mass m acted upon by a force F accelerate at rate F/m? Why *should* the pressure exerted by one mole of gas be nomically related to its temperature and volume according to the ideal gas law $pV = KT$? Why *should* the gravitational attraction between two massive bodies m_1 and m_2 be inversely proportional to the square of distance, d, between them? And if we attempt to render these laws more epistemically satisfying by deriving them from more basic laws, the problem is that there is no *a priori* reason why these more basic laws should be any more epistemically satisfying than the laws they underwrite.

Perhaps the idea is that once we have identified the ontologically basic natural laws, ones which underlie the workings of the universe, then total intelligibility will be ours; everything will fall into place, and epistemic satisfaction will be unbounded. The idea is that basic explanations would appeal to basic laws, and non-basic mechanistic explanations would be derivable from these basic laws. Suppose, now, that these basic laws had a kind of natural intelligibility: they immediately gave rise to epistemic satisfaction in human beings. Then it would be possible to have an account of the universe that yielded total intelligibility. The intelligibility, and the epistemically satisfying character, of the connection between rigid lattice structure and disposition to retain volume would follow from the general intelligibility yielded by the epistemically transparent nature of the basic laws. Every true explanation would be epistemically satisfying in the full-blooded sense, and this would derive ultimately from the epistemic transparency of the basic laws. This is quite a dream; one which I see no reason to believe is true. However, even if it is, it is of little relevance to the present discussion. If it were true, it would mean that epistemic satisfaction with regard to the molecular explanation of solidity and all explanations like it (i.e. non-basic explanations) would have to be postponed indefinitely; it cannot be attained in the absence of a fundamental theory of reality, one which identifies the epistemically transparent basic laws. On the other hand, if there is no basic level of reality, ultimate epistemic satisfaction would, presumably, have to be postponed not just indefinitely but eternally. Whichever of these alternatives turns out to be true does not matter. For it is pretty clearly true that we now, in the absence of such a fundamental theory, are quite happy to accept the molecular explanation of solidity, and countless other non-basic explanations, as perfectly adequate. We are quite happy to accept them, that is, as genuine explanations of what they purport to explain. And this means we cannot understand explanatory adequacy in terms of feelings of epistemic satisfaction.

On the basis of these considerations, I think we should be willing to countenance, albeit provisionally, the following idea. Conditions of adequacy for explanations cannot be explained in terms of epistemic satisfaction. The concept of explanatory adequacy, that is, cannot be explained in terms of this sort of *inner process*, at least not in the straightforward way envisaged. An explanation can be adequate even if it fails to elicit epistemic satisfaction. Epistemic satisfaction is, at most, a *typical accompaniment* of explanatory adequacy, but it is not constitutive of that adequacy because it is not necessary for that adequacy.

If this is correct, then it would be a mistake to hold up a reductive explanation of consciousness to these sorts of epistemic standards. It would be a mistake, that is, to understand the adequacy of a reductive explanation of consciousness as turning simply upon whether it elicits epistemic satisfaction. The case of consciousness is no different from other cases of reductive explanation in this regard. We *might* expect epistemic satisfaction to accompany an adequate explanation of consciousness, but we should not invest too much in this expectation. More importantly, we should not regard such epistemic satisfaction as *constitutive* of the adequacy of a reductive explanation of consciousness.

5   Proto-epistemic satisfaction

The above rejection of the claim that the concept of explanatory adequacy can be understood in terms of epistemic satisfaction is, of course, only part of the story. Remember, the adequacy of an explanation is, on the present construal, distinct from the correctness or truth of that explanation. To say that an explanation of event P is adequate is to say that we accept it as a genuine contender for a true explanation of P. It is an explanation that we are prepared to accept *might* be true, whether it in fact turns out to be; it is one, in short, that we are prepared to consider might be a worthy candidate for truth. This means that the rejection of the idea that explanatory adequacy can be explicated in terms of epistemic satisfaction must be accompanied with a positive account of in what terms the concept of explanatory adequacy *can* be explicated. What is required, that is, is a positive account of the factors in virtue of which we are able to recognise an explanation *as* the sort of thing that could be an explanation, true or otherwise. This is the task of the present section.

The factors involved in constituting the adequacy of an explanation are, I think, complex and manifold. And I cannot, in a work of this sort, do justice to all of them. Indeed, I shall not even mention the properly *formal* factors involved. Instead, I shall focus on the psychological factors involved, since these are, given the framework within which McGinn has located the dispute over consciousness, more pertinent to the present discussion. First, however, it is worth briefly mentioning one of the social factors that, I think, is quite centrally implicated.

By the time we reach adulthood, most of us are quite happy with the molecular explanation of solidity, and this is true whether or not we have made ourselves familiar with the arcane matters of wave dynamics. One reason for this, I think, is broadly sociological. When we first learn the molecular explanation of solidity, we are told quite simply, though perhaps not precisely in these words, 'That's the way it is; and you had better accept it if you want to get on.' After years of this sort of *reinforcement*, we start to think of the explanation as if it were completely natural, as if it wore its epistemic satisfiability on its sleeve. But underlying this illusion of naturalness are many years of social pressure. We are trained to think: rigid lattice structure, therefore solidity; and the epistemically satisfying character of the explanation derives not simply from the nature of the explanation itself, but from the years of training that have gone into making us see the explanation in this way. This appeal to social pressures and the reinforcement they occasion may seem somewhat fatuous. And, if this were the *only* explanation of our disposition to accept the molecular explanation of solidity, it would indeed be so. However, as we shall see shortly, social pressures are not the only thing that underwrites explanatory adequacy; they combine with certain features of the explanation itself. What is distinctly more fatuous, I think, is the naive idea that epistemic satisfaction is a property that quite simply and naturally attaches to some explanations and not to others independently of the societal framework in which these explanations are devised, propounded, and propagated.

With respect to the molecular explanation of solidity, the social pressures, whose aim is to induct us into the scientifically literate community, are combined with, and reinforced by, a certain natural quality of the explanation itself. This natural quality is not epistemic satisfaction as such, but a sort of inchoate, proto-version of this quality. I shall refer to this as *proto-epistemic satisfaction*, the core concept of which is to be explained in terms of the notion of analogy.

Many influential studies have emphasised the role of analogy in directing or facilitating scientific development and, in particular, of explaining familiar but intransigent phenomena in a new, unfamiliar, way. Many of our best theories have had their origins in a provocative initial analogy, one that is flawed in many ways, but that subsequently proved to be a fruitful vehicle of understanding (Kuhn 1957, 1962, Hesse 1966). This is not the time to develop a general account of the role played by analogy in scientific explanation. However, it is possible to point out, in a somewhat unsystematic, but still, I think, quite useful, way the connections between analogy and explanatory adequacy.

Consider, again, the molecular explanation of solidity. While the explanation may not occasion the sort of epistemic satisfaction associated with the molecular explanation of (some of) the macro-properties of graphite, the explanation of solidity does, I think, produce a form of enlightenment, one that is carried, to a considerable extent, by the relations between, on the one hand, properties of the reducing domain and, on the other, those of the reduced domain. Thus, suppose we accept that a given substance or structure is composed of atoms tightly bound together, and each oscillating about a fixed point. We can then, with relative ease, accept that the addition of energy to this structure might increase the frequency of this oscillation. And then, also, that the addition of sufficient energy might increase the oscillatory frequency to the extent that bonds break down, or that the atoms become less tightly bound together. And the addition of yet more energy might increase this breakdown further, and so on. So, *if* we accept that solids are made up of a rigid lattice structure of oscillating atoms, we can also see that the difference between this sort of structure and one where the bonds are more diffuse is something like, somewhat analogous to, the difference between a solid and a liquid. And the difference between a substance with slightly loose atomic bonds and one with very loose atomic bonds is something like, somewhat analogous to, the difference between a liquid and a gas. In other words, we can see that the relations between solids, liquids, and gases is something like, in many ways analogous to, the relations between varying strengths of atomic bond. And in virtue of this, the molecular explanation of solidity possesses a certain proto-epistemic satisfaction.

This is not, or not necessarily, epistemic satisfaction in the full-blooded sense associated with the molecular explanation of the dispositions of graphite. One might still be at a loss to see how a rigid lattice structure can retain its volume. However, the claim that explanatory adequacy is constituted by epistemic satisfaction is far too rigid, at least if epistemic satisfaction is understood as a type of 'Eureka!' feeling. Far more realistic, I think, is to regard the psychological states that, in part, constitute our recognition or understanding of an explanation as adequate as comprising a spectrum of views, ranging from the full-blooded 'Eureka!' feeling at one extreme, to a nebulous, imprecise form of proto-epistemic satisfaction at the other. While it is plausible to suppose that any explanation we recognise as adequate must elicit some psychological states in us, and be accepted as adequate by us in virtue of this, the precise nature of these might vary quite considerably from one explanation to another. Slack generated by lack of full-blooded epistemic satisfiability will, correspondingly, be taken up by the social forces that induct us into the scientifically literate community.

Once the forces of scientific induction have gone to work, analogy can be brought further into play to increase the level of epistemic satisfaction associated with particular explanations. For example, in increasing the epistemic satisfaction elicited by an explanation it is sometimes possible to employ observational facts likely to be familiar to the recipient of the explanation. In sieving rocks, for example, the rapid oscillation of the rocks in the sieve can create the impression of an unbroken, solid, surface. And so on. And, one might think, this is something like, somewhat analogous to, how an atomic lattice composed of mostly empty space might appear solid. And the sophistication of the analogies will increase with the degree of one's induction into the scientifically literate community.

There is nothing in any of this, of course, which requires that the analogies employed be true (the previous one, for example, is not). Our concern, in this chapter, is not the truth but the adequacy of explanations. We are concerned, that is, with how we come to recognise an explanation as one that *might* be true. I have argued that explanations come to be recognised as adequate because, at least in part, they occasion in us either epistemic satisfaction, or proto-epistemic satisfaction, or, perhaps more commonly, something in between. Epistemic satisfaction, in the full-blooded sense, is an accompaniment of some explanations but not others. Therefore, it is not constitutive of the concept of explanatory adequacy, nor does it explain in general how we come to recognise explanations as adequate. Rather, many explanations are recognised to be adequate ones because they possess a certain proto-epistemic satis-fiability, and this is reinforced by certain pressures accompanying one's induction into the scientifically literate community.

6   Mechanistic explanations and correlations

The other idea underlying McGinn's intuition, and the consequent rejec-tion of reductive materialism, is that an explanation of consciousness must proceed by way of a *mechanism*. The mere correlation of conscious pro-cesses with brain processes is not enough. Such correlations must not only be identified, they must be explained by way of an underlying mechanism.

In this section I shall try to show that it is extremely misleading to set up an opposition between mechanisms and correlations in this way. Mechanisms are not opposed to correlations; they are ways of *structuring* correlations. Any mechanism is, in all essentials, constituted by a series of correlations that are structured so as to make their explanandum more intelligible than it otherwise would have been.

Consider one example of a primitive mechanism at work. Once upon a time, there was a game called Mousetrap. The purpose of the game was to 'trap' a plastic mouse by making a cage fall on it. The falling of the cage was mediated by a complex mechanism involving, if I remember rightly, a metal ball, uneven stairs, seesaws, a bucket, a man who dived into the bucket, and so on. This mechanism was constructed as the game went on and, so poor was its construction, the metal ball generally exited the mechanism long before its purpose of making the cage fall on the mouse was accomplished. Playstation really is so much better. I cannot actually remember how the movement of the ball was begun, but let's suppose it involves pulling a lever which releases the ball. Then, if the mechanism functioned properly, the end result would be the cage falling on the mouse. Let's suppose we have managed to get hold of a superior version of this game, where the mechanism did generally function prop-erly (i.e. the metal ball did not exit prematurely, etc.). Then we would have a correlation between the pulling of the lever and the cage falling on the mouse. This correlation by itself, however, would not explain how the pulling of the lever effected the falling of the cage and the trapping of the mouse. In order to explain this, we need the intervening mechanism.

What knowledge of the mechanism does, in effect, is break down the original correlation (pulling lever – cage falling) into a structured series of smaller correlations (e.g., ball dropping on a plank – man being propelled into the air – man landing in bucket – cage being shaken off perch, and so on). And the reason this makes the original correlation more intelligible is that each intervening correlation is more immediately intelligible than the original one. This is the sort of enlightenment provided by mechanisms.

Mechanisms break down a correlation into a structured series of smaller correlations, where each of the smaller correlations is more readily intelligible than the original bigger one. This means, and this is the conclusion I want to emphasise here, that mechanistic explanation is not something radically opposed to, or different from, the identification of correlations. On the contrary, mechanistic explanation is a specific form of correlation-based explanation. It may be that a correlation between two items can be rendered intelligible by the uncovering of an underlying mechanism. But this is not to replace the correlation with something fundamentally different; it is to break down, and thus explain, the correlation by means of further correlations.

With this in mind, consider, again, the molecular explanation of solidity. The temptation was to think that we can lend this genuine full-blooded epistemic satisfiability by uncovering the relevant underlying quantum level mechanisms. If the above argument is correct, however, then these mechanisms cannot be regarded as fundamentally different from the original correlation. They are, in fact, a structured series of further correlations. Thus, the correlation between possession of a rigid lattice structure and solidity might be seen to break down into correlations such as those between ionic bonding and electrostatic attraction, which in turn may break down into correlations between the number of electrons in a given orbit and the disposition to exclude or attract further electrons, which may, in turn, be broken down into correlations concerning wave superposition, and so on. But at no point are we left with mechanisms that must be regarded as distinct from correlations. The breaking down of a correlation can only ever yield a further correlation; and it is structured series of such correlations that we call mechanisms. Mechanistic explanation, ultimately, is always a form of correlation-based explanation.

This claim flies in the face of what passes for common sense on these matters. That staunch defender of such sense, John Searle, claims that correlation is not enough for explanation: after all, the flash of lightning does not explain the clap of thunder (1997). This is, of course, true. However, nothing that has been said so far entails that all correlations are explanations. The claim is that at least some correlations are explanations. Thus pointing to a correlation that is not explanatory really misses the point. More importantly, the case of thunder and lightning is misleading, and the reason for this is indicative of the difference between those correlations that are explanatory and those that are not. The reason the flash of lightning does not explain the clap of thunder is that both are symptoms of the same underlying causal mechanism. This seems the wrong sort of correlation to have explanatory value. If we want to preserve the relevance of the discussion to the issue of

consciousness, then the type of correlations we need to consider are either (i) those obtaining between underlying causes and their effects – for
example, between a massive electrical discharge to earth from a cloud
of ionised water particles and a clap of thunder – or (ii) those obtaining
between an underlying supervenience base property and the properties
that supervene upon them – for example, between molecular structure
and solidity. And these are precisely the right sorts of correlations to have
explanatory value. And this, ultimately, is, if the above arguments are
correct, in virtue of the fact that such correlations are susceptible to being broken down into a series of sub-correlations. Thus, the correlation
between an electrical discharge to earth from ionised water particles and
a clap of thunder can be broken down: the discharge produces (and is
thus correlated with) heat; heat causes (and is thus correlated with) a
rapid expansion of the air surrounding the discharge; this rapid expansion sets up, and is thus correlated with, a compression wave, and so on.
To speak of the causal mechanism underlying the flash of lightning and
clap of thunder is to speak of this sort of structured series of correlations. It is correlations between underlying causal mechanisms and their
effects, or between supervenience base properties and the properties that
supervene upon them, that can have explanatory value. Correlations between the effects, or between the supervenient properties, themselves, of
course, typically do not.

It seems unlikely that anyone would want to claim that the relation
between consciousness and the brain is a relation between two symptoms
of the same underlying mechanism. The brain itself *is* the mechanism. Or
rather, certain processes in the brain are the mechanisms that produce
consciousness. So, to make Searle's analogy relevant, we would have to
focus on the correlation between, say, the clap of thunder and the underlying causal mechanism. But, then, this correlation does appear to be
explanatory.

7   Explaining consciousness

Abstracting from some of the unnecessary detail, we can state the principal conclusions of the preceding sections as follows:

(1) Mechanistic explanation works by breaking down a correlation into a structured series of smaller correlations. Mechanistic explanation is a species of correlation-based explanation.

(2) The explanatory adequacy of a correlation-based explanation does not require
that it elicit in us epistemic satisfaction in any full-blooded sense. Rather, all
that is required for an explanation to be recognised as adequate is that it elicit

proto-epistemic satisfaction (subject to suitable reinforcement involved in our induction into the scientifically literate community).

To these we can, I think, add a third principle:

(3) There is not *an* explanation of consciousness. Rather, there are several (perhaps many) explanations of consciousness: as many as there are features of consciousness that require explanation.

To see this, consider again the case of solidity. There is no such thing as *the* explanation of solidity. Rather, there are at least two. There is an explanation of rigidity and there is an explanation of the disposition to retain volume. There is no *a priori* reason for expecting that the two explanations will turn out to be the same. For, *prima facie*, an explanation of rigidity is not an explanation of the disposition to retain volume. That is why ball and wire models of molecules can be rigid without retaining volume. Quite generally, to talk of *an* explanation of X is often shorthand for talk of a number of explanations of distinct features of X. This, I think, is precisely what we should expect in an explanation of consciousness: distinct explanations (possibly) of phenomenality, subjectivity, non-relationality, and so on. This is not to say that there must be an explanation for each feature commonly associated with consciousness: common associations can be naive ones. Rather, the point is that the concept of consciousness almost certainly fragments, upon analysis, into several quite distinct concepts. To some of these concepts there will correspond a property that, the preponderance of evidence will suggest, we can legitimately regard as a property of consciousness; to others there correspond properties, perhaps, that will turn out to be in some way illusory. But, however many distinct and legitimate properties of consciousness the preponderance of evidence suggests there are, it is likely that separate explanations will be required for each of them.

Moreover, what is regarded as a single property of consciousness, phenomenality for example, might turn out, upon analysis, to fragment into a variety of distinct properties. And, if these properties are genuinely distinct, we should expect that a separate explanation will be required for each of them (this expectation might, in any particular case, turn out to be incorrect; but it is surely a legitimate expectation). Let us, now, apply principles (1)–(3) to an explanation of consciousness.

If (1) and (2) are correct, then the implications for our understanding of what is involved in an explanation of consciousness are fairly clear. Firstly, (1), in explaining consciousness, we need not regard ourselves as doing anything fundamentally different than identifying certain types of correlation between neural and conscious states. Secondly, (2), we need not require that these correlations produce in us any full-blown feeling of epistemic satisfaction; proto-epistemic satisfaction will do. Thirdly, (3) the principles expressed in (1) and (2) apply to every explanation of distinct features of consciousness.

Consider how this general model of explanatory adequacy can be applied to a specific attempt to explain consciousness: the much vilified, in philosophical circles, attempt of Francis Crick and Christof Koch to explain consciousness (1990). According to Crick and Koch, 40Hz oscillations in the visual cortex and elsewhere may be the fundamental neural feature responsible for conscious experience. This is because 40Hz oscillations play a crucial role in the *binding* of various sorts of information into a unified and coherent whole. Two different kinds of information about a visual scene – the shape and distance of an object, for example – may be represented quite separately, but Crick and Koch suggest that these separate neural representations may have a common oscillatory frequency and phase-cycle, allowing the information to be bound together by later processes and stored in working memory.

It is easy to see why this proposal has attracted so much criticism from philosophers. For, *prima facie*, this does not seem to be anything even remotely like an explanation of consciousness; it is not simply that it is not a correct explanation of consciousness; it does not even seem to be an explanation of consciousness at all. Crick and Koch may have provided a neurobiological model of how disparate information might be integrated in working memory. And it might, with suitable elaboration, be developed into an account of how information is integrated and brought to bear in the global control of behaviour. However, what it is not, it seems, is an explanation of phenomenal consciousness. Crick and Koch have, in fact, presented only an account of how a certain functional capacity – the capacity for integration of disparate information – is implemented in the brain. But this would be an explanation of phenomenal consciousness only if it could be shown, I think it is fair to say counterintuitively, that such consciousness could be reduced to a feature of, or function of, the capacity for binding. Much further argument is required; Crick and Koch have not presented such argument; and it is, indeed, difficult to see what such further argument might look like. Indeed, Crick and Koch later seem to concede that their account does not provide an explanation of phenomenal consciousness.[1]

---

[1] In a published interview, Koch is quoted as saying: 'Well, let's first forget about the really difficult aspects, like subjectve feelings, for they may not have a scientific solution. The subjective state of play, of pain, of pleasure, of seeing blue, of smelling a rose – there seems to be a huge jump between the materialistic level, of explaining molecules and neurons, and the subjective level' (*Discover*, November 1992: 96). Crick (1994: 258) also admits the possibility that science may not explain qualia, although he is more cautious than Koch.

However, if the general account of explanatory adequacy sketched here is correct, Crick and Koch may have been too quick to concede. Admittedly, their account does not yield anything like full-blooded epistemic satisfaction with regard to the production of consciousness. However, it may yield proto-epistemic satisfaction with regard, not to conscious experience itself, but to one important feature of it. Conscious experience is, so to speak, presented all at once; it is presented as irreducibly *gestalt*. Compare, for example, the conscious experience of a visual scene with a corresponding description of the visual features of that scene. The description is presented in articulated fragments, ordered spatially (if the description is written) or temporally (if the description is spoken). The conscious experience of the scene is not like that at all; it is presented, so to speak, all at once.

The model of Crick and Koch, I think, provides a certain degree of proto-epistemic satisfaction with regard to the gestalt character of conscious visual experience. And, again, to the extent that there is some sort of epistemic satisfaction here, this derives from a certain type of analogy. The gestalt character of experience is *something like*, somewhat analogous to, disparate information that has been bound together in appropriate ways. And to the extent that there is information that has not been bound, this will not play a role in constituting the specific content of the conscious visual experience. Thus, we can see, at least to some extent, that changes in the quantities and types of information that are bound together at any one time will systematically vary with changes in the content of the visual gestalt.

There is, of course, more to the character of conscious experience than its being gestalt. Nevertheless, this is clearly one feature of such experience, and the Crick and Koch model provides an explanation of why it should possess this character. This is not, of course, to say that their explanation is correct. But it is to say that it may be, in my sense, *adequate*; it is an explanation that *might* be true. It might be adequate in virtue of, at least in part, eliciting in us proto-epistemic satisfaction; we can see how the gestalt nature of conscious experience is somewhat like, somewhat analogous to, packets of information that have been suitably bound.

A proper explanation of consciousness would have to do the same thing for all the features of conscious experience that are deemed essential or otherwise worthy of explanation. There is no such thing as *the* explanation of consciousness; there are many explanations, as many as there are essential features of consciousness. But all we should require of each of these explanations is that they consist in correlations which elicit in us some form of proto-epistemic satisfaction. To hold them up to any higher standard is to be unnecessarily, and unfairly, stringent.[2]

[2] The following objection is inspired by arguments developed by Chalmers, though not to be found explicitly in his writings. The object runs like this. The example of an explanatory gap I have chosen to focus on involves a tacit appeal to a consciousness-dependent property. Thus, while there is indeed an explantory gap between molecular structure and solidity, this in no way counts against the claim that only in the case of consciousness is there an explanatory gap, because solidity, as that property is used here, is a consciousness-dependent property. The point is perhaps clearer with respect to a property such as heat. In this case, as Kripke and others have pointed out, it is important to distinguish heat from the feeling of heat. Heat, understood as molecular motion, is not consciousness-dependent, but the feeling of heat certainly is. Similarly, we must distinguish solidity from the feeling, and more generally, the appearance, of solidity. It could be claimed that all the above argument shows is that there is an explanatory gap between molecular structure and the feeling or appearance of solidity, but not between molecular structure and solidity itself. But, then, this in no way undermines the importance of the explanatory gap in the case of consciousness. On the contrary, it is simply another form of consciousness-based explanatory gap.

The problem with this objection, however, is that it either begs the question or is trivial. In the case of heat, for example, a reduction looks something like this. We might regard this reduction as beginning with an initial characterisation of heat as that which produces certain feelings in us. To say that something is hot simply means that it produces hot feelings in us, to say that something is cold means that it produces cold feelings in us. The next stage is to identify various non-phenomenal properties of the objects that produce these feelings, properties which might explain this capacity of, but that are at least correlated with, the objects in question. Thus, we discover a reliable correlation between molecular motion of a certain kind in these objects and the production of feelings hot or cold in us. Finally, heat is redefined simply as those molecular occurrences themselves. The initial characterisation of heat as that which produces certain feelings in us has now given way to a characterisation that does not mention the production of feelings or other subjective states. Heat is, therefore, said to be 'nothing but' molecular motion.

Given this rough model of what is going on in the reduction of heat to molecular motion, suppose we were to understand heat in the non-phenomenal (i.e. reduced) sense. Then the claim that we cannot know everything about molecular motion without knowing that molecular motion is hot is simply the claim that we cannot imagine knowing everything about molecular motion without knowing that molecular motion is molecular motion. In other words, the claim is trivial. However, suppose we were to understand heat in the non-reduced sense, the sense in which heat is consciousness-dependent, then his claim would be that it is impossible to know everything about molecular motion without knowing that molecular motion is hot. But it is this sort of claim that the arguments of this chapter have tried to undermine. Therefore, to simply assert it, as in this imagined case, is to beg the question against those arguments. The present objection, then, is either question-begging or trivial.

Nor will this situation be dramatically improved should we appeal to the distinction between properties and concepts. If the claim is that we cannot imagine knowing everything about molecular motion conceptualised as molecular motion without knowing everything about molecular motion conceptualised as molecular motion, then the claim is trivial. If, on the other hand, the claim is that we cannot imagine knowing everything about molecular motion conceptualised as molecular motion without knowing everything about molecular motion conceptualised as heat, then the claim is nothing more than an assertion and, as such, simply begs the question against the arguments developed in this chapter. Once again, then, the present objection is either question-begging or trivial.

4   Consciousness and higher-order experience

The previous two chapters examined the mind–body problem, understood here as the attempt to explain consciousness in physical terms. More precisely, it examined two important attempts to argue that this could never be done. It was argued that these attempts were less than conclusive. In this, and the following, chapter, the focus switches to what is sometimes known as the *mind–mind* problem: the attempt to explain consciousness in terms of mental states and relations between such states.

1   HOR models of consciousness

'Consciousness is the perception of what passes in a man's own mind.' Thus wrote John Locke three hundred years ago. And the naturalness of this intuition has scarcely been eroded by the passage of time. Consciousness, we are tempted to assume, does not consist simply in an ordinary mental state or process, but rather in our *awareness* of such a state or process. The consciousness of a mental state or process is something added to it, something that becomes attached to the state or process by, or in virtue of, our standing in a certain relation to it, specifically, our standing in a relation of awareness to this state or process. This natural intuition receives its most recent expression in what are known as *higher-order representation* models of consciousness.

Higher-Order Representation (HOR) accounts of consciousness have, in recent years, been developed by, among others, David Armstrong (1981), Paul Churchland (1989), David Rosenthal (1986, 1990), Peter Carruthers (1996, 1998), and William Lycan (1987). HOR theories are attempts to explain consciousness not, or at least not directly, in physical terms, but, rather, in mental terms: in terms of the relation between one mental state and another, distinct, mental state that is related, in an appropriate way, to the first. Broadly, speaking, the idea is that the consciousness of the former mental state consists in, or derives from, its standing in this relation to the other, and, if this other mental state is non-conscious, then this constitutes an explanation of consciousness in non-conscious, albeit mental, terms.

In order to understand HOR models of consciousness, we first need two preliminary distinctions. The first is that between *creature* and *state* consciousness. The second is the distinction between *transitive* and *intransitive* consciousness.

We ascribe consciousness to at least two distinct types of thing. On the one hand we ascribe it to creatures, on the other, to mental states. Ascriptions to the former are ascriptions of creature consciousness, ascriptions to the latter are ascriptions of state consciousness. The property of a state's being conscious, it is argued, is plainly different from the property of a creature's being conscious for the simple reason that mental states are states of creatures and the properties of such states cannot be the same as the properties of creatures which have them (Rosenthal 1986, 1990). HOR theories aim to explain not creature but state consciousness. If some mental states are, while some are not, conscious, this must, it is thought, be in virtue of some difference between conscious and unconscious ones, and the goal of HOR theories is to explain in what this difference consists.

Consider, now, the distinction between transitive and intransitive consciousness. We sometimes speak of our being conscious *of* something. This is *transitive* consciousness. Transitive consciousness is most naturally understood as a form of creature consciousness. Mental states are not conscious of anything; rather, creatures are conscious of things in virtue, at least in part, of possessing certain sorts of mental states. However, in addition to transitive consciousness, we also speak of an individual or state of that individual being conscious. This is *intransitive* consciousness. Intransitive consciousness can be ascribed to both creatures and mental states. A creature that is intransitively conscious is one that is awake as opposed to asleep, or sentient as opposed to non-sentient. A mental state that is intransitively conscious, on the other hand, is, roughly, and without wishing to beg any questions, one that we are aware of having rather than one of whose presence we are unaware.

The goal of HOR accounts is to explain intransitive state consciousness, and the core intuition underlying the account is that intransitive state consciousness is to be explained in terms of transitive creature consciousness. Roughly, a mental state possessed by creature C is intransitively conscious if C is transitively conscious of it. More accurately, a mental state of C is intransitively conscious if C is transitively conscious of it, but is so without relying on any inference or observation of which it is transitively conscious (Rosenthal 1990: 10). The exclusion of reliance on inference or observation is meant to rule out those cases where C discovers that it possesses a given mental state – say anger – through being persuaded by the testimony of others or by self-observation of its behaviour. And the restriction of these excluded processes to *conscious* inference or observation is meant to allow for the possibility – indeed probability – that some of the processes whereby we learn of our own mental states, without the mediation of others or self-observation, are processes of non-conscious inference.

Now, of course, what is required is an account of what makes us transitively conscious of our mental states. And here, HOR accounts diverge. According to one version of the HOR model, our transitive consciousness of any given mental state is to be explained in terms of a higher-order *experience* we have of this state. Since this experience is typically regarded as quasi-perceptual in character, higher-order experience models of consciousness are standardly built around the idea of *internal scanning*. The intransitive consciousness of our mental states consists in their being scanned by a higher-order perceptual, or quasi-perceptual, mechanism. This is the model of consciousness endorsed by Locke. More recently it has been advocated by Armstrong ('Introspective consciousness is a perception-like awareness of current states and activities in our own mind'), Lycan ('Consciousness is the functioning of internal attention mechanisms directed upon lower-order psychological states and events'), and Churchland ('Introspective consciousness . . . appears very similar to one's perceptual consciousness of the external world. The difference is that, in the former case, whatever mechanisms of discrimination are at work are keyed to internal circumstances instead of to external ones . . .'). HOR accounts which claim that the higher-order state is perceptual or quasi-perceptual in character, I shall refer to as HOP models. HOP models are the subject of this chapter.

The other version of HOR rejects the idea that consciousness is essentially perceptual, or quasi-perceptual, in character. Intransitive state consciousness, on this view, consists in the presence not of a higher-order perceptual experience, but of a *higher-order thought*. That is, according to what I shall call higher-order thought (HOT) accounts of consciousness, the intransitive consciousness of any given mental state, M, possessed by subject S consists in S having a thought to the effect that it has, or is in, M. HOT models have recently been endorsed by Rosenthal (1986, 1990) and Carruthers (1996, 1998) and also, to an extent, by Dennett (1991). HOT models of consciousness will be discussed in the next chapter.

At the outset, it is worth pointing out that although HOR models are often criticised for their failure, or alleged failure, to account for phenomenal consciousness, it is not clear that they are intended as accounts of such consciousness anyway. Armstrong, for example, does not mention phenomenal consciousness as such, and advances his HOP model as an account of introspective consciousness, which he contrasts with perceptual consciousness. And it is not clear that the concept of introspective consciousness, in Armstrong's hands, is intended to be equivalent to that of phenomenal consciousness. Lycan (1990), however, is quite explicit that it is not, and that he does not intend his HOP model as an account of phenomenal consciousness. His disavowal here relies on a partitioning of the problem of consciousness into a problem of awareness, on the one hand, and a problem of phenomenal character, on the other. Rosenthal is more equivocal. On the one hand, he explicitly separates consciousness from 'sensory quality', and says he is giving only a theory of the first. This suggests that phenomenal consciousness lies outside the scope of his account. On the other hand, he does make several remarks that *suggest* his model is to be understood as an account of phenomenal consciousness. He claims, for example, that a state is conscious when there is something that it is like to be in that state, which suggests that his subject is phenomenal consciousness after all.

In any event, if HOP models are not intended as accounts of phenomenal consciousness, then this must be because of the presumed possibility of separating issues of introspective awareness from issues of phenomenal character. Such a presumption can, I think, be questioned, but I shall not question it here. Rather, I shall simply assume, with Lycan, that HOP and HOT models are *not* intended as models of phenomenal, but of introspective, consciousness. And the criticisms I shall direct against these models will be criticisms of their capacity to account for introspective consciousness. One thing is clear: if they fail even as accounts of introspective consciousness, then they have no chance of accounting for phenomenal consciousness.

Two caveats, however, are in order. Firstly, although HOR models may be intended only as accounts of introspective, and not phenomenal, consciousness, included in the category of introspectible states are phenomenal states. Thus, it is possible to ask, without assuming that HOR models are in the business of explaining phenomenal character, whether or not they give a satisfactory account of our introspective access to essentially phenomenal states. Much of the focus of the following discussion will, in fact, be provided by phenomenal states.

Secondly, I shall assume that any HOR model purports to provide a general account of in what the consciousness of mental states consists. Loosely speaking, on any HOR model, consciousness is added to a mental state from the outside; that is, in virtue of its standing in a certain relation to a distinct, higher-order, mental state. This means that HOR models are committed to the claim that, taken in itself, *no mental state is essentially conscious*. They are committed to this claim, and not the anodyne assertion that *some* mental states are not essentially conscious. If some mental states were conscious without standing in a relation to a higher-order representation, then the generality of the HOR account would be undermined. And then the obvious question would be: if some mental states can be conscious independently of their standing in an appropriate relation to a higher-order perception or thought, then what is so special about such higher-order states? In particular, if a mental state M can be conscious independently of its standing in an appropriate relation to a higher-order state, then it is difficult to see how it can be the relation to higher-order states as such that bestows consciousness on mental states distinct from M.

2 The structure of HOP theories

The classic recent statement of the higher-order experience model of consciousness is undoubtedly provided by Armstrong, and his statement proceeds by way of a now classic example:

> After driving for long periods of time, particularly at night, it is possible to 'come to' and realize that for some time past one has been driving without being aware of what it is one has been doing. The coming-to is an alarming experience. It is natural to describe what went on before one came to by saying that during that time one lacked consciousness. Yet, it seems clear that, in the two senses we have so far isolated, consciousness was present... That is to say, there was minimal consciousness and perceptual consciousness... But something else is lacking: consciousness in the most interesting sense of the word ... What is it that the long distance truck driver lacks? I think it is an additional form of perception, or, a little more cautiously, it is something that resembles perception. But unlike *sense*-perception, it is not directed towards our current environment and/or our current bodily state. It is perception of the mental. Such 'inner' perception is traditionally called introspection or introspective awareness. We may therefore call this third form of consciousness 'introspective' consciousness. (1981: 59–60)

Minimal consciousness, for Armstrong, is roughly equivalent to intransitive creature consciousness: an individual is minimally conscious if it is awake as opposed to asleep, or sentient as opposed to non-sentient (1981: 55–6), because minimal consciousness consists in the presence of certain occurrent mental activities: perception, sensation, thinking, and the like. However, this characterisation is broad enough to incorporate dreams: as a form of mental activity, dreams are sufficient for minimal consciousness. Perceptual consciousness, on the other hand, consists in the awareness of what is going on in one's environment. As such, it entails minimal consciousness (since awareness is a form of mental activity) but is not entailed by minimal consciousness (since dreams are sufficient for minimal consciousness but not for awareness of environmental occurrences).

It is introspective consciousness, however, that, for Armstrong, is 'consciousness in the most interesting sense of the word'. It is clear that the long-distance driver is conscious in the minimal and perceptual senses: driving the car without crashing, after all, requires that various quite complex mental processes be executed, many of which will, quite obviously, be perceptual in character. Nonetheless, it is possible for these processes to occur in the absence of introspective consciousness, and, in the case of the long-distance driver, Armstrong suggests, these processes actually do occur in the absence of such consciousness. When the driver comes to, this awakening, Armstrong claims, consists in the supplementation of minimal and perceptual consciousness with introspective consciousness: a quasi-perceptual awareness of the mental.

It is worth spending some time isolating the structure of this argument, since, I shall argue, in this structure are concealed several presuppositions, most of which, I shall try to show, are untenable.

Firstly, consider exactly what sort of change accompanies, as Armstrong would have it, the supplementation of minimal and perceptual consciousness with introspective consciousness. That is, what difference is there in the character of the experience of the driver when he 'comes to'? It is sometimes forgotten that the fundamental change is one in the character of *externally* directed awareness. When introspectively conscious, the driver is not only seeing the road, which he also is when he is merely perceptually conscious, he is now also aware that he is seeing the road: aware of the oncoming vehicles, aware that the light is changing to red, and so on. In this instance, and I think more generally, introspective consciousness, as employed by Armstrong, is intended to explain some form of heightened, attentive, observant but, fundamentally, externally directed awareness (Guzeldere 1995: 796). The function of introspective consciousness is to *augment* perceptual consciousness: to make it more vivid, heightened, attentive, and so on. The onset of introspective consciousness alters the character of externally directed awareness, moving it, so to speak, from the footlights to the full glare of the spotlight of consciousness. But it should not be forgotten that this is still a change in the character of externally directed awareness. Thus:

(1) CHANGES IN THE CHARACTER OF EXTERNALLY DIRECTED MENTAL STATE M

explained in terms of:

(2) INTRANSITIVE CONSCIOUSNESS OF STATE M

That is, when the externally directed state, a perception of the road for example, becomes more heightened, vivid, attentive and the like, this is because, according to the HOP model, the perception has changed from being introspectively intransitively unconscious to introspectively intransitively conscious. The perceptual state was always, of course, intransitively conscious in the minimal and perceptual senses. However, something is added with the onset of introspective awareness. It now becomes intransitively conscious in one more way: introspectively. And it is the addition of this further form of intransitive consciousness that explains the alteration in the character of the externally directed awareness.

HOR models, of course, explain the intransitive consciousness of mental states in a particular way: in terms of transitive creature consciousness *of* those states. This is characteristic of all forms of higher-order representation model. That is, the intransitive consciousness of any given mental state, M, is to be explained in terms of:

(3) THE TRANSITIVE CONSCIOUSNESS OF M BY THE SUBJECT OF M

Where the HOP model differs from the HOT model, of course, is in the account it gives of this transitive consciousness. According to the HOP model, the transitive consciousness of a mental state M by the subject, S, of M is to be explained in terms of S possessing a higher-order experience, of a quasi-perceptual character, of M. That is, (3) is explained in terms of:

(4) HIGHER-ORDER PERCEPTION OF M

Having isolated the logical structure of the HOP model, we can now identify the presuppositions implicated in it.

3   Presuppositions of the HOP model

The most obvious presupposition implicated in the HOP model is the claim implicated in the move from (2) to (3): intransitive state consciousness can be explained in terms of transitive creature consciousness. The acquiring of intransitive consciousness by a mental state M is to be explained in terms of the subject of M becoming transitively conscious (by way of a higher-order experience) of M. Equivalently, what marks the difference between a mental state that is intransitively conscious and one that is not is that, in the former case but not the latter, the subject of the state is transitively conscious of it. I shall refer to this as the principle of the *primacy of transitive consciousness* (PTC):

Primacy of transitive consciousness: intransitive (state) consciousness can be explained in terms of transitive (creature) consciousness.

The second, and almost as obvious, presupposition of the HOP model is implicated in the move from (1) to (3): mental states can exist independently of our consciousness of them. If it is *changes* in the character of externally directed mental states that are to be explained in terms of these states becoming intransitively conscious, and if this, in turn, is to be explained in terms of the subject of those states becoming transitively conscious of them, then this entails that mental states can exist (i) independently of their being intransitively conscious and (ii) independently of their subject being transitively conscious of them. These two formulations are, of course, equivalent on all higher-order representation models since such models are characterised by the claim that intransitive state consciousness is to be explained in terms of transitive creature consciousness. I shall refer to this claim as the *independence condition*.

Independence condition: The presence of any given mental state, M, in a subject S, is independent of S being introspectively conscious of M.

This is a widely acknowledged entailment of the HOP model, and the reasons for this are intuitively clear. According to the HOP model, consciousness is not a property that is intrinsic to any given first-order mental state, but one that is added to it by its standing in an appropriate relation to a second-order perceptual or cognitive state, a state that is *of* the first-order state. Thus, first-order mental states are not essentially conscious ones. Indeed, neither are second-order ones. The HOP model (like its HOT cousin) attempts to reductively explain intransitive consciousness in terms of what is not intransitively conscious. The explanans is, in any given case, admittedly mental, but, if the model is not to be either circular or regressive, then the second-order state cannot be intransitively conscious. Thus, a presupposition of HOP accounts is the *independence* of mental states and consciousness. A mental state can, logically, exist independently of our being conscious of it. It becomes an intransitively conscious state when, and only when, there is a higher-order perception of it.

There is a further, less obvious, entailment implicated in the move from (1) to (3). According to the move, a change in the character of externally directed awareness is to be explained in terms of a change in internally directed awareness. Actually, the designations 'internal' and 'external' do not get quite to the heart of the issue. Perceptual awareness can, of course, be directed towards states of the body as well as the environment, and so in one clear sense need not be externally directed. What is crucial is the idea that changes in the character of environmental awareness, construed broadly enough to include states of the body as well as the world, are to be explained in terms of awareness or consciousness of those mental representations in virtue of which we are environmentally aware. Whichever way we formulate the move from (1) to (3), however, the core idea remains the same. Implicated in the move from (1) to (3) is the idea that the character of our experience of the environment (e.g. its level of vividness) is to be explained in terms of our awareness or consciousness of the properties in virtue of which we have that experience. That is, the way our experience seems to us (vivid, heightened, attentive or otherwise) is to be explained in terms of our awareness of the properties in virtue of which we have that experience. Equivalently, the character of our awareness of the environment (broadly construed) is to be explained in terms of our awareness of properties of the *vehicle* in virtue of which we have this awareness of the environment. I shall call this the principle of the *explanatory primacy of vehicles* (EPV):

Explanatory primacy of vehicles: changes in the character of our awareness of the environment are to be explained in terms of changes in our awareness of properties of the vehicle(s) in virtue of which we are aware of the environment.

All three principles, I think it is fair to say, have a certain *prima facie* plausibility. In the rest of this chapter, however, I shall argue that they should all be rejected.

4   The independence condition

According to what I have called the *independence condition*, the presence of any given mental state, M, in a subject S, is independent of S's being introspectively conscious of M. In many ways, it is this condition that lies at the core of the problems with the HOP model. As was noted above, if this model is to provide a general theory of intransitive state consciousness then it must be the case that all mental states are capable of existing independently of our consciousness of them. That is, the account requires not simply the uncontroversial claim that *some* mental states are capable of existing independently of our consciousness of them, it requires that *all* mental states be capable of existing independently of our consciousness of them. This is because the HOP account purports to provide a general model of consciousness according to which, roughly speaking, consciousness is added to a mental state by something outside that state: by a higher-order perception, or quasi-perception, *of* that state. If some mental states were essentially conscious, and were so independently of there existing a higher-order perception of them, then this would undermine the claim that it is transitive consciousness as such that confers intransitive consciousness upon our mental states.

It might be thought that the independence condition can be supported by observations from a variety of sources. Even before Freud, for example, it was well known that there is such a thing as self-deception about one's motives and attitudes. Just try reading Shakespeare. There is also anecdotal evidence: the athlete who does not realise he is in pain until put on the bench, etc., etc. Moreover, recent work in psychology has shown that, in certain circumstances, people are systematically mistaken about their reasons for actions, such claims often being the result of confabulation (Nisbett and Wilson 1977). In addition, there is neurological evidence. It is known that certain sorts of brain damage can lead to the sort of phenomena that seemingly confirm the independence condition. The most striking of these is *blindsight*. Here a person will deny that she can see anything in some portion of her visual field, yet when she is forced to make guesses about what is there, her correct response rate is significantly better than chance. Finally, there are specifically philosophical considerations, notably Armstrong's (1968) *distinct existences argument*. Introspective beliefs, judgements or awarenesses must be thought of as causal effects of the mental states that are objects of awareness. But, as Hume taught us, causes and effects must be distinct existences and, as such, only contingently connected.

These sorts of evidence all converge on the claim that the connection between mental states and our introspective consciousness of them is a contingent connection. This is not to deny that in many circumstances, probably most, we do have reliable introspective access to our first-order mental states and, consequently, that we can make introspective judgements and claims with a high degree of certainty. However, to the extent that we do have reliable introspective access to mental states and processes, this is a logically contingent fact about us.

However, upon further analysis, none of these sorts of reasons proves compelling. Consider, first, the philosophical reasons. The *distinct existences* argument advocated by Armstrong shows only that those mental states which are causal effects of a given mental state M must be logically distinct from M. It may be plausible to suppose that introspective beliefs and judgements about mental states are causal effects of those mental states. However, the present issue concerns our consciousness or awareness of our mental states, and not the beliefs and judgements we make about these states. It is possible to argue, of course, that such beliefs and judgements about M are essentially bound up with the intransitive consciousness of M, but to adopt this line is, in effect, to abandon the HOP model of consciousness in favour of an HOT model. This latter model will be the subject of the following chapter. That leaves us with awareness of our mental states. However, the claim that our awareness of M is a causal effect of M is unlikely to be accepted by anyone who does not already accept the HOP model of consciousness. To suppose that our awareness of M is a causal effect of M is tantamount to accepting the HOP model, and, therefore, its invocation at this point, in order to defend the independence condition, is simply question begging.

The anecdotal evidence is similarly less than convincing. In the heat of a sporting event, I might, temporarily, not notice an injury which, in other circumstances, would prove very painful. Does this mean that I have pain of which I am unaware? I can see no reason for accepting this. It seems at least equally as legitimate to say that although I have an injury that would, in other circumstances, be painful, at present, I am not in pain. The pain has been suppressed by the activity of various mechanisms, ones triggered by, say, large amounts of adrenalin coursing through my system, with the result that, at the time of injury, I actually feel no pain. Pain, of course, is a feeling. And if I feel no pain, I thereby have no pain. Or, at least, so it could be plausibly maintained. And, if this is correct, this sort of anecdotal evidence proves nothing.

Phenomena such as self-deception, and the fact that we are often mistaken about our motives, also prove nothing. No one, presumably, would want to claim that *all* mental states are essentially conscious. In particular, the propositional attitudes manifestly are not. So, the fact that we are, sometimes or even often, unaware of our motives and the like is no more surprising, and no more significant, than the fact that we are almost always unaware of (most of) our beliefs. Motives, like all other propositional states, are dispositional rather than occurrent in nature. HOP purports to provide a model of consciousness. Therefore, far more pertinent to its success or failure is whether it can provide an account of those states which are, or are commonly thought to be, far more closely bound up with consciousness than propositional attitudes. That is, the relevant issue is whether the HOP model can be successfully applied to *sensations*: pain, visual experience, sensory imagining, and the like. Remember, if HOP is to provide a *general* account of consciousness, one that applies to the consciousness of all mental states, and if HOP is to be thought of as providing a *reductive* explanation of in what consciousness consists, then it is committed to showing that *all* mental states are not essentially conscious. It cannot rest on the staggeringly obvious claim that some of them are not.

The case of blindsight is, *prima facie*, more interesting, because it purports to be a case of visual experience (i.e. a form of sensation) without introspective awareness of this experience. However, the evidence provided by this sort of case is, again, less than compelling. For to suppose that what we have in the case of blindsight is a case of visual *experience* is tendentious, and, without further support, almost certainly question begging. In particular, someone who rejects HOP will almost certainly deny this claim. What we have in a case of blindsight is a state that shares some – but certainly only some – of the causal features of a visual experience, but is not, itself, such an experience. The blindsighted subject, in other words, is not unaware of a visual experience but, rather, simply has a visual representation that is rather attenuated from the point of view of its causal role. So, once again, I think the phenomenon of blindsight ultimately provides no support for HOP.

If the above arguments are correct, then the independence condition receives rather less support from philosophical, anecdotal, psychological and neurological sources than might initially be apparent. The real problems, however, turn, not on its lack of support, but on two seriously problematic entailments.

Mindblindness

The independence condition entails the possibility of creatures that possess mental states of which they are never aware. For example, it entails the possibility of a creature that suffers intense pain its whole life but is never aware or conscious of this. That is, it entails the possibility of creatures who are what we might call *mindblind*: blind to their own mental states. If mindblindness is not a genuine possibility, the independence condition is false.

The idea of mindblindness derives from Shoemaker's (1994) account of what he calls 'self-blindedness' and is a conceptual extension of the idea of blindsight. In blindsight, it seems most natural to say, the person is blind to facts about her own mental condition, facts of which she would be aware if normal. She has perceptual consciousness of, say, the square in the missing part of her visual field, but she has no introspective consciousness of her perceptual consciousness. If, as the independence condition asserts, the connection between first-order mental states and our introspective consciousness of them is a contingent connection, then it would be possible, in some sense to be clarified shortly, that such blindness would be much more widespread. That is, if the independence condition is true, then it is logically possible that there be people who are blind to a wide variety of mental facts about themselves, facts to which normal people have introspective access. We can call such people *mindblind*.

In more detail, an individual is mindblind if (i) it possesses certain first-order mental states, (ii) it has the ability to conceive of such states, but (iii) it is blind with respect to their instantiation in it (cf. Shoemaker 1994). In order to be mindblind with respect to a certain kind of mental fact (understood as the instantiation of a mental state-type), an individual must have the ability to conceive of such a fact, just as a person who is literally blind will be able to conceive of those states of affairs she is unable to learn about visually. So lower animals who are precluded by their conceptual poverty from having first-person access do not count as mindblind. Moreover, it is only introspective access to mental facts that the individual is supposed to lack; it is not precluded that it should learn of them in other ways, e.g. in the way others might learn of them, through observation of behaviour.

Before we begin to assess the possibility of mindblindness, we must first sort out the status of this possibility. In particular, we need to establish whether HOP entails the (broadly) *logical* possibility of mindblindness, or whether it further entails its *nomological* possibility. Lycan is one who thinks that HOP entails only the logical possibility of mindblindness:

Massive unawareness of pain is probably nomologically impossible for organisms like us, in whom pain hooks up with cognition and conation in complex ways. It may well be nomologically impossible for organisms of any very complicated kind, since a system of internal monitoring may be required for any such beast to succeed in the real world. (1996: 18)

However, this is far too quick. In particular, Lycan's proposal faces two distinct problems. Firstly, as I shall argue shortly, his claim that pain hooks up with cognition and conation in complex ways is likely to prove too much: it is likely to show that mindblindness is not even a logical possibility. Thus, HOP would have to be rejected on the grounds that it entails a logical impossibility. Secondly, his point about internal monitoring being required for any creature to succeed in the real world proves too little. It in no way establishes that mindblindness is not a nomological possibility. To see this, one must remember that HOP is typically cashed out in terms of the notion of *internal monitoring*, and this is, indeed, the way Lycan understands HOP. But, for any case of conscious awareness, this entails the existence of two functionally distinct states instantiated in the brain; one a scanning, the other a scanned, state. But if these states are genuinely functionally distinct, and HOP is committed to the claim that they are, then they are, of course, also nomologically distinct. All that is required to separate the states is that we identify their causal roles and work out how to hive off one from the other. Suitable surgery would do the trick. This may not be technically possible, and as Lycan points out, may not be evolutionarily possible, but it must be nomologically possible if scanning and scanned states are functionally distinct.

However, in the arguments to follow, I shall take no stand upon whether HOP is committed to the nomological possibility of mindblindness. Instead, I shall try to show that mindblindness is not even a logical possibility. Therefore, since HOP is certainly committed to the logical possibility of mindblindness, HOP should be rejected.

The idea that a creature might spend its whole life in intense pain without ever being aware of this is a truly strange idea. But is it a logically impossible one? I think it is certainly possible to establish that we could never have any evidence to support the claim that a creature could be in pain in this way without realising it. As in the case of blindsight (a specific instance of mindblindness) discussed earlier, we could never have evidence supporting anything more than the claim that the creature instantiates a state that is functionally similar, along certain dimensions, to a state of pain. We could never have evidence that supports the claim that the creature actually is in pain of which it is unaware. But to show that a claim can have no supporting evidence is not to show that the claim is logically impossible.

However, it is, I think, possible to establish the impossibility claim by, broadly speaking, an extension of this type of argument. The idea is that once we appreciate how pain is bound up (as Lycan himself points out) with cognition and conation, then blindness with respect to pain will have a tendency to spread to these other states. The more this is so, the more attenuated will become the causal role of our putative pain state. In the end, we are left with something that is so attenuated, functionally speaking, that it cannot be regarded as a state of pain.

To see this, let us try to imagine an individual who cannot feel her pain, a person who is mindblind with respect to her pain. To imagine this, we have to imagine a person who has the intellectual, conceptual, etc. capacities comparable to ours, and she also, *ex hypothesi*, has pain, but she is introspectively blind to this pain she has. Her only access to her pain, therefore, is of a third-person nature: observing her own behaviour, or, perhaps, her own inner neurophysiological states. Moreover, we should not blithely suppose that she simply does not feel her pain. Pain is a feeling, and what she is introspectively blind to is precisely her feelings of pain.

Pain, of course, does not occur in a psychological vacuum. As Lycan points out, pain, like any other mental state, will connect up with cognitive and conative states in a variety of ways. A person who is in pain, for example, will typically judge that they are in pain, will typically dislike being in pain, will typically desire that the pain stop, will typically take steps to bring about the cessation of the pain, and so on. All these connections are part of the functional role of pain. So, to imagine someone who is blind with regard to their pain, we would have to imagine someone who possesses a state with this sort of causal role, or something very close to it, and then imagine them being unaware of this state.

So, in order to imagine this case of mindblindness, we have to imagine that, when the pain occurs, the person judges that she is in pain, actively dislikes something that is happening to her, desires that this thing end, and takes steps to bring about its cessation. Is she able to judge that she is in pain? Well, *ex hypothesi*, she is not aware of her pain. But, then, it is difficult to see how she could, *in any usual way*, judge that she is in pain. Similarly, it is difficult to see how she could be aware of the active disliking either. It is difficult to see, that is, how she could actively dislike something without knowing what it is. Similarly, she cannot desire that her pain go away unless she is aware of her pain. One can want not to have something while being unsure over whether one has it; but one cannot want to be rid of something, to not have it any more, unless one believes that one currently has it (Shoemaker 1994). Thus, it seems that her mindblindness with respect to pain must, if it is to be coherent, expand and cover more than just pain; it must cover all those states that have the pain as their intentional object. So, we cannot suppose that she is aware of her judging that she is in pain, aware of her disliking, nor can we suppose that she is aware of her desire that the pain cease.

It might be thought, however, that our imagined mindblind subject could work out that she is undergoing an episode of pain, since she possesses normal perceptual and conceptual capacities. Suppose that her judgement, dislike, and her desire to be rid, of the pain had their normal consequences. Thus, she takes some aspirin, calls the doctor's office for an appointment, and so on. It might be thought, on the basis of this behaviour, that it is possible for her to infer she is in pain. And such inference could provide the basis for her subsequent judgements, dislike, and desire. However, upon further analysis it is, I think, far from clear that she could, in fact, make the required inference. In order to do so, it seems, she would have to understand her behaviour *as* pain behaviour; and it is not at all clear that she could do this. It is possible for us, at least in some circumstances, to infer our mental condition from observation of our own behaviour; pain, anger or jealousy that might not be immediately obvious to us can be inferred from careful observation of our behaviour over a suitable period of time. However, it is likely that we are able to do this only because we have, at some time in the past, had more direct acquaintance with states of pain, anger or jealousy that we ourselves possessed. But our imagined mindblind subject has, *ex hypothesi*, had no such acquaintance with pain. But, then, what would she make of her own behaviour? She is performing various actions, and she has no idea why. To her it would presumably seem as if someone had taken control of her body. And, so it would appear to someone else, also. If we saw someone engaging in pain behaviour, visits to the medicine cabinet, calls to the doctor, etc., all of this interspersed with wonderings out loud about what this behaviour is all about, then the most likely hypothesis we would arrive at is multiple personality syndrome: two or more selves or personalities inhabiting one and the same body, one of which is in pain, aware of the pain, and acting accordingly, the other a prisoner in a body over which, at least temporarily, it has no control. But, then, this is not a case of mindblindness; for what the passive observer is blind to is not her own pain, but that of the other inhabitant of her body (Shoemaker 1994).

The moral is this. If we are to imagine a genuine case of mindblindness with respect to pain, then we have to be prepared to imagine a lot more. We have to imagine that the mindblind person is blind not only to her pain, but also to her judgements that she is in pain, to her dislike of the pain, to her desire to be rid of the pain, and to any state that is intentionally directed towards this pain. Furthermore, we have to suppose she will be blind to the reasons for her behaviour, and, thus, will have no idea why she is behaving in the way she is. Indeed, she will be blind even to the character of her behaviour; she will, in all likelihood, be unable to recognise pain behaviour as pain behaviour. When you take away introspective awareness of the pain, you take away all of this also.

What is left? Essentially, an extremely attenuated causal role. Our mindblind subject possesses a state that is caused by certain sorts of things, bodily damage of various stripes, and in turn causes various things, winces, grimaces and the like, that are involuntary and not motivated or rationalised by beliefs and desires. However, this functional role is so minimal, so attenuated relative to the standard functional role of pain, that there seems little or no justification for regarding it as a state of pain. Indeed, there seems little or no justification for regarding it as a mental state at all. Take away the awareness, and you take away everything that makes something a state of pain; indeed, you take away everything that makes the state mental. Therefore, mindblindness with respect to pain seems to be a logical impossibility. And, if this is correct, the independence condition cannot be sustained for cases of pain.

It might be thought that this objection can be overcome simply by claiming that it is an empirical question how much of the causal role of pain is carried by the first-order state itself, and how much is carried by the second-order awareness of pain (Lycan 1996). Lycan, for example, argues that it is possible that the sort of minimal causal role outlined above attaches to the state of pain itself, and that the remainder of this role, including, notably, the relations to judgement, dislike, desire, and will are added by the awareness of pain.

The problem with this response, however, is that it either begs the question or amounts to a rejection of HOP. To see this, remember that HOP purports to be an account of in what the consciousness of our mental states consists. Mental states are not essentially conscious, but consciousness can be added to such states when they stand in an appropriate relation to a distinct mental state. The problem posed by the impossibility of mindblindness, however, is that when we abstract away the awareness of, say, a state of pain, we also abstract most of the causal role of that state with the result that (i) there is little or no justification for regarding the remaining state as a token of the type pain, and (ii) there is little or no justification for regarding the remaining state as a mental state. If this is correct, then there is no way that awareness of pain can coherently be regarded as something that can be *added* to pain; if you take away the awareness then you also take away too much for the substrate to be regarded as pain. In other words, the problem for HOP raised by the impossibility of mindblindness is that awareness of pain is not something that can be added to pain; it is something that must be thought of as *constituting* pain. That is, pain is essentially introspectible; there is no pain without awareness of pain. But this means that the consciousness cannot be something added to pain from the *outside*, that is, by an extrinsic relation to a distinct mental state. Subtract the awareness, and there is nothing left to call pain. Therefore, there is no pain to which consciousness can coherently be added. Thus, to adopt this line of defence is, in effect, to give up on the idea that consciousness of a given mental state M is brought about by a higher-order experience of M. If M does not exist without consciousness, then consciousness cannot be added to M by its standing in an extrinsic relation to a distinct mental state.

The same sort of argument, an argument from *creeping mindblindness*, can also be applied to itches, tingles, and the like. Indeed, Shoemaker has argued that the argument can be developed not just for nonrepresentational sensational states, as pain, itches, tingles and the like are commonly understood to be, but also for perceptual experiences. Whether or not this turns out to be correct, however, does not matter for our purposes. If mindblindness is not a logical possibility for sensational states such as pain, itches, tingles, surely paradigmatic examples of states defined by qualia, then the independence condition cannot be sustained for such states. And, if the independence condition cannot be sustained for such states, the consciousness of those states cannot be thought of as something added from the outside, by way of a higher-order experience of those states. Such states would, on the contrary, be essentially conscious. Therefore, if this is correct, HOP cannot be regarded as a *general* model of the consciousness of mental states. And if it does not provide an account of the consciousness of pains, itches, tingles, and the like, what reason is there for thinking that it provides an account of the consciousness of other mental states?

False positives

The problem posed by mindblindness for the independence condition was that it seems to entail the possibility of conditions that are not, in fact, logically possible; for example the possibility of a creature that suffers intense pain its whole life but is never aware or conscious of this. There is also a converse problem: the possibility of a creature that is aware of being in intense pain its whole life without ever really being in pain. Such a situation would occur if an internal monitor fired without anything like proper cause; that is, in the absence of the appropriate first-order state. Mindblindness, in the case of pain, was pain without awareness of pain. The present problem is the awareness of pain without pain.

The problem stems from the fact that HOP (i) separates the first-order state of pain from the second-order awareness of pain and (ii) regards first- and second-order states as implemented in nomologically distinct neural structures (a given neural state and a distinct neural state whose function is to scan or monitor the former). From this two things follow.

Firstly, HOP is committed to the nomological possibility of there being awareness of pain without there being the pain that is the intentional object of this awareness. It is clear that this must, according to HOP, be regarded as a nomological possibility and not merely a logical one. This follows from the fact that internal monitors are nomologically distinct from those states they function to scan. It might be very unlikely that false positives of this sort occur, but HOP is committed to the claim that they are, nonetheless, nomologically possible.

Secondly, HOP is committed to the claim that it is awareness of pain that is (nomologically) possible in the absence of pain, and not just the vastly more innocuous claim that judgements that one is in pain are (nomologically) possible in the absence of pain. We are, presumably, all familiar with the idea that our judgements of the phenomenal states we are in can be mistaken. I think (judge) that I am experiencing a tickle, when, in fact, subsequent experience reveals that it was an itch. I think (judge) that the wine is tannic, when it is in fact, as subsequent experience reveals, acidic. However, HOP is committed to much more than this. HOP, of course, is not a higher-order thought model of consciousness. Consciousness, according to HOP, is added to a mental state by a higher-order experience, not a higher-order thought. It is, thus, committed to the nomological possibility of awareness of a phenomenal state, P, in the absence of P, and not simply the judgement that one is in P in the absence of P.

So, the question HOP must be able to answer in the affirmative is this: is the awareness of a phenomenal state P nomologically possible in the absence of P? It might be thought that we can quickly dismiss this possibility. Awareness of P is, presumably, an intentional state and, as such, essentially directed towards its object. One can no more have awareness of pain in the absence of pain, it might be thought, than one could have a belief that water is wet in the absence of water. This, however, is a little (but only a little) too quick.

Perhaps it is possible to amend the entailments of HOP in the following way. Whenever a monitor fires in the absence of the appropriate first-order neural state, then we do not have awareness as such, but, as we might put it, *quasi-awareness* (henceforth, *qu-awareness*). For example, when the relevant internal monitor fires in the absence of the appropriate first-order state, then we do not have awareness of pain as such (for there is no pain) but something that seems very like awareness of pain – a state that is phenomenally indistinguishable from awareness of pain.

This line of thought might be supported by an analogy with the case of belief. It is not possible to have a belief that water is wet in a world bereft of water, but it is certainly possible to have something very like it. It is possible to have a belief that retaw is wet, and such a belief may be subjectively indistinguishable for its subject from the belief that water is wet. Similarly, it might be thought, it might be possible to have a state subjectively indistinguishable from an awareness of pain – but which is not awareness of pain – in the absence of pain.

However this analogy breaks down upon further scrutiny. The reason why it is possible to have a belief subjectively indistinguishable from the belief that water is wet in the absence of water is that the former belief can be directed towards a substance – retaw – that is itself subjectively indistinguishable from water. To carry the analogy through, then, the proponent of HOP is going to have to explain the subjective indistinguishability of the qu-awareness of pain from the awareness of pain in terms of the qu-awareness being directed towards an object that is subjectively indistinguishable from pain. Thus, HOP will be committed to the claim that there is a state subjectively indistinguishable from pain but which is not itself pain. And this, it seems fairly certain, is not even logically possible. Any state that is subjectively indistinguishable from pain is pain.

Therefore, I think we should conclude that *false positives* – awarenesses or qu-awarenesses of phenomenal states in the absence of such states – are dubiously coherent. They do not appear even logically possible. However, HOP is committed to their nomological possibility. HOP, therefore, should be rejected.

This section has focused upon phenomenally individuated states, much of the discussion being concentrated upon pain. I have argued that HOP is committed to two claims which, at least with regard to such states, are logically impossible. The first is that of mindblindness, the second is that of false positives. Neither of these claims, I think, ultimately proves to be logically possible. However, it might be thought that much of the cogency of the arguments developed here derives from the phenomenal character of the states that have provided the focus for discussion. I concede this. In the next section, however, I shall try to show that there are serious problems with the idea that HOP models can provide an account of our introspective consciousness of *any* mental state, let alone ones that are phenomenally individuated. The problem here, however, is not with the independence condition but with the idea of the explanatory primacy of vehicles. And it is to consideration of this that we now turn.

5   The explanatory primacy of vehicles

According to the principle of the *explanatory primacy of vehicles*, changes in the character of our awareness of the environment (understood broadly enough to incorporate the body) are to be explained in terms of changes in our awareness of properties of the vehicle(s) in virtue of which we are aware of the environment.

To see why HOP is committed to this principle, consider, again, Armstrong's driver. This driver is, of course, always perceptually conscious of the road; this is what prevents him crashing. When he 'wakes up', however, his transitive perceptual consciousness of the environment is, according to Armstrong, augmented by the intransitive consciousness of his perceptual states. This intransitive consciousness of his perceptual states is brought about by there being a higher-order perception of them. And this higher-order perception is implemented by way of some form of neural scanning mechanism.

However, precisely what is it that this apparatus is supposed to explain? The driver, prior to his 'waking up', has transitive perceptual consciousness of the road. What function does the invocation of the intransitive consciousness of his perceptual states have? In other words, what is it that changes with the driver's revival such that this change is best, or appropriately, explained in terms of the intransitive consciousness of his mental states? And the primary change, here, seems to be a change in his *externally* directed awareness; that is, a change in his transitive perceptual consciousness. After his arousal, he is aware of the road in a way that he was not before. His transitive consciousness of the road is now attentive, observant, vivid, and so on, in a way that it was not prior to his waking up.

And according to HOP, this change in his *externally* directed awareness is appropriately explained in terms of a change in his *internally* directed awareness.

Therefore, according to HOP, changes in the character of the driver's transitive perceptual consciousness of the road are explained in terms of the acquisition of intransitive consciousness by the perceptual states in virtue of which he is conscious of the road. And the acquisition of intransitive consciousness by the perceptual states in virtue of which the driver is conscious of the road is explained in terms of his transitive consciousness of those states. And this inwardly directed transitive consciousness is, according to HOP, explained by way of a higher-order perception of those first-order states. Thus, HOP is committed to the claim that changes in the character of our externally or environmentally directed awareness can be explained in terms of changes in the character of our internally directed awareness; our awareness of the vehicles or states in virtue of which we have this externally directed awareness. However, HOP theorists are also, almost always, materialists. Both the first-order states and the second-order perceptual awareness of those states are physical states or processes. Thus, higher-order perception is typically explained in terms of internal scanning or monitoring of a first-order neural state by a higher-order neural state whose function is precisely to scan such states. Therefore, understood materialistically, HOP is committed to the idea that changes in the character of externally directed awareness, on the part of a subject S, can be explained in terms of scanning or monitoring of the internal neural states, or *vehicles*, in virtue of which S is externally aware. And this claim I have labelled the principle of the explanatory primacy of vehicles.

The principle of the explanatory primacy of vehicles is almost certainly false. Indeed, it seems to be simply a species of *vehicle/content confusion*. This type of confusion is commonplace and well understood. A vehicle of content, such as a neural representation of a state of affairs, need not possess all, or any, of the states of affairs it represents. A neural representation of a pink polka-dotted dress need not itself be pink or polka-dotted. Nor, less obviously, need a neural representation that occurs at a particular time, represent the time at which it occurs. The type of vehicle/content confusion exhibited by HOP, however, is of a slightly different form.

Suppose the driver became able to see, through innovative neurosurgery, real time magnetic resonance imaging, or mirrors, or whatever, the neural representations of road conditions in his brain, would this be sufficient to make him aware of those road conditions? It seems not; all he would become aware of are various sorts of neural activity. All one can become aware of by scanning or monitoring internal episodes are activities of the brain; because that is all that is there. The confusion, here, is to suppose that awareness of a state that represents P thereby yields awareness of P; and this seems to be a particular instance of a more general confusion.

As Dretske (1995) points out, no examination of the intrinsic, non-relational, features of a book – the type of paper, the type of font, the number of pages, etc., etc. – is going to tell us what the book is about. And no examination of the intrinsic feature of a photograph is going to tell us what the photograph represents. So, why should scanning or monitoring of brain states tell us anything at all about what those brain states represent? The mistake here, as Dretske points out (1995: 108) appears to be one of inferring that because mental representations (the vehicles of content) are in the head, we can become aware of what it is we think and experience by looking within, by experiencing what is inside. But this is the same mistake as inferring that because words are in books, the meanings are there also. An internal scanner would be as useful in becoming aware of what we are thinking and perceiving as a high-resolution camera would be in deciphering the meaning of coded text (Dretske 1995: 109).

In general, perceiving the intrinsic properties of meaningful symbols is not the way to perceive what these symbols are about. So why should perceiving meaningful brain states be a way of becoming aware of what those brain states are about? And so why should our coming to perceive a meaningful brain state provide an explanation for a change in the character of our awareness of what that brain state is about? It is possible to become engrossed in a book, so much so that one loses track of time, becomes unaware of events unfolding around one, etc. However, one does not become engrossed in a book by focusing more and more intently on the typeface occurring on the page in front of one.

Ultimately, I think, the principle of the explanatory primacy of vehicles requires a rather embarrassingly untenable assumption: that the intrinsic, non-relational, properties of representations somehow mirror, or resemble, the things which those intrinsic, non-relational, properties represent. That is, the principle of the explanatory primacy of vehicles rests on a resemblance theory of representation. It is Wittgenstein who has perhaps done more than anyone to undermine the influence of such theories, and the above argument against the explanatory primacy of vehicles employs an essentially Wittgensteinian device: *turning latent nonsense into patent nonsense*. According to the principle, alterations in the character of external awareness are to be explained in terms of a change in internal awareness; changes in the character of our access to environmental items are to be explained in terms of access to the intrinsic, non-relational, properties of states that represent such items. In order to see why this will not work, we bring it out 'into the open'. We examine, that is, whether it will work in a case where one external item (e.g. a book) represents another. Does our focusing on the intrinsic, non-relational features of one external item provide an appropriate explanation for our awareness of what those features represent? When we see quite clearly that it does not, this should lead us to strongly suspect that some sleight of hand has taken place with the internal version of the model. Somehow, we are tempted to suppose, internal perception of intrinsic, non-relational, features of representations is different from external perception of those features of representations. But such a temptation, as Wittgenstein has shown, involves a rapid descent into magic.

6   The primacy of transitive consciousness

According to the principle of the *primacy of transitive consciousness*, intransitive (state) consciousness can be explained in terms of transitive (creature) consciousness. It is easy to see that HOP is committed to this principle. According to HOP, a mental state is introspectively conscious only if it is intransitively conscious. That is, when we become introspectively conscious of any given mental state, that state becomes an introspectively conscious state in virtue of its becoming intransitively conscious. And, according to HOP, a mental state becomes intransitively conscious in virtue of there being a higher-order perception of it. It is the transitive consciousness occasioned by the occurrence of the higher-order state that makes the first-order state intransitively conscious. Thus, the intransitive consciousness of any given mental state is explained in terms of the transitive creature consciousness occasioned by the occurrence of a higher-order perception.

There is, however, an apparently serious problem with this model of intransitive consciousness. Transitive consciousness of an item P is, typically, not sufficient to make P intransitively conscious. It is possible for us to be transitively conscious of many things. And the vast majority of these things are not intransitively conscious. Our being transitively conscious of a rock or a tree does not make the rock or tree intransitively conscious. And when we focus on occurrences inside our body, the situation remains unchanged. And, as Dretske (1993, 1995) has pointed out, my being transitively conscious of my upset stomach, or a freckled patch of skin that has suddenly appeared, makes neither my stomach nor the skin patch intransitively conscious.

This shows that being transitively conscious of an item P is not, in general, sufficient to make P intransitively conscious. So, why suppose that it is my transitive consciousness of my first-order mental states that makes the states intransitively conscious? Here is Lycan's attempt to answer the question:

What is so special about physical states of that certain sort, that consciousness *of* them makes them 'conscious'? That they are themselves mental. Stomachs and freckled patches of skin are not mental. It seems psychological states are called 'conscious states' when we are conscious of them, but nonpsychological states are not.

This answer, however, seems manifestly inadequate. Presumably, HOP is in the business of providing an account of in what intransitive state consciousness consists. If this is so, what is required for HOP to be of any value is that it provide an explanation of why mental states become intransitively conscious in virtue of our transitive consciousness of them. What will not do, presumably, is the staggeringly cavalier assertion that, in effect: they simply do.

Once again, when we bring the model into the open, once we turn what is latent into what is patent, the explanation of intransitive consciousness in terms of transitive consciousness loses any plausibility. Any plausibility it seems to have derives from the fact that the internal transitive consciousness is hidden or internal. And, in philosophy, what is hidden quickly turns into what is magical. Thus, we are to suppose that internal transitive consciousness, transitive consciousness of our first-order mental states, is somehow different from external transitive consciousness, transitive consciousness of non-mental items, in that the former, but not the latter, is capable of making its objects intransitively conscious. But we are given no indication of why there should be this difference, nor of its basis. It must be magic.

7   What has gone wrong?

If the above argument is correct, then the attempt to explain intransitive consciousness in terms of transitive consciousness seems to be a nonstarter. However, as was made clear earlier, HOP models also assume that changes in the character of our transitive perceptual consciousness can be explained in terms of intransitive consciousness. That is, changes in the attentiveness, vividness, and the like, of our transitive perceptual consciousness are appropriately explained in terms of the perceptual states becoming intransitively conscious. This is what happens, for example, in the case of Armstrong's driver; his 'waking up' consists precisely in his perceptual states becoming intransitively conscious.

However, upon closer analysis, the appeal to intransitive consciousness to explain changes in transitive consciousness proves, I think, to be unnecessary.

According to HOP, Armstrong's driver is, in one clear sense, conscious of the road prior to his revival. He is, as Armstrong puts it, perceptually conscious, but not introspectively conscious. He is perceptually conscious in virtue of the fact that he has various perceptual states which, with respect to the road, guide his motor activity in appropriate ways. Thus, these perceptual states are states *in virtue of* which the driver is transitively conscious. Moreover, the second-order states that (allegedly) make first-order states intransitively conscious are, according to HOP, themselves states in virtue of which we are conscious of first-order states. Thus, quite obviously, central to the HOP model is the idea of transitive consciousness, and, it seems, a transitively conscious state is one *in virtue of* which we are conscious of something else.

However, once we allow the idea that there are states that make us conscious, states in virtue of which we are conscious of some other object, state, event or process, then why suppose that a necessary condition of a state's being conscious is that we be conscious of it? That is, why not simply say that for a state to be conscious is for it to make us conscious of some thing? On this view, one advanced by Dretske (1995), *conscious states are states with which we are conscious, not states of which we are conscious.* And this thought can be supported by the following diagnosis of the objections raised in the previous section.

Some people have cancer without being aware of it; others are aware of it. But this does not mean there are two forms of cancer, conscious and unconscious. Similarly, suppose some people were conscious of having experiences, while other people had them but were not aware of them (a claim central to the HOP model but which, I think, and given the arguments of section 4, are eminently questionable). This, by itself, should not mean that there are two sorts of experiences, conscious and unconscious ones, any more than it means there are conscious and unconscious cancers (Dretske 1995). What mistake has been made?

The mistake is ultimately one of confusing a property of the *act* of consciousness with a property of the *object* of consciousness. My being aware of my cancer does not make my cancer conscious, it makes *me* conscious of it. And, similarly, my being aware of an experience would not make my experience conscious, it would make *me* conscious of it. And I am conscious of it precisely because I instantiate an act of consciousness that is directed towards an object – my experience – in an appropriate way. Ultimately, the mistake made by HOP lies in a confusion of the act and the object of consciousness. An act of consciousness directed towards an object in an appropriate way makes me, the subject of the act, conscious of the object. It does not make the object conscious. The consciousness of the object is a property that derives from the act of consciousness, and attaches to the subject of this act in virtue of the act. It is not a property that attaches to the object of the act, the first-order mental state upon which the conscious act is directed.

The HOP model of introspective consciousness, then, ultimately rests on a confusion of the act and the object of consciousness, and sees properties which, in fact, attach to the former, or attach to a conscious subject in virtue of the former, as attaching to the latter. Perhaps this is not surprising. This is a pervasive confusion. We shall have cause to visit it again later. In fact, the entire second half of the book will turn around an attempt to avoid this confusion.[1]

---

[1] Why should this confusion be so pervasive? A passage from Carruthers, himself an HOR theorist, is, I think, particularly instructive: '... it is one thing to say that the *world* takes on a subjective aspect by being presented to subjects with differing conceptual and discriminatory powers, and it is quite another thing to say that the subject's *experience of the world* also has a subjective aspect, or that there is something which the *experience is like*. Indeed, by parity of reasoning, this would seem to require subjects to possess information about, and to make discriminations amongst, their own states of experience. And it is just this which provides the rationale for HOR-accounts ...' (1998)

Really? Then HOR accounts are in trouble. At least, this is what I shall try to show in part 2. Carruthers thinks that there is not only something that it is like to experience the world, there is also something that it is like to experience the experience. I shall argue that there is nothing that it is like to experience an experience. For there to be something that it is like to have an experience is simply for the experience to reveal the world to be a certain way. In virtue of having the experience, the world appears a certain way. Equivalently, but in a way that will seem cryptic prior to acquaintance with the arguments of part 2, there is no what it is like to reveal the world a certain way (other than the revealing of the world in another way). The what it is like of experience is the revealing.

5 Consciousness and higher-order thoughts

Higher-order thought (HOT) models of consciousness have been developed by Rosenthal (1986, 1990, 1993), Carruthers (1996, 1998), Gennaro (1996) and Natsoulas (1992), among others. According to such models, very roughly, a given mental state M is conscious if, and only if, the subject of that state possesses a thought about M, a thought to the effect that she has, or is in, M. Most attacks on the HOT model have tended to focus on the rather unfortunate entailments this account has, or is thought to have. Thus, Dretske (1995) argues, plausibly, that HOT theories rule out the possession of consciousness by non-human animals and children below the age of about three. I concur with these criticisms. However, in this chapter I shall argue that HOT accounts of consciousness face even deeper problems, problems of logical coherence. More precisely, I shall argue that HOT models face at least two distinct logical problems: *circularity* and *regress*. My focus will be provided by the developments of the model associated with Rosenthal and Carruthers, since these are probably the most well known, although similar arguments, I believe, apply to any of the theoretical articulations of this general account.

At the outset, however, a preliminary point concerning the status of HOT models is required. On the face of it, HOT models seem to sit rather uneasily on the borderline between two distinct endeavours, one conceptual, one ontological. On the one hand, there is the attempt to elucidate the *concept* of consciousness, of what it means for a mental state to be conscious. On the other hand, there is the attempt to identify the *property* in virtue of which mental states are conscious. There are very few, if any, proponents of HOT models, I think, who would be prepared to say that they are concerned *only* with the first project. But, against this, it would be armchair *hubris* of the very worst sort to present HOT models as *purely* empirical accounts of the way the brain goes about making states conscious. And when we turn to the writings of its principal protagonists, matters are not rendered significantly more transparent. Carruthers (1996: 147), for example, is clear that he sees the development of an HOT model as primarily an ontological endeavour, *but* as also, in part, a conceptual one. And certain claims by Rosenthal also suggest the conceptual nature of the HOT model.[1]

In fact, I think it is arguable that HOT models will eventually be revealed to be simply bastardised superimpositions of two very different projects and, as a result, a confused melange of two very different theoretical pictures. This, however, is *not* a claim I shall pursue here. Instead, I shall use the distinction between ontological and conceptual endeavours simply as a way of organising discussion. I shall assume that HOT models either are, or can be, *both* accounts of what it means for a mental state to be conscious *and* accounts of the property in virtue of which mental states are conscious. On either construal, HOT models are reductive in character. On the conceptual construal, HOT models attempt to explicate the concept of consciousness in terms of further concepts that do not contain this concept as a constituent. On the ontological construal, such models attempt to reductively explain the property of consciousness – the property in virtue of which mental states are conscious – in terms of properties that are not themselves conscious ones.

In the wake of well-known arguments associated with Quine and Wittgenstein, it is common to regard the distinction between conceptual and ontological investigations with some suspicion. I share this sentiment. However, organising the discussion in these terms does not, I think, commit us unduly to any division that has, or is alleged to have, fallen into disrepute. For, even if we accept the Quine/Wittgenstein arguments, it is still true that we are left with *some* form of distinction between conceptual and ontological investigations. It is simply that the relation between conceptual and ontological claims will now be understood in terms of a spectrum rather than a qualitative division, and the distinction will, accordingly, take the form of relative positions on this spectrum rather than a dichotomy. And it is only this minimal point that I shall require.

Whether understood as a conceptual or an ontological enterprise, I shall argue that HOT models run into serious logical difficulties. In each case, the problem is ultimately one of circularity, but the precise form this problem takes will vary depending on the emphasis of the HOT model.

---

[1] Here, I am thinking in particular of his assertion (to be explored further in section 2) that any account of mental state consciousness that appeals to mental states that are themselves conscious, will be trivial, uninformative and/or circular. The claim that features such as these are possessed by an explanation is typically explained in terms of the idea of the conceptual connectedness of explanandum and explanans. Thus, if Rosenthal wishes to safeguard HOT explanations of consciousness against triviality, circularity and uninformativeness, this suggests that he regards the development of an HOT model as, in part, a conceptual endeavour.

In section 2, I shall argue that the HOT model falls victim to what I shall call the problem of *circularity*. This type of problem arises most obviously when HOT models are understood as conceptual attempts to explicate what it means for a mental state to be conscious (but can also, I think, arise when such models are understood, ontologically, as attempts to say in what the consciousness of a mental state consists). In section 3, I shall argue that HOT models are subject to a problem of *regress*, and this form of the problem arises most obviously when such models are understood as part of the ontological enterprise of specifying in what the consciousness of a mental state consists. Either way, the prospects for HOT models of consciousness are, I shall argue, grim.

1   HOT models

In order to understand HOT models of consciousness, we first need to recall two preliminary distinctions introduced in the previous chapter. The first is that between *creature* and *state* consciousness. The second is the distinction between *transitive* and *intransitive* consciousness.

To recap. Firstly, we ascribe consciousness to at least two distinct types of thing. On the one hand we ascribe it to creatures, on the other, to mental states. Ascriptions to the former are ascriptions of *creature* consciousness, ascriptions to the latter are ascriptions of *state* consciousness. HOT theories aim to explain not creature but state consciousness. If some mental states are, while some are not, conscious, this must, it is thought, be in virtue of some difference between conscious and unconscious ones, and the goal of HOT theories is to explain in what this difference consists.[2]

Secondly, we sometimes speak of our being conscious *of* something. This is *transitive* consciousness. Transitive consciousness is most naturally understood as a form of creature consciousness. Mental states are not conscious of anything; rather, creatures are conscious of things in virtue, at least in part, of possessing certain sorts of mental states. *Intransitive* consciousness, on the other hand, can be ascribed to both creatures and mental states. A creature that is intransitively conscious is one that is awake as opposed to asleep, or sentient as opposed to non-sentient. A mental state that is intransitively conscious, on the other hand, is, roughly,

---

[2] However, from the perspective of opponents of the model, for example Dretske (1995), the assumption that the difference between conscious and non-conscious states is to be found in some difference in the states themselves is, very likely, the decisive movement in the conjuring trick (or, at least, one of them). Dretske argues that the difference between conscious and non-conscious states is to be found in the way subjects relate to those states, and not in the states themselves. In other words, the decisive movement underwriting HOT models is a confusion of *act* and *object* of consciousness. I concur wholeheartedly with Dretske on this point.

and without wishing to beg any questions (see note 1), one that we are aware of having rather than one of whose presence we are unaware.

The goal of HOT accounts is to explain intransitive state consciousness, and, as with HOP models, the core intuition underlying the account is that intransitive state consciousness is to be explained in terms of transitive creature consciousness. Roughly, a mental state possessed by creature C is intransitively conscious if C is transitively conscious of it. More accurately, a mental state of C is intransitively conscious if C is transitively conscious of it, but is so without relying on any inference or observation of which it is transitively conscious (Rosenthal 1990: 10).

Where HOT models differ from their HOP counterparts is in their account of what grounds this transitive consciousness. According to HOT models, we are transitively conscious of a given mental state when we have a thought about it. A mental state is intransitively conscious if it is accompanied by a thought about that state. The occurrence of such a thought makes us (non-causally) transitively conscious of the mental state; and so the state is an intransitively conscious state. Similarly, when no such higher-order thought occurs, we are unaware of being in the state in question, and the state is then not a conscious state. 'The core of the theory, then, is that a mental state is a conscious state when, and only when, it is accompanied by a suitable higher-order thought' (Rosenthal 1990: 13). There are certain constraints on the content of this higher-order thought. Most importantly, when a mental state is (intransitively) conscious, it is not simply that we are conscious of that state, it is that we are conscious of being in that state. Thus, the content of the associated higher-order thought must be that one is, oneself, in that mental state.

Within this general framework, HOT models can be developed in two importantly distinct ways, which, following Carruthers (1998), we can label *actualist* and *dispositionalist*. Very roughly, the core idea of actualist versions of the HOT account can be formulated as follows:

A mental state M possessed by creature C is intransitively conscious if C has an occurrent thought to the effect that it possesses M.

Rosenthal defends an actualist HOT account. He claims that the higher-order thought that confers intransitive consciousness on a mental state (or, as he would prefer, in which the intransitive consciousness of a mental state *consists*) must be both occurrent and, indeed, have the content of an assertion. Being simply disposed to have a thought about a state, according to Rosenthal, is not sufficient to make one conscious of it (1990: 15).

According to dispositionalist forms of the HOT model, however, the presence of an occurrent higher-order thought is not a necessary condition of a mental state being intransitively conscious. Rather, again very roughly:

A mental state M possessed by creature C is intransitively conscious if C is disposed to have a thought to the effect that it possesses M.

Carruthers endorses a dispositionalist form of HOT model. There are also further differences between Rosenthal's and Carruthers' accounts that need not detain us unduly. Carruthers' account has it that the higher-order thought is causally produced, or is disposed to be so produced, by the mental state that it makes conscious. Rosenthal, on the other hand, claims that assertion of a causal link is not part of the HOT model of consciousness as such, but may be appended to this model should certain other circumstances be found to obtain.[3]

As Rosenthal is keen to stress, according to the HOT model, whether actualist or dispositionalist, consciousness is an *extrinsic* property of mental states and not, as is commonly assumed, an intrinsic one. Roughly, very roughly, a property is intrinsic to an item if that item's having it does not consist, even in part, in that thing's bearing some relation to something else. Clearly, consciousness fails to satisfy this condition on both Rosenthal's and Carruthers' account. Whether or not a mental state M is (intransitively) conscious depends on whether the subject who has it also possesses a higher-order thought to the effect that they instantiate M. Consciousness is added to a mental state from the outside; its consciousness consists in there being a relevant higher-order thought about it.

2   The problem of circularity

Rosenthal is keen to point out that there is no logical circularity inherent in his development of the HOT model. Although the model, in effect, uses consciousness to explain consciousness, the type of consciousness implicated in the explanans is distinct from that contained in the explanandum. In the former, consciousness is transitive consciousness, a two-place property of one's being conscious of something. In the latter, consciousness is intransitive consciousness, a one-place property of being conscious.

Nevertheless, Rosenthal also points out that, unless certain conditions are met, circularity can lurk elsewhere. The HOT model is, of course, an

---

[3] Specifically, a causal theory of representation. He thinks what is crucial is what determines the reference of the higher-order thought, and if this should prove to be causal, we can amend the formulation of the HOT model accordingly. However, a specific answer to the problem of representation is, he claims, no part of a theory of consciousness as such.

attempt to explain consciousness in terms of mental states: the intransitive consciousness of a mental state M is explained in terms of the relation M bears to a distinct mental state. However, given that this is so:

It turns out that if all mental states were conscious states, it would be impossible to give any *nontrivial, informative,* explanation of the nature of state consciousness. (1990: 7; emphasis mine)

And again:

An explanation of what it is for mental states to be conscious will either appeal to mental states or it will not. Suppose now that all mental states are conscious, and that our explanation of what it is for mental states to be conscious does invoke mental states. Such an explanation will be *circular* since the appeal to mental states is then automatically an appeal to conscious states. Invoking the very phenomenon we want to explain *trivializes* the explanation and prevents it from being informative. (1990: 7; emphasis mine)

The claim that mental states are not essentially conscious is, therefore, a constitutive feature of Rosenthal's account. It should be remembered that his account requires not simply that *some* mental states be not essentially conscious – a comparatively uncontroversial claim to which most, I think, would be willing to assent – it requires that *all* mental states be not essentially conscious.[4] This is because HOT, like its HOP counterpart, purports to provide a general model of consciousness according to which, roughly speaking, consciousness is added to a mental state by something outside that state: by a higher-order thought to the effect that one is in that state. If some mental states were intransitively conscious independently of a higher-order thought, then the generality of the HOT model would be undermined. And then the obvious question would be: if some mental states can be intransitively conscious independently of a higher-order thought to the effect that one has them, then why cannot all mental states be conscious without such a thought? Thus, Rosenthal requires the thesis that no mental state is essentially conscious. That is, he is committed to what, in the previous chapter, I labelled the *independence condition*. And this means, if the arguments of the previous chapter are

---

[4] This makes Carruthers' (1996: 135–40) treatment of this issue inexcusably cavalier. Carruthers makes a case for the claim that perceptions and propositional attitudes can be unconscious, a relatively uncontroversial claim that, I think, few would deny. However, he then concludes the same chapter (5) by claiming that he has shown that *all* mental states can be unconscious. But what needs to be shown, and not simply assumed, if the HOT model is to be defended is that *all* mental states, processes and the like, can be unconscious. This is because, according to this model, consciousness is added to a mental state from the outside, by a higher-order thought. To me, it seems, to say the least, implausible that this general claim can be applied to all mental states. Discussions of sensory imaginings, for example, are noticeably absent from the writings of most HOT theorists.

anywhere near correct, that Rosenthal's position is in immediate trouble; for the independence condition is almost certainly false. However, beating Rosenthal over the head with the independence condition is, thankfully, not necessary. For even if the independence condition could be defended, this would not be sufficient for the HOT account to avoid the charge of circularity. To avoid this, Rosenthal needs to establish a much stronger claim: there are no logical connections *at all* between mental states and consciousness.

To see this, consider the language with which Rosenthal characterises the danger, to the HOT model, that lurks in the possibility that all mental states are essentially conscious. This possibility, if actualised, would render HOT models *trivial, uninformative*, and/or *circular*. Charges of triviality, uninformativeness and circularity are ones which find their most natural home in explanations that contain logical or conceptual connections between explanans and explanandum. The explanation of opium's capacity for inducing sleep in terms of its possessing a dormitive virtue is uninformative, trivial and circular because, the expression 'dormitive virtue' simply means 'tends to put people to sleep'.

However, if the notions of triviality, uninformativeness and circularity (henceforth, just 'circularity') are understood in this way, then an explanation will be circular if there are any logical connections between the concept expressed in the explanans and that expressed in the explanandum. The reason is that logical connections obey a principle of transitivity: if X is logically connected to Y and Y is logically connected to Z, then X is logically connected to Z. (It is not required that the logical connection between X and Z is the same as either of those between X and Y or Y and Z.)

Therefore, if we assume the standard view that the circularity of an explanation is to be defined in terms of the presence of logical connections between explanandum and explanans (and it is, to say the least, unclear what the alternative might be), then, given the transitivity of logical connectedness, the circularity of the explanation will follow the relations of logical connectedness.

In general, suppose we are proposing to explain the possession of property P by item x in terms of x's relation to a distinct item y. Then, in order to safeguard this explanation against circularity, it is not enough that we establish that y does not possess P, or does not possess P essentially. We must also establish that the concept of y is not connected, in virtue of its content, to the concept of P. In the case of the HOT model, P is intransitive consciousness, x is a mental state, and y is a higher-order thought to the effect that one has x. One way for this explanation to be circular would be for y to have P. However, there is another way: if the concept of y entailed the concept of P, or if it is impossible to understand the concept of y without understanding the concept of P. In this case, if the concept of a higher-order thought entails, or is in other ways logically bound up with, the concept of consciousness, then given the transitivity of logical connectedness, and given that circularity is defined in terms of logical connectedness, one would require prior possession of the concept of consciousness in order to understand the state that allegedly confers consciousness on mental state x. This explanation of the intransitive consciousness of x would, then, also be circular.

It is worth noting that this objection does not involve foisting on Rosenthal any unwanted or implausibly crude model of reductive conceptual analysis. In fact, it does not involve foisting anything at all on Rosenthal. The objection relies only on a claim that Rosenthal himself explicitly asserts: that an explanation of consciousness will be circular if it appeals to states that are themselves conscious. My point, then, is that if (i) we understand the notion of circularity in its usual way, namely as defined in terms of the notion of logical connectedness, and if (ii) the principle of the transitivity of logical connectedness is correct, then any account which appeals to states that have logical or conceptual connections to conscious states will be equally circular. If the danger is one of circularity (and Rosenthal is quite clear that it is) then this danger will be grounded in the existence of *any* logical connection between mental states and consciousness, and not necessarily a connection specifically underwritten by the claim that mental states are essentially conscious. So, two questions arise: (i) what might these further, less specific, logical connections be? and (ii) have we any reasons for endorsing them?

With regard to (i), at least three candidates suggest themselves. It might be claimed that while no mental states are essentially conscious, nevertheless all mental states are essentially such that they *could* become conscious. Or, we might weaken this still further and claim that while no mental states are essentially conscious, and while at least some mental states are such that they could never become conscious, nevertheless, for any token mental state M, M is a token of the same type as other tokens which are or could become conscious (McGinn 1997: 12). Or, even weaker still, we might claim that while no mental state tokens are essentially conscious, or need become conscious, or need even be a member of a type with other tokens that are conscious, a mental state must nevertheless be instantiated in a creature that is capable of consciousness (Clark 1993: 217–18).

With regard to (ii), the answer is that we have reason to endorse one or other of these formulations because of the need to inject a necessary element of chauvinism into our ascriptions of mental states. We are all familiar with the standard text-book objections to functionalism: Chinese rooms, Chinese nations, Zombies, Giant Lookup Tables, and the like. What these objections indicate, broadly speaking, is the need for our ascriptions of mental states to individuals to be constrained by considerations in addition to functional organisation and behavioural manifestation. And the most natural suggestion for in what these additional constraints consist is some sort of relation to consciousness of the sort outlined in response to (i). Thus, to take just one example, in an influential treatment of the status of folk psychology, Clark (1993: 189–219) argues that two conditions must be met in order for an organism to be counted as possessing a belief: a normativity condition and a consciousness condition. The consciousness condition, very roughly, is that it is impossible for a being to count as grasping a concept unless it is capable of having a conscious experience involving it (1993: 217). This entails that it is conceptually impossible for a representational state to exist unless it is instantiated in a creature that has the capacity for conscious experience. And without this sort of condition, our ascriptions of mental states to organisms will lack sufficient chauvinism to be plausible, and so run into the sort of objections listed above. So, once again, we have a logical connection between mental states and consciousness. Admittedly, this connection is not as straightforward as the implausible 'all mental states must be conscious' variety. But it is a logical connection nonetheless, and thus threatens the HOT model with circularity no less than more straightforward versions.

Worse still for Rosenthal, he effectively concedes that there are logical connections between mental states and consciousness. He concedes this in his attempt to disarm a particular temptation for thinking that mental states are essentially conscious (1990: 6). The temptation derives from the thought that there must be some way of demarcating what is mental from what is not, and consciousness provides the most likely demarcatory candidate. In response to this temptation, Rosenthal writes:

We can satisfy our need for a uniform mark of the mental by having a single property in terms of which we fix the extension of 'mental'. We need not also have a single property that all mental states exhibit. As a way of fixing this extension, consciousness very likely does provide a single mark of the mental. We fix the extension of 'mental' by way of conscious mental states, even though not all mental states are conscious. (1990: 6)

But fixing the extension of the word 'mental', obviously, is fixing the content of the concept of the mental, and if we appeal to conscious mental states in fixing this extension, then we appeal to consciousness in delineating the concept of the mental. Therefore, Rosenthal accepts that there are logical or conceptual connections between mental states and consciousness.

And this, in effect, means that Rosenthal's explanation of consciousness in terms of higher-order thoughts is going to be circular after all. The question of whether or not mental states are essentially conscious is not the question most directly relevant to the issue of circularity. Rather, it is whether there are any logical connections between mental states and consciousness. Of course, if mental states were essentially conscious, then there would be such a logical connection. But, as we have seen, there are other ways for logical connections to be underwritten. Not only does Rosenthal fail to rule out such connections, he in fact tacitly endorses them. And considerations pertaining to the chauvinism inherent in mental state ascriptions suggest that these logical connections are independently plausible.

In responding to this problem, there seem to be four options available to Rosenthal.[5] The first option is, in effect, to abandon the idea that the HOT model is an attempt to elucidate the *concept* of consciousness. If one understands the model simply as an attempt to identify the property of consciousness, the property in virtue of which mental states are intransitively conscious, then one might be able to accept, with equanimity, the idea that one cannot understand the HOT model without prior grasp of the *concept* of consciousness. This problem is a serious one, it could be argued, only if one takes HOT models to be in the (conceptual) business of explicating the concept of consciousness, and not the (ontological) business of specifying the property of consciousness. This proposal will be dealt with in the next section. There, I shall argue that HOT models, understood in this latter way, run into what is, essentially, an analogous problem; a problem of regress.

If Rosenthal wishes to maintain that HOT models are, in part, attempts to explicate the concept of consciousness, then there appear to be three further options available to him. The first option might be to claim that he is using the concept of circularity in a non-standard way, in particular, in a way that renders it independent of the notion of logical connectedness. This would require that Rosenthal find a way of specifying the content of the concept of circularity that makes this concept independent of the notion of logical connectedness. I have no idea how this could be done, and Rosenthal certainly gives no indication that he is interested in this option.

---

[5] Actually, there are five. But I assume that denying the transitivity of logical connectedness is not a realistic option.

The second option is to admit the circularity, but deny that it is vicious. Logical circles that are wide enough, we are sometimes told, need not be vicious ones. The option, however, seems unpromising for the simple reason that the circle inherent in Rosenthal's model does not seem to be a wide one. On either of the three accounts, suggested above, of the relation between the concepts of mental states and that of consciousness, in order to understand the former one needs to understand the latter. Logical circles do not, it seems, get much tighter.

The third option is probably the most promising, but takes some unpacking. Broadly speaking, the option involves abandoning the claim that an account of intransitive state consciousness that involves appeal to intransitive state consciousness is thereby a circular account. This, of course, contradicts Rosenthal's stated position, but it is, nonetheless, a possible option. In fact, not only is it a possible option, it seems to be the one that is actually endorsed by Carruthers.

With regard to the issue of circularity, Carruthers' account differs radically from that of Rosenthal. Rosenthal insists that the higher-order thought in which the intransitive consciousness of a mental state consists cannot, on pain of circularity, itself be intransitively conscious. Carruthers, on the other hand, is quite happy with the idea that the higher-order thought that confers intransitive consciousness on a mental state is itself intransitively conscious (although this claim is rendered somewhat murky by his insistence on the dispositional nature of the thought; presumably the idea is that if the thought is occurrent, then it is or can be also intransitively conscious). In response to the charge of circularity, Carruthers replies that this is really no problem for we can give a *recursive* explanation of intransitive state consciousness. That is:

Any mental state M, of mine, is conscious = M (level 1) causes the belief (level 2) that I have M, which in turn causes the belief (level 3) that I believe that I have M, and so on; *and every state in this series, of level n, causes a higher-order belief of level n +1.* (1996: 165, emphasis his)

Now, on the face of it, this seems quite staggering in its complacency. For, with respect to consciousness, surely what we are after is not a recursive explanation but a *reductive* one. That is, the efforts of the diverse group of philosophers interested in this subject in the past couple of decades have been concerned with the possibility of *naturalising* consciousness: explaining what consciousness is in more basic terms, by appeal to objects, properties, relations, or whatever, that are *not* themselves conscious, or, at the conceptual level, explicating the concept of consciousness in terms of more basic concepts. Of course, we can give a recursive explanation of consciousness; whoever thought otherwise? But to attempt *only* such an explanation is, in effect, to give up on the attempt at providing a reductive explanation of consciousness; it is to give up on the project of naturalising consciousness in the above sense.

It would, perhaps, be unfair to accuse Carruthers of such a basic error. What underlies his above remarks, I think, is a far more respectable project. The recursive explanation of consciousness, of the sort outlined above, functions in much the same sort of way as does, for example, a Ramsey sentence in traditional functionalist accounts of mental state types. In such accounts, the reduction of mental state types was effected not by the Ramsey sentence itself, but by identification of the filler of a causal role – a role specified by the Ramsey sentence – with a physical state (that realises the same causal role). Carruthers is entitled to make a similar point: that the explanatory reduction of consciousness is effected not by the recursive explanation of consciousness, but by the subsequent identification of a cognitive architecture that realises or underwrites the roles specified in the recursive explanation. The reductive aspect of Carruthers' account lies here; in the identification of the relevant cognitive architecture, and not in the recursive specification itself.

Carruthers' strategy avoids the problem of circularity, then, but only because he changes the function of the appeal to higher-order thoughts in the explanation of intransitive state consciousness. On Carruthers' model, unlike Rosenthal's, the appeal to such thoughts, in itself, does not function reductively. That is, the appeal does not even attempt to explain the nature of consciousness in terms of items that are not conscious. However, what this does mean is that if Carruthers' model is to be of any interest, the reductive element of the model must be incorporated elsewhere, by the identification of a suitable cognitive architecture capable of underwriting the roles specified by the recursive explanation. To specify such an architecture, therefore, would be to specify the properties in virtue of which a mental state is intransitively conscious; it would be to specify the properties that make a given mental state intransitively conscious, or (alternatively), the properties in which the intransitive consciousness of a mental state consists.

This means, in effect, that this final option reduces to a version of the first option: the denial of the claim that the purpose of the HOT model is conceptual analysis and the assertion that its purpose is ontological reduction. That is, HOT models, on this view, are attempts not to explain the concept of consciousness but to identify the property of consciousness, the property in virtue of which mental states are intransitively conscious. It is to an assessment of HOT models understood in this way that we now turn. I shall argue that, understood in this way, such models suffer from a problem of *regress*.

3   The problem of regress

If construed as an ontological attempt to identify the property that makes mental states intransitively conscious, the HOT account faces a rather unpleasant dilemma. HOT models try to ground the intransitive consciousness of a mental state M in a given subject S in the simultaneous possession, by S, of a first-person indexical thought to the effect that S possesses M. For example, my pain is intransitively conscious if, and only if, I possess a thought to the effect that I am in pain. But then an obvious dilemma arises. Either the higher-order thought that I am in pain is itself intransitively conscious or it is not. If it is, and if its being intransitively conscious is what grounds the intransitive consciousness of the pain, then the HOT model clearly faces a regress. The property that confers intransitive state consciousness has not been identified but deferred. So, suppose now that the higher-order thought is not intransitively conscious. Then, among other things, I will not be aware of having this thought. So, I will not be aware of thinking that I am in pain; I will, in effect, have no idea that I am thinking this. But, then, how is my thinking that I am in pain supposed to ground the intransitive consciousness of my pain? How can my thinking that I am in pain make me conscious of my pain if I have no idea that I am thinking that I am in pain?

Rosenthal is well aware of this sort of objection. It is, after all, a stunningly obvious one. But his reply is, I think, less than satisfactory. He writes:

This objection disregards the distinction between transitive and intransitive consciousness. HOT's confer intransitive consciousness on the mental states they are about because it is in virtue of those thoughts that we are transitively conscious of those mental states . . . So a HOT can be a source of consciousness for the mental state it is about because the HOT is a transitive state of consciousness; it does not also need to be an intransitive state of consciousness. (1990: 16)

But this, of course, is not an answer to the objection, but merely a restatement of the HOT model. What we need to understand is how an intransitively non-conscious thought can make another state intransitively conscious. To this objection, Rosenthal merely writes:

One might insist that this misunderstands the objection about a source of consciousness; such a source must be conscious in just the way conscious states are conscious. But without some independent justification, this claim begs the question at hand, since on the HOT theory a state's being intransitively conscious just is one's being transitively conscious of it in a suitable way. (1990: 16)

Now it is unclear to me, to say the least, who is begging the question here. But, in any event, it is possible, I think, to satisfy Rosenthal's demand for independent justification as follows.

Consider my thought that Ouagadougou is the capital of Burkina Faso (a didactically useful thought gratefully acquired from Stephen Stich many years ago and updated to keep track of recent political developments in Africa). When this thought is intransitively conscious, that is when I am aware of having it, the thought makes me aware that Ouagadougou is the capital of Burkina Faso. What about when it is not intransitively conscious? Does it make me aware that Ouagadougou is the capital of Burkina Faso then? It seems not. That is why I am not, in the relevant sense, aware that Ouagadougou is the capital of Burkina Faso most of the time.[6] Now clearly, the instantiation of the relation of *being the capital of* by Ouagadougou and Burkina Faso is not the sort of thing that can itself be intransitively conscious. Therefore, the instantiation of the relation is something of which I am transitively conscious. And what makes me transitively conscious of this is the fact that my thought itself is intransitively conscious. If it were not, then it is difficult to see how it could make me transitively conscious of the relation between Ouagadougou and Burkina Faso.

This intuitive idea can be generalised. Thoughts are, of course, representational states. And it is a truism that to be aware of a thought is, in part, to be aware of what it represents. Almost as truistic is the idea that one of the differences between an intransitively conscious thought T and one which is not is an awareness of what T represents. That is, intransitively conscious thoughts are distinguished from intransitively non-conscious thoughts by way of the transitive consciousness of what they represent. Intransitively conscious thoughts are ones which make us transitively conscious of what they represent, and intransitively non-conscious thoughts are ones which do not make us transitively conscious of what they represent. This account of the difference between intransitively conscious and intransitively non-conscious thoughts is not, of course, supposed to be non-circular, but rather is intended to highlight the conceptual connections between intransitive consciousness of a thought and transitive consciousness of what it represents.

[6] Of course, in one sense of 'aware', I am aware that Ouagadougou is the capital of Burkina Faso all the time. 'Aware', in this sense, means, roughly, 'being informed of'. It should be clear that this is not the sense of awareness relevant to the present issue. The HOT model is an account of consciousness, not an epistemological theory about the conditions under which one can be said to be informed about some fact.

The moral seems to be that thoughts can indeed make us transitively conscious of things. But they can do so only when they themselves are intransitively conscious. And Rosenthal has given us no reason for supposing that higher-order thoughts are any different from first-order thoughts in this regard. Understanding how an intransitively unconscious thought that I am in pain can make me transitively conscious of a pain is just as difficult as understanding how the intransitively unconscious thought that Ouagadougou is the capital of Burkina Faso can make me transitively conscious of the relation between Ouagadougou and Burkina Faso. But if thoughts can make us transitively conscious of mental states only when those thoughts are intransitively conscious, and if it is our higher-order thought-mediated transitive consciousness of mental states that makes those states intransitively conscious, the HOT model finds itself, once again, facing the problem of regress.

It might be thought the HOT account can avoid this conclusion. In particular, it might be thought that a distinction drawn by Carruthers (1996: 54) could be pressed into service here. The distinction is between non-conscious mental states that are *dormant* and those that are *activated*. Most of my representational mental states, including the belief that Ouagadougou is the capital of Burkina Faso, lie dormant most of the time. I have them, but they have no effect on my current mental processes. And this is, of course, because representational states are dispositional. Sometimes, however, these states become active, as when one acts so as to satisfy a desire, or to form new beliefs on the basis of present ones.

The distinction might be thought to give the HOT model a way of avoiding the problem of regress. It could be argued that while representational states that are both non-conscious and dormant do not make us aware of what those states represent, representational states that are non-conscious but active do make us so aware. And, if this is correct, we can avoid the problem of regress if the higher-order thoughts that bestow intransitive consciousness on the states they represent are non-conscious but active.

This line of argument certainly looks plausible when we consider the well-known cases of non-conscious perception of the sort involved in driving along a familiar road, walking across the living room, doing the washing up, and so on. If these are indeed examples of non-conscious perception,[7] then they certainly also seem to make us aware, non-consciously, of our surroundings. So, we seem to have examples of mental

---

[7] This has been challenged by Dennett (1991: 137) and Kirk (1992: 35) who regard these sorts of cases as examples of near-instantaneous memory loss.

states that are non-conscious but which, nonetheless, make us aware of what they represent.

However, when we switch our attention to other examples of representational states, the plausibility of this picture evaporates. The HOT model is, of course, not a perceptual (i.e. HOP) model of consciousness, and, indeed, is incompatible with a perceptual model. So, more germane to the present issue is not whether there are non-conscious perceptions that make us aware of what they represent, but whether there are non-conscious thoughts that do this. And, I think, the answer, here, is clearly that there are not.

Consider what is involved in thinking, unconsciously, that, say, my dog is seriously ill. This thought, we will suppose, is active, in Carruthers' sense, thus exerts an influence on my current mental processes. The genesis of this thought need not concern us unduly, but we might suppose that I have subliminally picked up on certain tell-tale signs of serious illness, without, consciously, recognising them for what they are. Therefore, assuming I am attached to my dog, I might find myself doing various things: giving him more expensive and appetising meals than usual, taking him for longer and more enjoyable walks, etc. I might also find myself feeling various things, unexplained senses of melancholy, or whatever. But, it seems, what makes my thought that my dog is seriously ill an intransitively non-conscious one is precisely the fact that I am not aware of the content of this thought; I am not aware of the fact that my dog is seriously ill. Thus, I am doing these things, but have no idea why. And, as soon as I become aware of this content, as soon as I become aware of the fact of serious illness in my dog, my thought, of course, becomes a conscious one. Indeed, this seems to be precisely what makes it a conscious thought. With regard to thoughts, if not with regard to perception, the intransitive consciousness of a thought and the transitive consciousness of what it represents go hand in hand: one does not find one without the other.

If this is correct, then intransitively unconscious thoughts do not yield transitive consciousness of what they represent. In order for us to be conscious of what a thought represents, the thought itself must be intransitively conscious. It would, in fact, be very surprising if the dormant/active distinction yielded a way of avoiding the problem of regress, for the distinction marks a difference in the role a representational state can play in mental processing, and it is certainly difficult to see how we are going to get from this to any substantive claim about representation itself. More concretely, the key feature of active but non-conscious representational states is that they influence our occurrent mental processing, hence our behaviour, *without* making us aware of what it is they represent. It is their role in influencing our mental processing that makes them active, but, crucially, it is the fact that they do not make us aware of what they represent that makes them non-conscious.

So, once again, intransitively unconscious thoughts do not yield awareness of what they represent. So it is difficult to see how an intransitively unconscious higher-order thought can yield consciousness of the mental states it is about. The only way, it seems, to get such awareness is to make the higher-order thought intransitively conscious. And then we are simply back to the problem of regress.

Carruthers' official response to the problem of regress, however, rests not on the dormant/active distinction, but on the actualist/dispositionalist distinction outlined earlier (1996: 194ff.). As we have seen, according to actualist versions of the HOT account, the intransitive consciousness of a mental state M, possessed by creature C, consists in the actual presence of a higher-order thought in C to the effect that C currently possesses M. Dispositionalist accounts, however, reject this condition. According to the standard dispositionalist account, intransitive state consciousness of M consists in C's being *disposed* to have a thought to the effect that it has M. And, according to Carruthers, and *pace* Rosenthal, the higher-order belief that C is disposed to have to the effect that it possesses M must be a conscious one. And this, as we have seen, and as Carruthers acknowledges, leads to a regress: an infinitely nested set of conscious beliefs. In order to avoid this regress, Carruthers argues, we must reject an actualist HOT model in favour of a dispositionalist one.

Carruthers believes dispositionalist HOT accounts avoid this problem because he has a particular (and, I think, peculiar) understanding of what the regress problem actually is. The problem of regress is, according to Carruthers, essentially a problem of *cognitive overload*. Actualist HOT models, since they are committed to explaining intransitive mental state consciousness in terms of the presence of a conscious higher-order thought, will lead to an infinite regress of nested conscious beliefs. And any cognitive system would, of course, be incapable of storing an infinite set of actual (i.e. occurrent) beliefs.[8] Carruthers' answer is to move from an actualist to a dispositionalist HOT account since there is no problem, he argues, in understanding how a cognitive system could instantiate an infinite number of dispositional higher-order thoughts.

The answer to the question of in what intransitive state consciousness consists, on the dispositionalist account, is, then, this. Intransitive state consciousness consists in an infinitely nested set of dispositional higher-order thoughts to the effect that (i) one is in mental state M, (ii) one

---

[8] See Carruthers (1996: 166). This is not the only source of overload that troubles Carruthers. Another derives from the richness of our experience and the resulting necessity of a belief for every aspect of our experience of which we can be conscious (1996: 167–8).

believes that one is in mental state M, (iii) one believes that one believes that one is in mental state M, (iv) one believes that one believes that one believes that one is in mental state M, and so on *ad infinitum*.

There are, I think, several problems with the dispositionalist gambit, but I shall develop just one of them. Suppose mental state M, possessed by me, is accompanied by an occurrent or actual higher-order thought to the effect that I possess M. Then, on both an actualist and a dispositionalist account, M is an intransitively conscious mental state. Suppose, now, that M is not accompanied by an actual higher-order thought to the effect that I am in M, but has a disposition to produce such a thought in me in appropriate circumstances. Then, on the dispositionalist, but not on the actualist, account, M is intransitively conscious. In fact, on the dispositionalist account, M is conscious in precisely the same way and to precisely the same extent as in the first case. This is because, on the dispositionalist account, it is the presence of the disposition to cause the higher-order thought that is crucial and not whether, in any particular case, the disposition is actualised.

Therefore, if the dispositionalist version of HOT, like its actualist counterpart, is in the business of giving an account of in what intransitive state consciousness consists, then it seems committed to the claim that mental states are made intransitively conscious by way of a disposition (or that their intransitive consciousness is constituted by a disposition). And intuitively, this seems very wrong on at least two scores. Firstly, an intransitively conscious experience, for example, seems categorical in a way that dispositions are not. A conscious experience is something actually taking place in me. It does not seem the sort of thing that could be constituted by a disposition: a tendency for something to take place in me. The conscious experience *as* of, say, a loud trumpet seems, at least *prima facie*, to be either something I am having or something I am not having at any given time. And this does not seem the sort of thing that can be captured in terms of certain dispositional facts about myself. (This is, of course, distinct from the question of whether it actually is a loud trumpet I am hearing, as opposed to something that could be mistaken for a loud trumpet. The present point concerns the having of an experience with a given phenomenological character.) On the face of it, there seems almost as much difficulty in understanding how a conscious experience could be constituted by a *disposition* to produce a higher-order thought as by, say, a disposition to behave in various ways. Phenomenologically, conscious experiences are categorical in a way that seems to make them incapable of being constituted by dispositions. The question of the nature and status of conscious experience is, of course, a controversial one. Nevertheless, it seems that an adequate defence of the claim that conscious experience is constituted by a type of disposition cannot be developed in the absence of a general defence of the view that we are fundamentally and systematically mistaken about the phenomenological character of our experiences.[9] One finds no such defence in the work of Carruthers.[10]

Secondly, and more importantly, there seem to be severe difficulties in even making sense of the claim that dispositions can actually *make* anything be a certain way. Dispositions are simply not the sorts of things that can make a particular item have a property P. They are descriptions of that item's tendency to acquire P under certain circumstances. It is not the brittleness of an object that makes it break upon falling. Rather, its brittleness is simply its tendency to break in these sorts of circumstances. What makes the object break is not its brittleness but a certain underlying categorical molecular structure. And, if this is correct, it is, to say the least, unclear how a disposition to instantiate a higher-order thought can even be the right sort of thing to make a mental state intransitively conscious.

The nature of dispositions is, of course, disputed. And it might seem that Carruthers could avoid this problem by adopting an alternative account of dispositions. Armstrong, for example, has argued that dispositions are identical with the physical structures in which they are instantiated. On this view, brittleness, for example, is in fact a particular type of molecular structure. And, if this is true, dispositions, after all, can be the sort of thing that can make a particular item behave in a certain way or acquire a certain property.

The problem for Carruthers, however, is that this alternative account of dispositions is not available to him. The reason, in a nutshell, is that what is crucial to Carruthers' account is that higher-order thoughts are *non-categorical* in character, and Armstrong's account is, in essence, a categorical view of the nature of dispositions. If there is to be any substance at all to the distinction between actualist and dispositionalist versions of the HOT account, then dispositions cannot be assimilated to structures that are actually present, in categorical form, in the items that possess them. Adopting Armstrong's view of dispositions would, then, collapse the distinction between actualist and dispositionalist versions of the HOT account.

To see this, consider again Carruthers' stated reason for adopting the dispositionalist account. Carruthers argues that dispositionalist versions of the HOT account are to be preferred to their actualist alternatives

---

[9] Of the sort, perhaps, developed by Dennett (1991).

[10] I seriously doubt if such a defence would even be coherent. The general theme, presumably, would be that we are mistaken in thinking that the phenomenal character of our experience is categorical; it only *seems* that way to us. On the face of it, however, this theme seems unintelligible, since the phenomenal character of our experience is, precisely, the way it *seems* to us. We should, I think, be extremely suspicious of any appeal to an appearance/reality distinction for phenomenal character.

because the latter, but not the former, face a problem of *cognitive over-load*.

> There would appear to be an immense amount which we can experience con-sciously at any one time ... Actualist HOR theories purport to explain this dis-tinction [the distinction between conscious and non-conscious experience] in terms of the presence, or absence, of a HOR targeted on the percept in ques-tion. But then it looks as if our HORs must be just as rich and complex as our conscious perceptions, since it is to be the presence of a HOR which explains, of each aspect of those perceptions, its conscious status. And when one reflects on the amount of cognitive space and effort devoted to first-order perception, it becomes hard to believe that a significant proportion of that cognitive overload should be replicated in the form of HORs to underpin consciousness. (1998: 12)

The way to avoid this problem, Carruthers claims, is to go dispositionalist. Dispositionalist forms of the HOT account can 'neatly avoid the cognitive overload problem'.

> They merely have to postulate a special-purpose short-term memory store whose function is, *inter alia*, to make its contents available to HOT. The en-tire contents of the store – which can in principle be as rich and complex as you please – can then be conscious even in the absence of a single HOT, provided that the subject remains *capable* of entertaining HOTs about any aspect of its contents. (1998: 12)

But the contents of dispositional higher-order thoughts can be 'as rich and complex as you please' without precipitating cognitive overload only because these thoughts are there in dispositional, rather than categorical, form. Therefore, if Carruthers adopts the view of dispositions associated with Armstrong, this strategy will not be available to him, because then the higher-order thought will, in effect, be there in categorical form (in the same way that the molecular structure which, on Armstrong's view, is identical with brittleness is there in categorical form). And then the problem of cognitive overload will not have been avoided.

So, the idea that a disposition, in the non-categorical sense required by Carruthers, can *make* a state intransitively conscious is an extremely mysterious one that, on the face of it, seems to make little sense. Is there any way the dispositionalist can avoid this conclusion? Carruthers' at-tempt to deal with this sort of objection is, I think, instructive. In fact, Carruthers does not even consider the problem that dispositions are not the sort of things that can bring about, or be responsible for, the pos-session of a property by any given item. He is, however, willing to allow that conscious experience is categorical in a way that seems to make it ill-suited to being constituted by dispositions. So, consider his response to this problem. He writes:

But the reply to this is easy. For there *is* something categorical taking place in me whenever I have a conscious experience, on the above account – the perceptual information is actually in there in the short-term memory store C, which is defined by its relation to higher-order thought. (1996: 172, emphasis his)

The question, however, is not whether there is anything 'categorical taking place in me whenever I have a conscious experience'. The question is whether this categorical occurrence is what is responsible for the intransitive consciousness of mental states. And it is this question that seems to impale Carruthers on the horns of a serious dilemma.

Suppose he answers this question in the negative. Then the categorical something that is taking place within me is not what grounds the intransitive consciousness of my mental states. And then we are simply back with the problems of explaining (i) how dispositions to have a given thought could be responsible for the categorical nature of my conscious experience, and (ii) how dispositions could ever be responsible for anything at all. So, to answer the question negatively does not allow us to avoid the dilemma. On the contrary, it places us more firmly on one of its horns.

Suppose now that Carruthers answers the question in the affirmative. The categorical something that is taking place within me *is* what grounds my intransitive state consciousness, and hence is what explains its seemingly categorical character. To give this answer is, in effect, to abandon the dispositionalist version of the HOT account. The categorical something taking place within me that grounds the intransitive consciousness of my mental states is not a disposition, but a piece of information present in my short-term memory store. So, intransitive state consciousness is not constituted by a disposition after all.

I think it should be concluded that dispositionalist versions of HOT are inherently unstable and, in any event, cannot do the work required of them. We are left, therefore, with actualist versions. And these, if the arguments of this chapter are correct, lead to an infinite regress.

6   The structure of consciousness

1   Introduction

If we want to understand the peculiar problems consciousness poses for attempts to slot it into the natural order, then we have to understand what is peculiar to, or about, consciousness. In the remainder of the book, I want to press a certain claim, one that, I shall argue, has enormous ramifications. What is peculiar to consciousness is its *structure*, in particular, its *dual* structure. Consciousness can be both *object* and *act* of experience. Metaphorically speaking, consciousness can be both the *directing* of awareness and that upon which awareness is directed. Consciousness can include both experiential features *of* which we are aware, and experiential features *with* which we are aware. This bifurcation lies at the core of consciousness; consciousness is essentially hybrid, and this, I shall argue, is the basis of its peculiarity.

The hybrid character of consciousness brings with it the possibility of ambiguity in our interpretation of its central features. For example, as we saw in part 1, a conceptual device that has assumed particular importance in explaining the character of consciousness is the notion that there is *something that it is like* to be conscious, or to undergo conscious experience. However, if consciousness is, indeed, essentially hybrid in character, then this introduces the possibility of quite distinct interpretations of the what it is like of conscious experience. On one interpretation, the what it is like of our experience is something *of* which we are aware in the having of that experience; it is one of the items with which we are consciously acquainted when we have that experience. On the other interpretation, the what it is like of our experience is not something *of* which we are aware, but something *with* which we are aware; it is a feature of our experience in virtue of which we are, for example, aware of the world as being thus-and-so. This is not, at present, to say that either or both interpretations are correct – that is a matter for the next chapter – but, rather, that the possibility of both interpretations is implicated in the hybrid nature of consciousness.

This chapter is concerned with establishing the hybrid character of consciousness and, consequently, the possibility of distinct interpretations of its constitutive features. I shall also try to show that most recent discussions are not sufficiently sensitive to the hybrid nature of consciousness. Indeed, most, if not all, recent discussions operate with a conception of consciousness as essentially an object, rather than an act, of awareness. Consciousness is explicitly or implicitly assimilated to the sort of thing that can be an object of conscious experience. While this assimilation, in itself, is not strictly mistaken, I shall argue, it does leave us with an incomplete conception of consciousness. Moreover, it can result in further assimilations which are, I shall argue, straightforwardly mistaken. Thus, the assimilation of consciousness to an object of experience results in the identification of the what it is like of experience as an item of which a subject is aware in the having of experience. And this latter assimilation, I shall try to show in chapter 7, is mistaken.

At root, however, the problem with ignoring the hybrid status of consciousness, and, as a result, assimilating consciousness to an object of consciousness is that *many* things can be objects of consciousness. Some of these things are conscious – as when we introspectively direct our attention towards an experience we are currently having; most are not. But only consciousness can exist as the directing of conscious experience. Thus, it might be expected that if we are to identify what is most distinctive about consciousness, we must focus on the fact that consciousness is the act of experience as well as an object. Thus, also, it might be expected that, if we want to adequately grasp the *peculiar* problems that consciousness poses for attempts to locate it in the natural order, we must focus on consciousness as the act of experience, and not as an object.

2   Consciousness as object of consciousness: empirical apperception

Before the advent of consciousness, the world and its component parts were simply objects. Not objects of consciousness, of course, since there was none. Nevertheless, before consciousness evolved, the world was made up of physical particulars – objects, events, processes, and the like – with physical properties – shape, motion, mass, and the like – and both these sorts of item were *potential* objects of consciousness: the sorts of things that could become objects of consciousness should it ever arise. Consciousness is the fault line that splits reality asunder. The world now contains not just objects, but also subjects. The world now contains not just items towards which awareness can be directed, it also contains the directing of awareness itself.

The most significant aspect of consciousness, I shall try to show, is its structure, its *hybrid* character. Consciousness can be both act and object of experience. Using the somewhat metaphorical notion of *directing*, we might say that consciousness is not only the directing of awareness but *can* be that upon which awareness is directed. Consciousness is not only the act of conscious experience, it can be experience's object.

To say that it is possible for consciousness to become an object of consciousness is simply to express an idea that is, at least apparently, pretty ordinary: *empirical apperception is possible*. We can be, and often are, aware of what it is we are thinking, feeling, wanting, and so on. Apperception, as I shall use the term, simply denotes whatever process, or, in all probability, *class* of processes, is responsible for subjects of consciousness being aware of the conscious states they instantiate. Largely due to the influence of Kant, apperception became associated with a representation of self, thus with *self*-consciousness.[1] However, that is not how I shall use the term here, at least not if this is understood in terms of the acquisition and deployment in reasoning of a self-concept. The term 'apperception', as employed here, might be thought to approximate to 'introspection'. However, I propose to reserve this latter term for one specific form of apperception: hence I require the more general denomination.[2] There are, in fact, two quite distinct forms of apperception; one relatively quotidian, one curiously neglected in recent times. The first is *empirical*, the second *transcendental* apperception. This section deals with the former.

Empirical apperception, as I shall use the expression, is characterised by two claims. Firstly, it is a process in virtue of which a subject is aware of either the mental states (events, processes) or of the facts she instantiates. The distinction between states, events and processes on the one hand, and facts on the other, is, as we shall see, not insignificant. Indeed, it generally corresponds to quite different ways of understanding the nature of the apperceptive process in question. Secondly, the apperceptive process is

---

[1] This is because Kant, at least on some of the manifold interpretations of Kant, thought that transcendental apperception amounted to nothing more than the thought of (or perhaps ability to have the thought of) a thinking subject that persists through time. The notion of transcendental apperception, as employed in later sections of this chapter, differs significantly from this Kantian version.

[2] Things are a little muddy here. It may well be that empirical apperception is nothing more than introspection. However, I shall not assume that this is so. Locke, for example, who adopts a perceptual model of consciousness, also distinguishes degrees of consciousness. Thus, one possibility is that introspection in any full-blooded sense, that is, where one deliberately and attentively focuses on one's mental goings on, may be identified only with heightened degrees of perceptual consciousness. To avoid these sorts of complications, I propose not to assume that introspection is the only form of empirical apperception. What is crucial to future discussion is the numerical distinctness of the act of apperception from the mental state thus apperceived, and not the essentially terminological issue of whether this should be labelled introspection.

numerically distinct from the states or facts that it reveals to the subject. The first condition is, arguably, common to all forms of apperception. It is the second condition that renders the apperceptive process specifically empirical in character.

John Locke provides a good place to begin any account of empirical apperception. As we saw in chapter 4, consciousness, according to Locke, is 'the perception of what passes in a man's own mind' (1690: II, i, 19). As such, it comprises two distinct mental acts: (i) ideas in one's mind, or processes defined over such ideas, and (ii) a perception of these ideas or processes. The perception of ideas, for Locke, is an act numerically distinct from the having of the ideas themselves. The claim that ideas in one's mind are distinct from one's perception of those ideas is one that is dubiously compatible with Locke's insistence that 'thinking consists in being conscious that one thinks', hence that thinking cannot exist without consciousness of thinking. Nevertheless, the numerical distinctness of idea from consciousness of that idea is, apparently, forced upon Locke by his perceptual model of consciousness.

Introspection is the most familiar form of empirical apperception. Thus, in one clear sense, talk of consciousness becoming an object for itself is just a way of recording the relatively mundane claim that introspection is possible. I say *relatively* mundane, because while the existence of introspection is not in dispute, its nature very much is. There are, that is, very different accounts of in what one's introspective access to one's own conscious states consists. Some accounts, object perception models providing the most obvious example, are pretty clearly designed along Lockean lines. On a simple object perception model introspection will have essentially the same dyadic structure as perception, a structure constituted by a content bearing state whose directedness towards its intentional object is effected by way of some sort of causal relation. Other models of introspection, however, are quite different. Dretske (1995), for example, defends a *displaced* perception model of introspection. On this account, very roughly, our introspective access to our own conscious states is a function of our experiential access to, typically, environmental items. The principle is similar to learning about, for example, the amount of petrol in one's gas tank through perception of the petrol gauge. These two models are quite different, not only in terms of their basic structure but also in terms of their consequences. On an object perception model, for example, introspection affords us access to mental objects, events, or processes.[3] On a displaced perception model, however, introspection, it

[3] There is nothing in this that is incompatible with materialism, of course, provided that we are willing to identify such objects, events or processes with physical objects, events or processes.

seems most natural to say, affords us access not to mental objects, events or processes but to mental *facts*. Our awareness is (typically) of an environmental object, but this affords us information about, or allows us to acquire knowledge of, a mental fact.

The above examples, of course, by no means exhaust the possible accounts of introspection. Fortunately, at least at the outset, there is no need to adjudicate between competing models. So, at least to begin with, I shall assume the intuitive view that in introspection, and in empirical apperception more generally, we become aware, *in some sense*, of our conscious states, but I shall remain neutral on the question of in what this awareness consists (object perception, displaced perception, etc.). In line with this neutrality, I shall speak of conscious *items*, where this is intended to be neutral between mental objects, events, processes and mental facts. Moreover, my talk of *awareness* of conscious items should be understood in a sense sufficiently broad to incorporate the sort of information acquired through displaced perception of non-mental objects. That is, to be aware of, in the sense used in this chapter, means to have acquired the relevant sort of information about, where, firstly, the notion of *about* is neutral between *of* and *that* and, secondly, where the notion of relevance is to be cashed out in terms of one's favoured model of introspection.

Therefore, to claim that consciousness can become an object for itself is simply to claim that it is possible for some conscious beings, such as ourselves, to become aware of, in the sense of acquiring the relevant sort of information about, conscious mental items that we ourselves possess or instantiate. To claim that consciousness can be an object, or become an object, for itself, is simply to claim that introspection is possible.

3   Transcendental apperception

In the First Replies to the objections raised against his *Meditations of First Philosophy*, Descartes claims that 'there can be nothing within me [as a thinking thing] of which I am not in some way aware' (CSM II: 77).[4] This view is reiterated in the Fourth Replies: 'The fact that there can be nothing in the mind, in so far as it is a thinking thing, of which it is not aware ... seems to me self evident ... We cannot have any thought of which we are not aware at the very moment when it is in us' (CSM II: 171). Along with McRae (1965: 183), I take these, and numerous similar

---

[4] René Descartes, 'Objections and replies to *Meditations of First Philosophy*', in *The Philosophical Writings of Descartes*, 2 vols., trans. John Cottingham, Robert Stoothoff and Dugald Murdoch, Cambridge, Cambridge University Press. I shall refer to the Cottingham, Stoothoff and Murdoch translations of Descartes as CSM I and II.

assertions, to indicate that for Descartes all thought is accompanied by apperception of some form. However, there are two different ways of interpreting Descartes's claim.

On one reading, Descartes is claiming that every act of consciousness is accompanied by a second, numerically distinct, act of consciousness. That is, Descartes is claiming that every act of consciousness is accompanied by empirical apperception of that act; this apperception having the original act as its object. Bernard Williams (1978) reads Descartes in this way, and this results in his accusation that Descartes confuses mere consciousness with reflective consciousness. For Williams, Descartes's claim that all consciousness is self-consciousness is equivalent to the claim that every act of consciousness requires making a reflexive judgement about oneself.

On the other reading, Descartes is seen as claiming that every act of consciousness is one with a consciousness of itself. According to Aquila (1988), for example, 'Descartes proposes an *identification* of a certain kind of self- or inner-directed consciousness with a certain kind of cognition or perception of which it is a consciousness' (1988: 547). If a subject is conscious of an external object, for example, then the subject's consciousness of herself as conscious of that object is not distinct from her consciousness of that object. Understood in this way, Descartes is not claiming that every act of consciousness is accompanied by an act of empirical apperception. His claim, rather, is that every such act is accompanied by one of *transcendental* apperception.

Like anything that is to count as apperception, transcendental apperception is a process in virtue of which a subject is aware of either the mental states or of the mental facts she instantiates. However, unlike its empirical cousin, the act of transcendental apperception is not numerically distinct from the mental act (or fact) of which it makes its subject aware. Although the idea of transcendental apperception may be present, at least implicitly, in Descartes, it is most closely associated with Kant.

Kant, as is well known, distinguishes two types or modes of apperception: empirical and transcendental. Like Locke, Kant seems to adopt a quasi-perceptual mode of the former. Empirical apperception, he tells us, is 'consciousness of self according to the determinations of our state in inner perception' (A 107).[5] Empirical apperception, Kant claims, occurs through 'self-affection'; we are affected by ourselves because of our faculty of inner sense (B 156), and this is the faculty by means of which the mind intuits its inner states. Empirical apperception 'yields no intuition

---

[5] Here I follow standard practice by referring to the first and second editions of Kant's *Critique* by the letters A and B respectively.

of the soul itself as an object' (A 22/B 37). Rather, it yields consciousness of one's states of consciousness.

While Kant's account of empirical apperception seems, fairly clearly (or as clear as it is possible to get when interpreting Kant), the perceptual model, his account of transcendental apperception is quite different. This account is based on the relation between apperception, consciousness of objects, and the concept of synthesis. The idea of synthesis is, in the first instance, linked to consciousness of objects. Synthesis of a manifold of intuitions (roughly, sensory data) requires the use of the concept of an object in general. In virtue of this requirement, synthesis produces consciousness of objects and, hence, of an objective world. Consciousness of objects is then linked to transcendental apperception via the idea of synthesis. The idea, in broad outline, is this. Transcendental apperception, in itself, has no contents. The only way for the self to be conscious of itself, then, is by means of a contrast between, on the one hand, its pure identity and unchangingness and, on the other, the constant variety and change in the contents of experience. However, it is, according to Kant, only if the data presented to sensibility are conceived of – via synthesis – as constituting relatively permanent items that the experiencing subject can distinguish itself as distinct from them, since this requires that the order of subjective representational states is distinguishable from the order of the represented items. And this, in Kant's view, amounts to the idea of a subject's series of representations jointly constituting a course of experience through an objective world. Thus, it is through the unifying of the sensory manifold brought about by the activity of synthesis that the self comes to consciousness both of itself and of its objects. That is, it is only through consciousness of self and object simultaneously that consciousness of either can be attained. Consciousness of self and consciousness of objects are connected by synthesis because synthesis necessarily produces both. An objective synthetic unity of experience is correlative with the transcendental unity of apperception because the conditions under which an experienced world is constituted as an intelligible synthetic unity are the same as the conditions by which an experiencing consciousness is constituted as a unitary self.

Thus, for Kant, all conceptual representation of an objective world is self-conscious. What transcendental apperception ultimately amounts to, for Kant, is not awareness of one's mental states, nor is it the awareness of the self as an object; rather, it is the representation of the identity of the self through time. It is the possibility (or, on some interpretations, the actuality) of such representation that must accompany every conscious act.

For our purposes, what is important is that transcendental apperception is not a process whereby the self is made into an object of
consciousness. Nor, unlike empirical apperception, does transcendental apperception make states of the self into objects of consciousness. By
separating transcendental from empirical apperception, Kant makes it
clear that transcendental apperception is awareness of self not as an object of consciousness but as a *necessary condition of consciousness*. Equivalently, transcendental apperception is not a *dyadic* relation, of the sort
that might obtain between consciousness and its object. Therefore, neither can it be constructed out of, or explained in terms of, such relations.
Thus, transcendental apperception cannot be explained as a form of intentional relation. Nor, for the same reason, can it be explained as a
form of knowledge. For, certainly *prima facie*, knowledge conforms to
the sort of dyadic structure – the act of knowing and the object known –
that makes it an unsuitable tool for understanding transcendental apperception. The awareness that transcendental apperception yields is not a
species of knowledge, at least as this is commonly understood.[6]

The existence of a form of transcendental apperception implicit in every
conscious act is also asserted by Sartre, although Sartre's account differs
significantly from that of Kant. For Kant, transcendental apperception is,
essentially, the representation of a thinking subject that persists through
time. For Sartre, on the other hand, transcendental apperception pertains
not to representation of a persisting self but to specific modes or acts of
consciousness.

Crucial to Sartre's position are the closely related distinctions between (i) *positional* (or *thetic*) consciousness versus *non-positional* (or *non-
thetic*) consciousness, and (ii) *reflective* and *pre-reflective* consciousness. It
is sometimes supposed that these distinctions are equivalent. In fact, they
cross-classify each other.

For Sartre, every act of consciousness has both a positional and non-
positional aspect. Suppose I am looking at a seagull outside my study
window. Then my consciousness of the seagull is positional consciousness, the seagull is 'posited' as the object of my consciousness. Sartre
argues that consciousness is essentially intentional. Thus, all consciousness is necessarily positional consciousness. However, according to Sartre
also, 'every positional consciousness of an object is at the same time
a non-positional consciousness of itself' (1943: liii). This can be explained in terms of the distinction between pre-reflective and reflective
consciousness. My positional consciousness of the seagull is, ordinarily,

---

[6] For support for this claim, see especially the First Paralogism, *Critique of Pure Reason*,
A 341–8. The claim that transcendental apperception is a non-cognitive, non-intentional,
relation is also defended by Dieter Heinrich (1989).

pre-reflective consciousness, where this is understood as consciousness directed towards something other than itself. However, suppose I attempt to focus my attention on my consciousness of the seagull. In this case, I have reflective, positional, consciousness of my consciousness of the seagull, and the consciousness that is doing the reflecting remains non-positionally conscious of itself.

Sartre's pre-reflective consciousness is a form of transcendental apperception as characterised in this section. There are, indeed, striking similarities between Sartre's pre-reflective consciousness and Kant's account of transcendental apperception. No reflection is involved in this mode of self-consciousness for either Sartre or Kant. For both it is a non-cognitive, non-intentional, and crucially non-dyadic mode of self-awareness. Moreover, both transcendental apperception for Kant and pre-reflective consciousness for Sartre yield awareness not of an object of consciousness but of a necessary condition of consciousness.

Most importantly, Sartre is quite clear on two things. Firstly, pre-reflective consciousness is a mode of awareness of one's conscious acts, hence it is, on the present characterisation, a form of apperception:

> However, the necessary and sufficient condition for a knowing consciousness to be knowledge of its object, is that it be consciousness of itself as being that knowledge. This is a necessary condition, for if my consciousness were not consciousness of being consciousness of the table, it would then be consciousness of that table without consciousness of being so. In other words, it would be a consciousness ignorant of itself, an unconscious – which is absurd. This is a sufficient condition, for my being conscious of being conscious of that table suffices in fact for me to be conscious of it. (1943: xxviii)

The type of awareness yielded by pre-reflective consciousness, then, is awareness of itself as a specific act or mode of consciousness (e.g. a perception of a table). That is, pre-reflective consciousness is, as Sarte puts it, 'consciousness conscious of itself as consciousness of an object' (1943: xxx).

Secondly, pre-reflective consciousness is not numerically distinct from the act of positional consciousness. This is a claim consistently asserted by Sartre in both *The Transcendence of the Ego* and *Being and Nothingness*. Thus, in the former we are told, for example, that 'To be and to be aware of itself are one and the same thing for consciousness' (1936: 83). And, in the latter, it is emphasised over and over again that the existence of pre-reflective consciousness does not break the unity of consciousness. Every positional consciousness of an object *just is* a non-positional consciousness of itself: 'We understand now why the first consciousness of consciousness is not positional; it is because it is one with the consciousness of which it is consciousness' (1943: xxx).

It is for this reason that pre-reflective consciousness cannot be regarded as a form of knowledge. The fact that pre-reflective consciousness is not numerically distinct from the consciousness of which it is consciousness means, indeed, that it cannot be explained in terms of any form of dyadic relation. Any attempt to explain it in these sorts of terms would lead to an infinite regress:

> The reduction of consciousness to knowledge in fact involves our introducing into consciousness the subject–object dualism which is typical of knowledge. But if we accept the law of the knower-known dyad, then a third term will be necessary in order for the knower to become known in turn, and we will be faced with this dilemma: Either we stop at any one term of the series – the known, the knower known, the knower known by the knower, etc. In this case, the totality of the phenomenon falls into the unknown; that is we always bump up against a non-self-conscious reflection and a final term. Or else we affirm the necessity of an infinite regress ... which is absurd. (1943: xxviii)

That is, if we conceive of the relation between the pre-reflective consciousness and the consciousness of which it is consciousness in terms of a dyadic model we end up with either a regress or a final term in the series, a final term which is not consciousness and which, Sartre thinks, therefore cannot ground the consciousness of the terms in the series. To avoid this we need to accept that 'there must be an immediate, non-cognitive relation of the self to itself' (1943: xxix).

To emphasise the indivisibility of pre-reflective consciousness from positional consciousness, Sartre recommends a syntactic intervention.

> We understand now why the first consciousness of consciousness is not positional; it is because it is one with the consciousness of which it is consciousness. At one stroke it determines itself as consciousness of perception and as perception. The necessity of syntax has compelled us hitherto to speak of the 'non-positional consciousness of self'. But we can no longer use this expression in which the 'of self' still evokes the idea of knowledge. (Henceforth we shall put the 'of' inside parentheses to show that it merely satisfies a grammatical requirement.) (1943: xxx)

Whatever pre-reflective consciousness does involve, then, it is clear that it does not involve the positing of consciousness as an object of consciousness. Pre-reflective consciousness is a mode of awareness of one's (positional) conscious acts, hence qualifies as a form of apperception. However, it is not numerically distinct from these positional conscious acts. Thus, it is a form of transcendental, not empirical, apperception.

The concept of transcendental apperception is one that has been curiously neglected in recent philosophy of mind. Perhaps, at least in part, this is because it is a notoriously obscure concept, one whose content can, I think, legitimately be questioned. Sartre has several interesting phenomenological and transcendental-phenomenological arguments for asserting the existence of pre-reflective consciousness, or transcendental apperception as I have called it. However, it may well be that Sartre's way of explicating the content of this concept may, in the final analysis, prove not entirely consistent.[7] To the extent that it is visible in recent analytic philosophy of mind, discussion of transcendental apperception occurs in mutated, though importantly related, forms, for example non-conceptual self-consciousness realised in proprioceptive and ecological specifications of the self and its states (see Evans (1982), Bermudez (1998), Wider (1997) and Hurley (1998)).

In any event, this chapter, and much of the argument of the remainder of this book, turns on consciousness in its dual capacity as act and object of experience. In particular, I am going to be concerned with what sorts of features of conscious experience can be made into objects of such experience. But transcendental apperception, as we have seen, is certainly not a process whereby consciousness is made into an object of experience. Therefore, it is not directly relevant to the arguments to be developed in the remainder of this book. Depressingly, therefore, I shall continue in this tradition of neglect. This is unfortunate; for me as much as anyone else. For reasons that will, perhaps, become clear later, things would be so much easier if I could assume some robust and widely accepted concept of transcendental apperception. It would, for a start, make the arguments to follow so much easier to swallow.

Furthermore, I think a good case can be made out for the claim that many of the more implausible positions on consciousness in recent philosophy of mind can be traced to a confusion of transcendental with empirical apperception. Higher-order representation models of consciousness provide an obvious example. Indeed, many of the sacred cows of recent discussions of phenomenal consciousness, in particular the idea that we *know* what it is like to have an experience, may be traceable back to the same confusion. But that this is so is not something I shall assume in this book. There is, I think, no general consensus on whether transcendental apperception exists, let alone what it is. And the arguments to be developed in the following chapters will be controversial enough without relying on any controversial premises. Accordingly, I shall make only fleeting, and non-essential, use of the idea of transcendental apperception in the chapters to follow. At most it will be employed as a means of backing up arguments to be developed in those chapters; it will not be employed as the basis of those arguments. And, in particular, when I talk of consciousness, or features of consciousness, being made into objects of

---

[7] For an excellent discussion, see Kathleen Wider, *The Bodily Nature of Consciousness*, chapter 3.

conscious experience, I shall assume that this occurs by way of empirical apperception. And when I talk of empirical apperception, I shall have in mind, almost exclusively, *introspection*.

4   Consciousness as experiential act

To claim that consciousness can be an object of conscious experience amounts to nothing more than the fairly quotidian claim that introspection is possible. To talk of consciousness as the *act* of experience is, again, to record a relatively mundane idea. When we become aware of (i.e. acquire the relevant sort of information about) conscious items that we possess or instantiate, these conscious items cannot, by themselves, exhaust the nature of consciousness. This seems to be a necessary truth about consciousness. Consciousness consists not just in the conscious items of which we are aware, consciousness consists also in the awareness of these conscious items. There is nothing in this claim that entails a higher-order representation theory of consciousness. The claim is not that in order to be conscious we have to be conscious of a conscious item, say by having a (non-conceptually individuated) experience of that item, or by having a (conceptually individuated) thought that one possesses that item. The claim, here, is not one about the necessary conditions of being conscious, nor does it entail any such claim. Rather, the claim is that whenever one is conscious, *whatever is required for that*, one's consciousness is necessarily *not* exhausted by the items of which one is conscious. Consciousness consists in more than the items of which we are consciously aware, it consists also in the awareness of these items.

Since some of the theses that future chapters will try to derive from this claim will be considered by many to be radical, it may be worthwhile at this time to drive home the utter domesticity of these claims. When we are aware of a non-mental item, an environmental object for example, no one would suppose that our consciousness is *exhausted* by this item. Some might want to claim that the environmental item is a *constituent* of our conscious experience of it, and this is a claim with which I have a considerable degree of sympathy. No one, however, would want to claim that the environmental item exhausts our consciousness of it. And this is exhibited in our use of the term *of*. Not only is there the object of our awareness, there is our awareness of it. Similarly, when we are aware of conscious items rather than environmental ones, we should resist any temptation to suppose that our consciousness is exhausted by the items of which we are aware. Not only are there the conscious items of which we are aware, there is our awareness of these items. One need not be committed to any particular model of consciousness, or, indeed, any particular model of introspection, to appreciate this claim.

The claim that consciousness is not exhausted by its objects, even when those objects are conscious states, is one defended forcefully by Sartre:

Thus consciousness (of) belief and belief are one and the same being, the characteristic of which is absolute immanence. But as soon as we wish to grasp this being, it slips between our fingers, and we find ourselves faced with a pattern of duality, with a game of reflections. For consciousness is a reflection (*reflet*), but qua reflection it is exactly the one reflecting (*réfléchissant*), and if we attempt to grasp it as reflecting, it vanishes and we fall back on the reflection. (1943: 74–5)

Indeed, for some modes of consciousness – which he labels *being-for-others* and *impure reflection* – Sartre would go so far as to claim that consciousness cannot be made an object at all. Underlying this claim is his celebrated dictum that *consciousness is not what it is and is what it is not*. When we try to focus our attention on our consciousness, there is at least one aspect of that consciousness that necessarily evades our focusing – the focusing of attention itself. One aspect of consciousness, that is, always evades our conscious grasp. The result is that consciousness is a 'decompression of being'; consciousness is characterised by an essential 'fissure'. Or, as Sartre more famously expresses it, consciousness is essentially infected with *nothingness*:

Nothingness is always an elsewhere. It is the obligation for the for-itself never to exist except in the form of an elsewhere in relation to itself, to exist as a being which perpetually effects in itself a break in being. This break does not refer us elsewhere to another being; it is only a perpetual reference of self to self, of the reflection to the reflecting, of the reflecting to the reflection. (1943: 78)

The intuitive idea that consciousness is not exhausted by its objects, even when those objects are conscious items, can be given somewhat more precise expression by way of a distinction between what I shall call *actualist* and *objectualist* conceptions of consciousness. Suppose one focuses one's attention on one's consciousness, and in doing so becomes aware of various mental items – thoughts, feelings, desires, sensations, and the like – which possess various properties: a thought might be compelling, a feeling irritating, a desire troubling, and so on. When one thinks of consciousness as a collection of these sorts of items, possessing these sorts of properties, one is thinking of consciousness from, as I shall use the expression, the *objectualist* perspective. Consciousness viewed from this perspective is a collection of conscious items and properties. To think of consciousness from the objectualist perspective, therefore, is to think of consciousness as if it were an object of consciousness; it is to think of it as the sort of thing towards which consciousness can be directed. And such a conception is, Sartre's reservations notwithstanding, quite legitimate. Consciousness can be conceived of as an object of consciousness; consciousness can become an object for itself in the sense outlined above.

Consciousness, however, cannot be *identified* with what is revealed from the objectualist perspective because what is revealed from this perspective cannot exhaust consciousness. Consciousness is not only what is revealed from the objectualist perspective, it is also the adopting of an objectualist perspective. That is, consciousness is also the adopting of the perspective from which consciousness is seen to comprise a collection of items and properties. To think of consciousness as the directing of awareness rather than that upon which awareness is directed is to think of consciousness as the *adopting* of an objectualist perspective, either towards itself or towards external items. And to think of consciousness as the adopting of an objectualist perspective, rather than as what is revealed from this perspective, is to think of consciousness from, as I shall use the expression, the *actualist* perspective. And to think of consciousness from an actualist perspective is to think of consciousness as act, rather than object, of experience.

The idea of thinking of consciousness from a perspective has, to be sure, a certain awkwardness. At the end of the preceding paragraph, I was thinking and writing about consciousness conceived of from the actualist perspective. But in doing so, I was necessarily adopting an objectualist perspective towards it. It is only possible to think about things – to make them objects of one's thought – by adopting an objectualist perspective towards them. This follows from the characterisation of the notion of an objectualist perspective given above. Thus, in thinking about consciousness conceived of from the actualist perspective, I am thinking about consciousness from the actualist perspective from the objectualist perspective. And this reveals an unfortunate but inevitable ambiguity in the idea of thinking about consciousness *from* a perspective. In thinking about consciousness from the actualist perspective one is also, it seems, thinking about it from the objectualist perspective. And, if this were not confusing enough, it seems that one must think of consciousness from the objectualist perspective in order to think of it from the actualist perspective.

There is, of course, no deep incoherence here. The problem is ultimately one of logical types. We can, for example, distinguish between first- and second-order adoptions of a perspective. Then we can say that in writing about consciousness conceived of from the actualist perspective, we are adopting a second-order perspective towards a first-order perspective on consciousness. Somewhat less awkwardly, we can flag the potential ambiguity by way of the following linguistic device. Henceforth, instead of talking about thinking of consciousness *from* the actualist or objectualist perspective, I shall instead talk of actualist and objectualist *conceptions* of consciousness. Talk of a conception of consciousness, here, denotes a first-order perspective towards consciousness. And the subject matter of this chapter consists in actualist and objectualist conceptions of consciousness, and in the difference between them. In addressing these issues, we must, of course, adopt an objectualist perspective towards them, for the objectualist perspective is precisely that perspective from which something can be seen as an object of thought. But this is a second-order perspective: a second-order objectualist perspective towards first-order actualist and objectualist conceptions of consciousness.

5   What it is like

As we have seen, in most recent discussions of consciousness, the idea that there is something that it is like to be conscious, or to undergo a conscious experience, figures quite centrally. The significance of consciousness for materialism, it is generally accepted, is that for an organism to be conscious means that there is something that it is like to be that organism. And it is the *what it is like* of conscious experience that is often claimed not to be susceptible to materialist analysis or explanation. However, I shall argue that just as it is possible to distinguish two distinct conceptions of consciousness – actualist and objectualist – so too is it possible to distinguish two corresponding interpretations of the notion of the what it is like of conscious experience.

The interpretation of the notion of what it is like that is oriented around the objectualist conception I shall refer to, obviously enough, as the *objectualist interpretation*. The objectualist interpretation treats the what it is like of conscious experience as an object of consciousness; as one of the things *of* which one is aware when one has such experience. On the objectualist construal, to say that there is something that it is like to be in pain, for example, means that any individual who is in pain will be consciously acquainted with a certain object – the what it is like of being in pain. The what it is like of conscious experience, that is, is understood as an object of conscious acquaintance, and any organism that undergoes a conscious experience that possesses, or is defined by, a phenomenology will thereby be acquainted with this object.

Two points should be noted here. Firstly, to say that what it is like is an *object* of conscious acquaintance is *not* to say that it is an object as opposed to an event, process, or fact. Nor is it to claim that it is a particular as opposed to a property. If we think of consciousness as both a directing of awareness and as that upon which awareness can be directed, then the objectualist interpretation simply claims that the what it is like of conscious experience is something upon which awareness can be directed. It is one of the things *of* which one is aware when one has a conscious experience. And this claim, in itself, is compatible with its being a particular or property, an object or an event or process.

Secondly, to understand what it is like to undergo a conscious experience to be an object of consciousness does not prejudge any questions about the scope of the notion of what it is like. As we saw in chapter 1, it is possible to adopt broad or narrow interpretations of the scope of 'there is...'. Some, for example, may adopt a very broad conception of its scope, such that there is something that it is like to be a bat, or to be a human. On the objectualist interpretation, this would mean that there is some object of conscious acquaintance and that all (conscious) bats are acquainted with this object. An even broader conception might claim that there is something that it is like to be conscious (e.g. Flanagan 1992: 87). Again, on the objectualist construal this would mean that there is some object of conscious acquaintance and that all conscious creatures are acquainted with this object. It is, of course, possible to narrow considerably the scope of this sort of claim. Thus, one might claim that what it is like is associated not with being conscious in general, nor with being a particular species of conscious organism, but, rather, with types of experience. An objectualist construal of this claim would entail that for every type of conscious experience there is some object of conscious acquaintance such that a creature which undergoes this type of experience is acquainted with that object. One might narrow the scope even further and claim that what it is like associates only with particular tokens of types of experience. On this view, for example, while there is no one thing that it is like to be in pain, there is something that it is like to suffer a particular token of pain, and, on the objectualist interpretation, when one suffers this token, one is acquainted with the what it is like to undergo this token. My suspicion is that narrower construals of the concept of what it is like are more plausible, but I shall not presuppose this here. The objectualist understanding of what it is like as an object of conscious acquaintance is, accordingly, neutral on the question of with what this object is associated.

The *actualist* interpretation of the concept of what it is like is underwritten by the actualist conception of consciousness, and differs significantly from the objectualist interpretation. According to the actualist interpretation, what it is like is not an object of consciousness but, rather, a feature or complex of features that exist in the directing of consciousness towards a quite distinct object. This may sound cryptic, but the principle underlying it is quite simple. To make this principle clear, consider actualist and objectualist interpretations of what it is like to be in, for example, terrible pain.

According to the objectualist interpretation, what it is like to be in terrible pain should be understood as an object of conscious acquaintance. When one is in terrible pain, then, among other things, one stands in a relation of conscious acquaintance to the what it is like to be in terrible pain. The what it is like to be in terrible pain is one of the objects of one's consciousness, one of the things of which one is aware when one is in terrible pain. On an actualist interpretation, on the other hand, one is not consciously acquainted with any object of what it is like. Rather, when one is in terrible pain, one stands in a certain relation to, let us suppose, bodily damage. And it is one's standing in this relation that feels terrible. What one is aware *of* here, is the bodily damage, although, of course, one is not necessarily aware *that* it is bodily damage (cf. Dretske 1995: 102). And it is the directing of one's awareness towards this object that feels terribly painful. The what it is like to be in terrible pain, on this construal, is not an object of consciousness; it is, rather, a feature or complex of features that is possessed by, and exists in, the directing of consciousness towards a quite distinct object.

One way of fleshing out this general idea is in terms of the sort of representational account of pain developed by Tye (1990, 1995). This type of account will be discussed in a lot more detail in chapter 9, and, there, I will not agree with every aspect of it. Here, I make no attempt to evaluate the model, but merely use those very general aspects of the account with which I do agree; they provide a useful way of developing the general idea of actualism about what it is like.

In broad outline, let us suppose that there are various bodily mechanisms that have evolved in order to detect bodily damage. Such mechanisms, in virtue of their evolutionary history, have what Millikan (1984, 1993) calls a *proper function*, the proper function of detecting bodily damage. The proper function of some mechanism, trait, or process is what it is *supposed* to do, what it has been *designed* to do, what it *ought* to do. Let us also suppose that among these mechanisms are ones whose proper function is to detect tokens of relevant types of bodily damage. Then, according to the representational account of pains, when a particular mechanism M has the proper function of representing bodily damage D and fulfils this function by going into state S, then state S of M represents D.

According to this form of representational view, the representation of bodily damage is *non-conceptual* (Tye 1990: 333). According to this model, a subject is, in any particular case, conscious *of* a tokening of bodily damage, and is aware of this tokening in virtue of possessing a mechanism with a certain proper function. However, the subject is not conscious *that* it is a tokening of bodily damage. That is, the relevant type of consciousness is what Dretske (1993) has called *thing* consciousness as opposed to *fact* consciousness.

Given this framework, it is possible to neatly distinguish objectualist and actualist accounts of what it is like. Both accounts can share the idea that when a subject feels pain that subject is aware *of* a tokening of bodily damage, but not, necessarily, aware *that* her body is undergoing that tokening. But according to the objectualist account, the subject in addition to being conscious of a tokening of bodily damage is also conscious of the what it is like to undergo that bodily damage. That is, the what it is like to undergo the bodily damage is one of which the subject is aware when she has that experience. And this is precisely what the actualist account denies. Rather, on this latter account, the subject is conscious only of the bodily damage, and it is her consciousness of the bodily damage that feels painful. The painfulness of her experience exists, that is, in the directing of her consciousness towards the tokening of the bodily damage; it is not something upon which that consciousness is itself directed.

Equivalently: according to the actualist interpretation, the what it is like of conscious experience is not something of which we are aware but something *with* which we are aware in the having of the experience. The term 'with' should be understood phenomenologically rather than causally. The bodily damage is the object of which we are aware. But we are not, typically, aware of this bodily damage *as* bodily damage; our awareness of it is thing-awareness rather than fact-awareness. Rather, the bodily damage is represented by us or, as I prefer, *revealed* to us, in a certain way: as painful. On the actualist interpretation, the what it is like of conscious experience is what, phenomenologically speaking, reveals to us the objects of our awareness in the way they are revealed.[8] What it is like to be in pain is not, itself, an object of consciousness but something that exists in the taking of bodily damage as the object of consciousness and revealing, or representing, this object as painful. More generally, the what it is like of conscious experience is not an object of consciousness but something that exists in the taking of a distinct, non-phenomenal, item

[8] Note that this is not equivalent to saying that the what it is like of conscious experience is the way in which objects of consciousness are revealed. Rather, it is what constitutes the revealing of objects in the way in which they are revealed. The identification of the what it is like with the way in which objects of consciousness are revealed is what I shall, in chapter 9, refer to as *mode representationism*. I shall reject this position. For present purposes it is sufficient to point out that this is a form of objectualism rather than actualism. The way objects are presented is still a (potential) object of consciousness. One can be aware not only of the objects presented in conscious experience but also of the way in which they are presented, for this simply amounts to awareness of the manifest properties of the objects.

as such an object and revealing this object to be thus-and-so. Indeed, the what it is like to undergo a conscious experience is not only something that exists in the revealing of a non-phenomenal object of consciousness to be thus-and-so, it is, in a sense to be explored later, that which constitutes the revealing of this object in such a way.

To adopt an actualist interpretation of the notion of what it is like to be in pain is, of course, not to deny that there is something that it is like to be in pain. It is simply to deny that what it is like to be in pain is an object of consciousness. And this is, at most, a reinterpretation of the notion of what it is like to be in pain, not a denial of that notion's validity. On the actualist interpretation, the what it is like of conscious experience is just as real as on the objectualist interpretation. It is simply that the former interpretation denies that this real feature of the world is an object of consciousness. It belongs to the actualist conception of consciousness, to consciousness as a directing of awareness, not to consciousness as that upon which awareness is directed.

Both actualist and objectualist interpretations of what it is like can make room for the idea that conscious experiences are subjective, perhaps essentially so. They do so, however, in very different ways. On the objectualist interpretation, the subjectivity of conscious experience derives from the fact that the object of consciousness – the what it is like of conscious experience – is such that it can only be experienced or apprehended from a single point of view. The subjectivity of conscious experience, that is, derives from the nature, the subjective nature, of an object that is grasped in the having of that experience. On the actualist interpretation, on the other hand, the subjectivity of conscious experience derives not from the object of experience, but from the fact that only one organism can be hooked up to the object of consciousness in the appropriate way. Thus, in the case of pain considered above, the object of consciousness is bodily damage. And the subjectivity of experience derives not from the subjectivity of bodily damage itself. Bodily damage is a perfectly objective feature of the world. Rather, the subjectivity of experience derives from the fact that one, and only one, experiencing subject can be connected – hooked up – to this bodily damage in the appropriate way. That is, the difference between objectualist and actualist explanations of subjectivity amounts to this. On the objectualist interpretation, the subjectivity of conscious experience derives from the nature – the subjective character – of an object grasped in the having of the experience. On the actualist interpretation, the subjectivity of conscious experience derives from the nature of the relation between an experiencing subject and the object of that subject's consciousness.

6   The ubiquity of objectualism

While it is possible to distinguish both objectualist and actualist interpretations of the concept of what it is like, it is fairly clear that most, and perhaps all, of recent discussions of consciousness presuppose, implicitly or explicitly, an objectualist interpretation of this concept. Consider, first, explanatory gap arguments.

Explanatory gap arguments

Thomas Nagel, in his seminal (1974) paper 'What is it like to be a bat?', develops the following argument against materialism:

1. 'Fundamentally, an organism has conscious mental states if and only if there is something that it is like to be that organism – something it is like *for* the organism.' (166)
2. 'If physicalism is to be defended, the phenomenological features of experience must themselves be given a physical account.' (167)
3. 'But when we examine their subjective character it seems that such a result is impossible. The reason is that every subjective phenomenon is essentially connected with a single point of view, and it seems inevitable that an objective physical theory will abandon that point of view.' (167)

With respect to the purposes of this chapter, the principal problem with this argument is that it is crucially ambiguous. Since it is possible to distinguish actualist and objectualist conceptions of consciousness, so, consequently, is it possible to distinguish two distinct interpretations of the notion of *what it is like*. One interpretation is oriented around the actualist conception of consciousness; the other, perhaps more familiar, interpretation is oriented around the objectualist conception.

The ambiguity in Nagel's argument arises in premise 1, and goes on to infect the remainder of the argument. To claim that 'an organism has conscious mental states if and only if there is something that it is like to be that organism' is ambiguous between the actualist and objectualist interpretations of what it is like. If the arguments of the previous section are correct, the what it is like of conscious experience can be understood as an object of conscious acquaintance, or it can be understood as a feature that exists in the directing of consciousness towards a quite distinct object. The former interpretation identifies what it is like as belonging to the objects of consciousness. The latter sees what it is like as belonging to the directing of conscious awareness, and not to the objects upon which this awareness is directed.

While the argument is ambiguous in this sense, it is reasonably clear that Nagel is operating with an objectualist interpretation of what it is like. The following passage is, I think, particularly telling:

For if the facts of experience – facts about what it is like *for* the experiencing organism – are accessible only from one point of view, then there is a mystery how the true character of experiences could be revealed in the physical operation of the organism. (1974: 172)

There are two points relevant here. Firstly, the what it is like of conscious experience is assimilated to the category of *facts*. Secondly, these facts are identified as being of a peculiar variety – they are accessible only from a particular point of view. That is, Nagel's account of subjectivity rests on the idea that there are certain things – experiential facts – that, by their nature, are accessible only from a certain point of view. Since they are accessible, they are objects of consciousness. And the explanation of subjectivity, then, is that these objects of consciousness have a certain property, the property of being apprehensible only from a certain point of view. Subjectivity, thus, derives from the nature of an object of consciousness. And this is, as we have seen, an objectualist rather than an actualist explanation of subjectivity. Therefore, it seems that Nagel is committed to an objectualist interpretation of what it is like.

A similar commitment to an objectualist interpretation of what it is like is also to be found in critics of Nagel. Flanagan, for example, a defender of the constructive materialist approach towards consciousness, writes:

The first source of trouble is Nagel's claim that moving away from the phenomenological surface inevitably takes us 'farther away' from 'the real nature of the phenomenon'. Why think that how consciousness seems gets at its real nature? . . . Unless one thinks that the conscious mind is diaphanous one should not think that its real nature is revealed fully by first-person appearances. (1992: 161)

Again, this pretty clearly presupposes an objectualist conception of consciousness. Flanagan conceives of consciousness as something that appears, and raises the question of whether the way that consciousness appears to us is revelatory of its real nature. This question, however, makes no sense for an actualist conception of consciousness since, on this conception, consciousness is, as we might say, the appearing and not what appears. And if, as the actualist interpretation claims, the what it is like of conscious experience exists only in the directing of consciousness towards its objects, then any focusing on these objects themselves must take us 'farther away' from the 'real nature' of what it is like.

Implicit commitment to an objectualist understanding of consciousness is also to be found in McGinn's influential arguments against constructive materialism. For example, one of McGinn's central arguments (the hidden structure argument) runs, essentially, as follows.

1. There is some property, P, of consciousness which relates it to the brain in an epistemically satisfying way.
2. Thus, if we can identify P (*qua* P), this will allow us to explain how consciousness is produced by the brain.
3. However, P is cognitively closed to us. The very nature of our concept-forming capacities means that we cannot conceptualise P, thus cannot identify P *qua* P.
4. Therefore, we cannot explain how consciousness is produced by the brain.

This argument, however, pretty clearly presupposes that consciousness is an object of conceptualisation. That is, consciousness is an object to which our concept- and category-forming apparatus can be applied. We relate to our consciousness as an object that can be conceptualised in various ways, and only the correct manner of conceptualisation – a manner which, given our limited cognitive repertoire, is beyond us – will yield an explanation of how consciousness is produced by the brain. It is objects of experience that are, or can be, conceptualised in various ways. We are able to conceptualise a noise as middle C on a piano only because it is an object of our awareness, something of which we are aware. An accomplished wine taster is able to conceptualise a wine as oaky as opposed to fruity, full bodied as opposed to light, only because the wine is the object of his awareness. Therefore, to regard consciousness as an actual or potential object of conceptualisation, as something that can be conceptualised in a variety of non-equivalent ways, is to regard consciousness as an object of conscious acquaintance. It is to adopt an objectualist conception of consciousness. Thus, given that McGinn regards the what it is like of conscious experience as constitutive of that experience as such, it is also to adopt an objectualist interpretation of what it is like.

Knowledge arguments

Knowledge arguments against the reductive explanation of consciousness also, pretty clearly, presuppose an objectualist conception of consciousness, hence an objectualist understanding of what it is like. Consider Jackson's (1982) classic statement of the argument.

We are to imagine that we live in an age of a completed neuroscience, an age where we know everything there is to know about the physical processes within our brain responsible for our behaviour. Mary has been brought up in a black and white room and has never seen any colours except black, white and shades of grey. However, despite this, she is the world's leading neuroscientist, knowing, in particular, everything there is to know about the neurophysiology of colour vision. That is, she knows everything there is to know about the neural processes involved in visual information processing, the physics of optical processes, the physical makeup of objects in the environment, etc. But she does not know what it is like to see colour. Thus, Jackson argues, when she leaves her room for the first time and sees a bright red object, she learns something new; she learns what it is like to see red. Now she knows something she did not know before – what it is like to see something red – and this new knowledge could in no way have been constructed, or derived, from her previous knowledge.

This scenario invites us to regard the what it is like of conscious experience as something that can be known. What it is like is, here, regarded as an actual or potential object of knowledge. And this is to adopt an objectualist interpretation of what it is like: objects of knowledge are logically distinct from the acts whereby subjects know about them. Knowledge, that is, has a genuinely dyadic act–object structure. Consequently, if what it is like is an object of knowledge, something that can be *known*, it must, also, be an object of consciousness. At this point, my aim is not to argue against this understanding of what it is like, but to point out that it is not the only possible one.

As we saw earlier, Sartre closely associates the idea that we have *knowledge* of our conscious states with the idea of *reflective* or *positional* consciousness. However, he rejects the idea that this form of consciousness is what makes any given conscious state conscious. Rather, the fundamental relation a conscious state bears to itself (or, as Sartre would prefer, *within* itself) is one of pre-reflective or *non-positional* consciousness. Every positional conscious act is also essentially characterised by a non-positional consciousness (of) itself, where the parenthesised 'of' indicates that non-positional consciousness is intrinsic (*immanent*) to the state itself and does not possess the sort of extrinsic, relational, character characteristic of reflective consciousness (e.g. introspection). And Sartre is very clear that the concept of knowledge, being extrinsic and relational in character, is entirely inappropriate for capturing or characterising the concept of pre-reflective consciousness.

However, Sartre would go further than this. There are certain features of consciousness in its pre-reflective state that are lost when consciousness becomes reflective. Such features, then, cannot become objects of knowledge. This emerges in his discussion of the nature of reflection (1943: 150–70) and, in particular, of what he calls *impure* reflection.

Sartre's discussion of reflection is organised around the following framework. Firstly, in any act of reflection, the consciousness reflected on is pre-reflectively conscious of itself; that is, it is both a positional consciousness of an object distinct from itself and a non-positional consciousness of itself. Secondly, the act of reflection is itself pre-reflectively conscious of itself; that is, it is a positional consciousness of the consciousness upon which it reflects and non-positional consciousness of itself. Thirdly, the act of reflection consists in the transformation of the non-positional, pre-reflective, consciousness of the original act to positional consciousness of itself. However, even though Sartre accepts the framework itself, he is also very clear that not every property of the original positionally conscious act can become an object of reflection. Impure reflection, for example, is the attempt 'to apprehend the reflected-on as in itself in order to make itself be that in-itself which is apprehended' (1943: 159). That is, in impure reflection, the reflective consciousness tries to view the consciousness reflected on as an object. That is why Sartre views impure reflection as a form of *bad faith*: the 'abortive attempt on the part of the for-itself to be another while remaining itself' (1943: 161). Impure reflection is the attempt to separate the consciousness reflected upon from itself while also claiming that it is that very same consciousness. Most obviously, this applies to what Sartre calls the ego, understood as the totality of the states and properties and actions of a person. Consciousness is, necessarily, not the ego; rather, it is what apprehends and also constitutes the ego. The ego, Sartre says, is a shadow cast by consciousness. It is created by consciousness's attempt, at the level of impure reflection, to give itself an outside and claim that this outside is strictly identical with oneself. But this cannot be done. Such consciousness is not consciousness of consciousness *as* consciousness; the ego is not consciousness but, as Sartre puts it, a transcendent object.

More importantly for our purposes, Sartre applies the same reasoning to states of consciousness. In *The Transcendence of the Ego* he gives the example of hatred. Although hatred exists in acts of consciousness, it transcends any one moment and has a permanence that the acts themselves lack. It is given, according to Sartre, as continuing even when the person who hates is absorbed in other things and has no consciousness that reveals the hatred. 'Hatred ... is a transcendent object' (1936: 63). The hatred that is the object of reflection is not at all the same thing as the hatred non-positionally aware of itself in the original act of consciousness.

My purpose here is not to evaluate these claims, or the arguments Sartre gives for them. My purpose, rather, is to use them as illustrative of a general claim that will be clarified and defended in the chapters to follow. There are certain aspects of conscious states that cannot be captured or explained in terms of an extrinsic relation such as reflective consciousness. There are certain features of consciousness that are *immanent* to it. They exist only in the directing of positional consciousness towards its objects, and in that positional consciousness's non-positional consciousness of itself. They are not things towards which consciousness, in reflective mode, can be directed. These features are ones of which we cannot have *knowledge*. Their relation to conscious states is too *immanent*, too close, for them to be explained in terms of the knowledge conscious states might have *of* them.

It is here that Sartre finds a *prima facie* unlikely bedfellow in Wittgenstein:

It can't be said of me at all (except perhaps as a joke) that I *know* I'm in pain. What is it supposed to mean – except perhaps that I *am* in pain? (1953: 246)

The idea that our consciousness of our own conscious states is, in some sense, too 'close' to the states themselves to count as a case of knowledge is, at least in part, what lies behind this notorious claim. And one can develop this idea in terms of the distinction between actualist and objectualist conceptions of consciousness. Knowledge, and the associated idea of giving reasons justifying one's claim, is appropriate to objects of consciousness. Here we can ask the traditional questions concerning the epistemic relation one bears to the objects of one's consciousness: to what extent is the connection warranted? Is this warrant sufficient to count as a case of knowledge? And so on. However, the concept of knowledge, and the associated idea of giving reasons justifying one's claim, are not appropriate to those features that exist not as objects of consciousness but, rather, in the directing of consciousness towards quite distinct objects. Such features are not objects of consciousness and so do not stand in an epistemic relation to consciousness. They do not belong to the domain of giving reasons.

Therefore, if knowledge arguments are to work, then the what it is like of conscious experience must be regarded as an object of consciousness. If it is not, then Mary cannot be said to acquire new knowledge, to learn something new, when she first has colour experiences. Knowledge arguments, then, presuppose an objectualist interpretation of what it is like. However, as we have seen, it is not clear that the what it is like of conscious experience must be understood in this way. The alternative is to regard what it is like not as an object of conscious acquaintance but as a feature of conscious experience that exists in the directing of such experience towards a quite different object of acquaintance.

7 Summary

Consciousness has a dual structure. Consciousness can not only be the object of conscious experience, it can also be the subject of that experience. There are, that is, two distinct conceptions of consciousness: objectualist and actualist. There are, correspondingly, two distinct interpretations of the idea that there is something that it is like to undergo a conscious experience. Most, and perhaps all, recent discussions of consciousness, however, presuppose an objectualist understanding of consciousness and, consequently, an objectualist understanding of the what it is like of conscious experience.

7   What it is like

The previous chapter distinguished two distinct conceptions of consciousness. According to the objectualist conception, consciousness is assimilated to an object of conscious experience; consciousness is an object towards which conscious experience can be directed. According to the actualist conception, on the other hand, consciousness is assimilated to an act of conscious experience. Consciousness, here, is not an object towards which conscious experience is directed; it is the directing itself of that experience. There is nothing illegitimate about either of these conceptions; consciousness has precisely the sort of dual structure that enables it to be both subject and object of conscious experience.

The dual structure of consciousness, the fact that it admits of both actualist and objectualist interpretations, however, carries over and infects the concept of the what it is like of conscious experience, which many take to be constitutive of conscious experience as such. Since the concept of consciousness admits of both actualist and objectualist interpretations so too does the what it is like of conscious experience. According to the objectualist interpretation of this latter concept, what it is like is an object of conscious acquaintance. When one undergoes an experience that is defined by a phenomenology, then one of the things with which one is consciously acquainted, one of the things of which one is consciously aware, is the what it is like to have that experience. According to the actualist interpretation of what it is like, on the other hand, the what it is like of conscious experience is not an object of conscious acquaintance. It is not one of the things of which one is aware when one has an experience. Rather, the what it is like of conscious experience is something that exists in the directing of experience towards a quite distinct, and non-phenomenal, object.

While it may be true that both actualist and objectualist interpretations of consciousness are equally legitimate, it does not follow that both interpretations of the notion of what it is like are equally legitimate. The reason for this is that actualist and objectualist aspects of consciousness might have, and presumably do have, associated with them quite distinct features. If this is so, then it might turn out that the what it is like of conscious experience is a feature that an experience possesses in virtue of its actualist aspect but not its objectualist one. Or vice versa. What it is like, that is, might be associated with the directing of conscious experience and not with that upon which conscious experience is directed. Or it might be associated with (or be) that upon which conscious experience is directed and not the directing itself of that experience.

Nothing that was said in the previous chapter, of course, was intended to adjudicate between actualist and objectualist interpretations of the notion of what it is like. That chapter was only concerned with establishing the distinctness and, perhaps, *prima facie* viability, of the interpretations. Adjudicating between the interpretations is the function of the present chapter. I shall argue that, with respect to the what it is like of conscious experience, the actualist interpretation is to be preferred to the objectualist alternative. What it is like is an aspect of conscious experience that exists only in the directing of such experience towards a non-phenomenal object. It is not itself an object of such experience.

The argument for this claim has three strands. Firstly, it will be argued that the objectualist interpretation of what it is like should be rejected on the grounds that it is incompatible with materialism. Secondly, it will be argued that the actualist interpretation allows us to explain certain central features of the what it is like of conscious experience, features that the objectualist interpretation renders mysterious. Thirdly, a diagnosis will be offered of why we are so tempted to regard what it is like as a feature towards which our conscious experience can be directed, one upon which our conscious gaze can fall.

1   Against objectualism

In sections 2–4, it will be argued that objectualism commits us to the rejection of materialism. Thus, if one wants to be a materialist, one cannot adopt an objectualist interpretation of what it is like. The argument, in outline, runs as follows:

1. According to the objectualist interpretation, what it is like to undergo a conscious experience should be understood as an object of consciousness.
2. If what it is like is an object of consciousness then it is either a phenomenal particular, a phenomenal property, or a representational property.

3. The claim that what it is like is a phenomenal particular entails the rejection of materialism.
4. If what it is like is a phenomenal property, then it cannot plausibly be regarded as an object of consciousness.
5. If what it is like is a representational property, then it cannot plausibly be regarded as an object of consciousness.
6. Therefore, if what it is like is an object of consciousness then it can, consistent with materialism, be neither a phenomenal particular nor a phenomenal property nor a representational property.
C. Therefore, if materialism is true, what it is like cannot be an object of consciousness.

In other words, regarding what it is like as a phenomenal property or a representational property is incompatible with objectualism. Therefore, objectualism, consistently understood, is committed to regarding what it is like as a phenomenal particular. And, therefore, objectualism, consistently understood, is committed to the rejection of materialism. So, if we want to be materialists, we must abandon the objectualist interpretation of what it is like.

2   What it is like as a phenomenal particular

To claim that what it is like is an object of consciousness is, as was made clear earlier, not to claim that it is an object. Many things, and not just objects, can be objects of consciousness: events, processes, properties, characteristics, etc. can all be objects of consciousness. What makes something an object of consciousness is not the ontological category to which it belongs but whether or not it is the sort of thing upon which consciousness can be directed. And in this regard there appear to be just two possibilities: an object of consciousness can be a particular or it can be a property. We can be aware of particulars – objects, events, processes, substances and the like – but we can also direct our attention towards the properties that such particulars possess.

I shall assume that these two options are exhaustive. If this is correct, then if we regard what it is like as an object of consciousness, we are, it seems, going to have to regard it as a particular or as a property. Consider, first, the implications of viewing what it is like as a particular.

The principal problem with regarding what it is like as a particular is that, if we do, we are going to have to regard it as a *phenomenal* particular. And this cannot be accommodated within a materialist metaphysic. Suppose we are looking at a particular visual scene, one containing, say, a pink polka-dotted dress. Our consciousness can, of course, be directed towards this object; it can be an object of our consciousness. In addition, there is, let us suppose, something that it is like to see a pink polka-dotted dress. And according to the objectualist interpretation of what it is like, this means that we are also consciously acquainted with an object distinct from the dress, and this object is the what it is like to see a pink polka-dotted dress. It is our acquaintance with this latter object, so it is claimed, which marks the difference between our conscious experience of the dress and, for example, the unconscious perception of the dress exhibited by a zombie. What it is like, as an object of consciousness, is thus distinct from any external physical item. Now, if we are asked what it is like to experience a pink polka-dotted dress it seems that, at the very least, we are going to have to say things like 'it seems pinkish', 'it seems polka-dotted' and so on. And on the objectualist construal of what it is like, where this is understood as a particular, we can either explain this by claiming that the what it is like must actually have properties such as being pink and being polka-dotted, or by claiming that it *apparently* has such properties. For reasons that will become clear shortly, the second option is not available to the defender of the objectualist interpretation of what it is like. That is, as I shall argue shortly, claiming that the what it is like only apparently has the properties we experience (or appear to experience) in undergoing a conscious experience is incompatible with viewing it as an object of conscious acquaintance. Thus, we are left with the claim that, in the above case, the what it is like of seeing a pink polka-dotted dress actually has the properties of being pink and being polka-dotted. The phenomenological character of our experience of a pink polka-dotted dress – a character shared by experiences as diverse as perceptions, hallucinations, illusions, etc. – is explained in terms of our being consciously acquainted with an object – the what it is like of these experiences – which actually has the properties we seem to experience when we perceive, or seem to perceive, the dress. More generally, on the objectualist construal that regards what it is like as a particular, we explain the phenomenological character of a conscious experience of an item I by claiming that we are consciously acquainted with a particular P which really has the properties we either experience, or seem to experience, when we experience I. And a particular P, which really has the properties that we either experience, or seem to experience, when we experience a distinct item I, is a *phenomenal particular*.

This objectualist and particularist account of what it is like, of course, is not equivalent to the classical sense-datum account of perceptual experience. The key difference is that sense-datum accounts make phenomenal particulars the *only* direct objects of conscious perceptual acquaintance. The objectualist, particularist, account of what it is like, on the other hand, is neutral about the existence of other direct objects of conscious perceptual acquaintance. It claims only that among those objects is a phenomenal particular, the what it is like to see a pink polka-dotted dress. Thus, the objectualist, particularist, account of what it is like is, whereas classical sense-data theories are not, compatible with the claim that the dress is a direct object of conscious perceptual acquaintance (it is also, of course, compatible with the denial of this claim).

That materialism is incompatible with the existence of phenomenal particulars is well known, and has been at least since the time of Hobbes. The problem in the above case, for example, is that there is nothing in the brain which *really* has the properties of being pink and polka-dotted. So, if a phenomenal particular really has these properties, then this precludes its identification with anything in the brain. A materialist might, arguably, be able to get away with the existence of irreducible phenomenal properties. But commitment to phenomenal particulars is, effectively, constitutive of dualism. So, if we are to adopt the objectualist interpretation of what it is like we cannot, consistently with materialism, regard what it is like as a particular.

3   What it is like as a phenomenal property

There are various well-known materialist strategies for dealing with the apparent existence of phenomenal particulars. And these strategies can, broadly speaking, be divided into two sorts. The first type of strategy covers a spectrum of distinct positions, but all of these are united by the idea that it is possible to eliminate quantification over such particulars by recasting it as quantification over phenomenal *properties*. The second type of strategy may allow that quantification over phenomenal particulars can be eliminated in favour of quantification over phenomenal properties, but adds to this the additional claim that quantification over phenomenal properties can itself be eliminated in favour of quantification over *intentional* or *representational* properties. The phenomenal, that is, ultimately reduces to the representational. This section considers strategies of the first sort.

Classical adverbialist approaches to experience provide one good example of the attempt to eliminate quantification over phenomenal particulars in favour of quantification over phenomenal properties (Ducasse 1942; Chisholm 1957; Sellars 1963; Aune 1967; Cornman 1971). According to such approaches, having an experience is not, as a particularist position would have it, a matter of experiencing a particular (immaterial) object, but, rather, experiencing in a certain manner. A statement of the form:

P has an F sensation

is allotted an adverbial reconstruction:

P senses F-ly

or:

P senses in an F manner

Thus, statements that purport to be about phenomenal particulars: pains, after-images, and the like, are, in fact, statements about the way or mode in which a person is experiencing. And the notion of a way or mode of experiencing is explained in terms of properties of the act of experiencing; i.e. phenomenal properties.

A related approach is to be found in Smart's (1962) elimination of phenomenal particulars (although Smart himself is also hostile to the idea of irreducibly phenomenal properties). Suppose we are tempted to believe in a phenomenal particular which, as we see it, really has the property of being polka-dotted. Smart's strategy involves replacing this particular with a state or process such as seeing, imagining, or after-imaging. There is now no phenomenal particular but, rather, a state or process that has phenomenal properties. And to say that a process possesses the phenomenal property P is to make the materialistically unproblematic claim that the process is such that when a subject S undergoes it, it appears to S that she is experiencing P. To say that a process possesses the phenomenal property of being polka-dotted, for example, is to say that when a subject undergoes this process it seems to this subject that she is experiencing something polka-dotted.

Not all materialist accounts of phenomenality, of course, adopt these classical lines. And constraints of space do not allow me to survey the various alternatives. For our purposes, however, it is not the details of each particular strategy that are important, but their common reliance, in one form or another, on the notion of a phenomenal property. That is, any account that relies on the notion of a phenomenal property, and which seeks to provide an objectualist interpretation of the notion of what it is like using the notion of a phenomenal property, will be subject to the arguments to follow.

Given the availability of an appeal to phenomenal properties, then, it might be thought that it is possible to give a materialistically acceptable account of the notion of what it is like, and still understand this as an object of conscious acquaintance. That is, it might be thought that we can render an objectualist interpretation of what it is like compatible with materialism by construing it as a phenomenal property, or complex of such properties, possessed by a process occurring in the brain. In undergoing a conscious experience, we become aware not of a phenomenal particular but of a phenomenal property.

This objectualist account of what it is like must also, however, be rejected. There are two distinct types of reason that could underlie this rejection because there are two distinct interpretations of the concept of a phenomenal property.

On the first interpretation of the notion of a phenomenal property, the possession by state S of the phenomenal property of being P means that S really is P. The possession by S of the phenomenal property of being polka-dotted means that S really is polka-dotted. One hesitates to call this an *interpretation* of the concept of a phenomenal property. It is almost certainly a misunderstanding, rather than an interpretation, of that concept. But whether or not this is correct, it is fairly clear that, on this 'interpretation', the invocation of phenomenal properties is no more materialistically acceptable than the invocation of phenomenal particulars. If the possession by a state or process of the phenomenal property of being polka-dotted means that the state or process really is polka-dotted, this will again preclude its identification with anything occurring in the brain. Indeed, on the present 'interpretation' of the concept of a phenomenal property, the existence of phenomenal properties seems to entail the existence of phenomenal particulars. If a phenomenal property is an object of consciousness, then the instancing of such a property will also, presumably, be an object of consciousness. And if the possession by a state S of the phenomenal property of being P means that S actually is P, then the instancing of P in S will be just one more object of consciousness, just one more item toward which the inner gaze can be directed. Under these circumstances, the instancing of the phenomenal property would be a phenomenal particular. However, even if this latter claim is not correct, it is still fairly clear that the present attempt at providing a materialistically acceptable objectualist interpretation of the notion of what it is like fails. The attempt (i) rests almost certainly on a misunderstanding of the concept of a phenomenal property and (ii) presents materialism with precisely the same difficulties as arose with phenomenal particulars.

There is, of course, a far more plausible interpretation of the concept of a phenomenal property, and it is this interpretation that should be employed by the materialist. On this interpretation, to say that state S possesses phenomenal property P is not to say that S really is P. It is to say that S appears to be P; that is, that S has the property of *appearing to be P*. This interpretation of the concept of a phenomenal property does not lead to the reintroduction of the problems posed for materialism by phenomenal particulars. However, understanding the concept of a phenomenal property in this way rules out the objectualist interpretation of what it is like. That is, the claim that what it is like is an object of consciousness, the understanding of this object as a phenomenal property, and the present understanding of phenomenal property, form an inconsistent triad. The reason for this is that the property of appearing to be P cannot be a genuine object of consciousness. The property of appearing to be P attaches to the *apprehension* of the object of consciousness; it is not itself an object of consciousness.

To see this, let 'P' represent a property: say the property of being at a gas station in Nebraska. Then, the phenomenal version of this property, phenomenal P (henceforth ph-P) is the property of appearing to be at a gas station in Nebraska. And let us suppose that ph-P is satisfied by a certain individual: Elvis. To say that Elvis satisfies ph-P, then, is simply to say that Elvis has the property of appearing (to be) at a gas station in Nebraska. The question is: is ph-P a genuine property of Elvis? And it is pretty clear that it is not. It would be implausible to suppose, whenever someone has a hallucination of Elvis as being at a gas station in Nebraska, that Elvis acquires a new property: the property of appearing to be at a gas station in Nebraska. The property of appearing to be P is no more a genuine property of Elvis than the property of being believed by Elvis to have an atomic weight of 79 is a property of gold.

'Appears' is, of course, an elliptical predicate, and the corresponding property of appearing is a relational one. To say that Elvis appears at a gas station is to say that he appears to someone (at some time). Moreover, to say that Elvis has the property of appearing to be at a gas station in Nebraska is not to attribute a property to Elvis at all; it is to attribute a property to the person who hallucinates Elvis at the gas station. That is, to say that Elvis has ph-P is simply to say that I (or someone) experiences Elvis as P. That is, ph-P is a property that attaches to the *experiencing* (presumably hallucinatory experiencing) of Elvis, not to Elvis. That is, ph-P attaches to the *act* of consciousness, to consciousness as the *directing* of awareness, and not to the object upon which consciousness is directed.

Let us now replace Elvis with a process, E, of experiencing. E, let us suppose, possesses phenomenal property Q (i.e. ph-Q). That is, E has the property of appearing to be Q. However, as in the case of Elvis, to say that E has ph-Q is not to attribute any genuine property to E. Rather, to say that E has ph-Q is simply to say that I (or someone) experiences E as Q. Being ph-Q is not a property that attaches to E, it attaches to my experiencing of E. That is, ph-Q is not an introspectible property of E, something that the act of introspection might target. It is a property that attaches to the experiencing or introspecting of E rather than to E itself. It is not an introspectible property of E, but one that attaches to the introspect*ing* of E. In other words, it is not a property of the object, but of the act, of consciousness.

To say that a process has the property of appearing to be P is misleading. What we are in fact saying is that the process appears P. And this equivalent locution makes it clear that whatever property is involved here attaches not to the process itself but to the *apprehension* or grasp of this process. But this means that, when phenomenal properties are understood in this way, they cannot be part of the object of consciousness. The property of appearing a certain way, that is, cannot be an object of consciousness. Properties of appearing a certain way are not things upon which awareness can be directed. Rather, they are properties that exist *in* the directing of awareness upon its objects. Properties of appearing a certain way are not among the objects of consciousness, they attach to consciousness as the directing of awareness rather than to consciousness as that upon which awareness is directed. Thus, we are led back to an actualist interpretation of what it is like.

This argument, if correct, also shows why it is not possible to couple an understanding of what it is like as a phenomenal *particular* with the understanding of such particulars as only *apparently* possessing the properties constituting the phenomenological character of an experience. Once again, this would be to deny that what it is like can be an object of experience and lead us back to an actualist interpretation of that notion. To say that what it is like is an object of consciousness that only apparently has the properties constitutive of an experience's phenomenological character is, in effect, to deny that what it is like can be an object of consciousness.

Therefore, it seems that on any remotely plausible interpretation of the notion of a phenomenal property, such properties are not objects of conscious awareness. They exist only in the directing of consciousness towards quite distinct, and, if materialism is true, non-phenomenal, objects. Phenomenal properties attach to consciousness as directing of awareness; their domain is the actualist conception of consciousness. Thus, to explain the notion of what it is like in terms of phenomenal properties is to abandon the objectualist conception of what it is like.

It is perhaps worth pointing out that to say that a phenomenal property does not genuinely attach to the state or process that 'has' it is not to deny that this state or process *does* possess various properties that are *responsible* for the production of that property, at least in part. When one stands in an appropriate relation to bodily damage, for example, one might be in awful pain. One might want to describe what is going on by saying that this bodily damage has the property of appearing awfully painful. But this, as we have seen, is disingenuous. Rather, what is going on is that, when one stands in an appropriate relation to this bodily damage, one experiences it as awfully painful. And, in this case, there certainly are various properties of the bodily damage, properties that are genuinely possessed by this damage, in virtue of which, in part, we experience it in this way. The point is, however, that these are not themselves phenomenal properties. They are properties in virtue of which, in part, one experiences the bodily damage as awfully painful. They are not the awful painfulness itself. This latter property attaches to the apprehension of the bodily damage, not to the bodily damage itself.

The situation so far, then, appears to be this. We have been examining whether what it is like to undergo a conscious experience should be conceived of as an object of consciousness; that is, whether it should be understood as belonging to the objectualist conception of consciousness. And it does not seem that it can be legitimately conceived of in this way. On the one hand, what it is like cannot be understood as a phenomenal particular, since this would commit us to abandoning materialism. On the other hand, what it is like cannot be understood as a phenomenal property. Combining an objectualist construal of what it is like with the claim that this is a phenomenal property yields two possibilities. On one interpretation, understanding what it is like as a phenomenal property is just as materialistically problematic as understanding it as a phenomenal particular, and might even entail the existence of phenomenal particulars. On the other, more plausible, understanding of the notion of a phenomenal property, we would be forced to recognise that phenomenal properties are not to be found among the objects of conscious acquaintance but, rather, attach to the apprehending of such objects by conscious subjects. And this is tantamount to rejecting the objectualist interpretation of what it is like. Either way, it is difficult, to say the least, to hang on to the idea that what it is like is both an object of conscious acquaintance and a phenomenal property.

4   What it is like as a representational property

There is another gambit available to those materialists who want to hold on to an objectualist interpretation of what it is like. This is to adopt one or another form of *representationism*: the view, roughly, that the phenomenal character of experience is reducible to its representational content. On this view, then, the what it is like of a conscious experience is neither a phenomenal particular nor a phenomenal property but, rather, an *intentional* or *representational* property of that experience (Dretske 1995; Tye 1995). The idea, here, would be that the problems posed for the objectualist interpretation of what it is like stem from the phenomenality of the property with which it is identified, and if we excise this phenomenality, in favour of representationality, then these problems might be avoided.

Representationism is, of course, not an uncontroversial doctrine. There are well-known objections to the representationist attempt to reduce phenomenal character to representational content. Firstly, although this is a claim I do not accept, it is common to hold that while some phenomenally characterised states – perceptual experiences providing a paradigmatic example – are representational ones, many are not. Bodily sensations – itches, tingles, pains, orgasms – are held by many to be examples of states that have phenomenal but not representational character (McGinn 1982; Searle 1983; Block 1995). If this is correct, then there seems to be no prospect of a general reduction of the former to the latter. Secondly, even in the case of states that are uncontroversially both phenomenal and representational, there are well-known problems with the attempt to reductively explain their phenomenal character in terms of their representational character, as the recent proliferation of *swampman* and *inverted earth* discussions seems to indicate (Block 1990, 1996). In chapter 9, I shall examine the representationist account in more detail. Here, however, my purpose is not to evaluate its plausibility but, rather, to examine its compatibility with the objectualist understanding of what it is like. That is, I shall be examining the question of whether the representational properties of an experience are items of which we are aware in the having of that experience. I shall argue that they are not.

It might be thought that this negative claim could be established very quickly, on the basis of the arguments presented in the previous section for the claim that the phenomenal properties of experience are not items of which we are aware in the having of experience. For if phenomenal properties are, as argued above, not objects of consciousness, and if, as representationism claims, phenomenal properties reduce to representational ones, then it is very difficult to see how representational properties can be objects of consciousness either. However, I shall not rely on the non-objectual status of phenomenal properties argued for above, but, rather, seek to independently motivate the idea that representational properties are not objects of consciousness. That is, I shall try to show that, irrespective of the status of phenomenal properties, the representationist should not regard representational properties as objects of consciousness.

The claim to be defended in this section, then, is this: the representational properties of any experience, E, are not properties *of* which we are aware in the having of E. Rather, they are properties *with* which we are aware, in the having of E, of the public objects and properties that E is of or about. That the representational properties of experience are not objects of conscious acquaintance flies in the face of received wisdom in certain quarters. Tye, for example, writes:

Standing on the beach in Santa Barbara a couple of summers ago on a bright, sunny day, I found myself transfixed by the intense blue of the Pacific Ocean. Was I not here delighting in the phenomenal aspects of my visual experience? And if I was, doesn't this show that there are visual qualia? I am not convinced. I experienced blue as a property of the ocean not as a property of my experience. My experience itself certainly wasn't blue. Rather it was an experience that represented the ocean as blue. What I was really delighting in, then, were specific aspects of the *content* of my experience. It was the *content*, not anything else, that was immediately accessible to my consciousness and that had aspects that were pleasing. (Tye 1992: 160. Emphases mine)[1]

However, I shall argue that, *pace* Tye and others, representational properties, properties constitutive of the content of an experience, should not be regarded as objects of conscious acquaintance. Not only is there nothing in representationism as such which requires that representational properties be construed as objects of consciousness but, more importantly, to regard them as such would undermine one of the principal motivations of representationism.

According to Tye, it is the *content* of experience that is immediately accessible to consciousness. This could, taken in itself, mean one of at least three things, only one of which, however, is suitable for representationist purposes.

1. *Empiricist content.* There is a traditional empiricist way of construing talk of experiential content according to which this consists in the ideas or other mental entities one has in one's mind when one has experiences. The content of my perceptual experience of the Pacific Ocean is, on this construal, simply the various ideas that pass before my mind when I perceive this ocean. This conception of experiential content reached its twentieth-century culmination in sense-datum accounts of such content. I perceive the Pacific Ocean off Santa Barbara in virtue of perceiving, or otherwise being conscious of, the appropriate sense-data. Such data thereby provide the content of my experience of this stretch of the Ocean. This is, emphatically, not what Tye means by content. Indeed, the representationist view endorsed by Tye is typically set up explicitly in opposition to sense-datum accounts.
2. *Russellian content.* According to Russell, singular propositions are those which would not be available to be expressed at all if the objects

---

[1] Echoing these sentiments, Chalmers writes: '... when we have an experience, we are aware of the *contents* of the experience. When we experience a book, we are aware of the book; when we experience a pain, we are aware of something hurtful; when we experience a thought, we are aware of whatever it is that the thought is about' (1996: 221).

to which their component expressions referred did not exist (Russell 1905). This was the result of their comprising predicate-expressions conjoined with logically proper names. Such names he regarded as genuinely referring expressions: ones which must be taken as referring if they are to have sense. The objects to which such expressions referred were, for Russell (1917), objects of acquaintance, and he (usually) thought such objects were one or another variety of sense-data. What goes by the name of 'Russellian' content, today, however, differs significantly from Russell's conception. Most importantly, the connection with sense-data has been abandoned; the objects of 'acquaintance' constituting the availability of a singular proposition are regarded as public objects and properties. To talk of the Russellian content of an experience, then, is to talk of content that is constituted by the environmental objects and properties which that experience is about. Again, this is not the notion of content required by Tye in the above passage. If we adopt a Russellian notion of content, then the claim that we are aware of the content of our experience is nothing more than the claim that we are aware of those public objects and properties our experience is about.[2] It is difficult to see how the what it is like of experience could be identified with content in this sense.

3. *Representational content.* Tye is, in fact, quite clear that when he talks about the content of an experience he is talking about what is usually called *representational* content. This is to be expected, since by far the most prevalent construal of the notion of content today is the representational construal. In this sense, the content of an experience is to be identified with the representational properties of that experience. These are properties of the experience, and hence not to be identified with any environmental objects or properties. They are, rather, the properties the experience has of representing things to be a certain way.

For our purposes, it is important to clearly distinguish each form of content, even though it is only representational content that is required by Tye's representationism. For I want to argue that (i) there is little temptation to suppose that representational content is an object of consciousness, one of the things of which we are aware in the having of an experience, unless we confuse representational with Russellian content, and, more importantly, (ii) if we do regard representational content as an object of consciousness, then any advantage representational content has

---

[2] Even with a Russellian concept of content, Tye's claim that the content of our experience is *immediately* accessible to us is insufficiently defended. For the claim seems to rest on the implicit assumption that in being aware of a part or aspect of the content of an experience we are thereby aware of the entire content of that experience.

over empiricist content immediately disappears. The representationist, then, is not only not committed to the objectualist interpretation of content, he should, in fact, reject that interpretation. The representational content of an experience is not something of which we are aware in the having of that experience. I shall begin with discussion of claim (ii), and the question of the justification for the representational interpretation of content over its empiricist competitor.

Empiricist, or sense-datum, views of content provide us with a *mediational* conception of the relation between experience and the world. Our immediate experience is awareness of certain non-physical, or mind-dependent, entities, sense-data, which are not to be identified with public objects and properties in the world around us. In virtue of this immediate experience, we are then mediately aware of, or *as* of, these public objects and properties. Experience of the world is mediated by way of experience of sense-data.

It is this mediational conception of the way experience relates to the world that leads to two serious problems for empiricist accounts of experiential content.

1. When we reflect on our experience, that is, when we introspect, we do not encounter the sorts of items sense-datum accounts indicate we should encounter. As I write this passage, I can look out of my study window, across the field and down to the ocean, I can see the early morning mist rising, shrouding the trees. I may attend to the bickering seagulls in the sky above me, or, closer to home, the way the droplets of dew cling to the grass outside my window. But I can also reflect on what it is like for me to be staring at the mist and the seagulls and the dew. That is, I can direct my attention on my experience of these items. What is noticeable is that when my attention is thus turned inwards, the mist and seagulls and dewdrops are not replaced by some other entities, ones belonging to the inner realm of the mind. Rather, I focus on my experience by perceptually attending to the external items themselves, and reflecting on this while I do it. Experience is, in this sense, *transparent* or *diaphanous* (Moore 1903). Thus, in one sense, reflection on experience reveals *less* than we would expect on the basis of the sense-datum account.

2. When we reflect on our experience we encounter items that sense-datum accounts indicate we should not expect to encounter. We encounter public objects and properties, not their private, mind-dependent, intermediaries. In one sense, then, reflection on experience reveals *more* than we would expect on the basis of the sense-datum account.

Thus, the phenomenon of experiential transparency creates two problems for empiricist, or sense-datum, accounts of experiential content.[3] Firstly, there does not seem to be some private entity corresponding to each object of perception, or a subjective quality to correspond to each perceived feature of such objects. When we try to introspectively focus on such private entities or qualities, all we are presented with are worldly, mind-independent, objects and properties. This presents the sense-datum account with the burden of explaining how conscious visual experience can actually be of sense-data when it appears to be of mind-independent objects and properties.

Secondly, the public, mind-independent, objects of perception and the properties of those objects are not banished from one's consciousness just because one shifts one's attention from how things are in the environment to how things are experientially. And this presents the sense-data account with the burden of spelling out just how the postulation of purely private, subjective, entities as objects of consciousness can explain how mind-independent objects come to be objects of this consciousness.

Sense-datum accounts of content suffered widespread rejection through, in no small part, their inability to shoulder these burdens. However, if we regard the representational content of an experience as something of which we are aware in the having of that experience, then representationism will suffer from analogues of these problems.

Consider the first problem. The problem is that introspection seems to reveal less than would be expected if the sense-datum account were true. Introspection reveals the existence not of private subjective entities and qualities, but of public objects, events and properties. However, if we regard the representational account as claiming that the representational properties of experiences are the objects of immediate conscious acquaintance, then a *tu quoque* response is available to the defender of the sense-datum account. The sense-datum theorist, that is, might concede that introspection does not make manifest the existence of sense-data, but point out that neither does it make manifest the existence of representational properties. If we take the phenomenon of experiential transparency seriously, then we must allow that all introspection in fact makes manifest are public objects and properties. But these can constitute the content of an experience only in a Russellian, and not in the required representational, sense. So, the sense-data account is no worse off than the representational account in this regard.

Consider, now, the second problem. The problem for the sense-datum account is, essentially, one of explaining how mind-independent objects

---

[3] Here I am indebted to Martin's excellent discussion in 'The transparency of experience', http://www.nyu.edu/psas/dept/philo/courses/concepts/martin.html.

and properties can figure in an account of what experience is like. To see the problem here, it is useful to compare the ease with which sense-datum accounts can explain the contents of illusory or hallucinatory experience, on the one hand, with the difficulty they have with veridical experience on the other. The sense-datum account of the content of illusory or hallucinatory experience is straightforward: the experiencing subject is aware of various mind-dependent entities that do not, in such cases, reflect what is present in the world. The problem for sense-datum accounts was that they were expressly constructed with cases of illusion or hallucination in mind and that they were unable to go on and explain how experience can, in veridical cases, latch on, or relate, to the world. The experiencing subject is, in effect, left behind a *veil* of sense-data.

Consider, now, how the representationist will handle non-veridical experience. The basic strategy involves an appeal to an analogy with belief or judgement. A belief, for example, is a representational state and, as such, can represent a particular state of affairs whether or not that state of affairs obtains. One can believe there is a blue expanse in front of one even if there is not. And, applying this model to the case of perceptual experience, we can say that an experience can be of (or as of) a blue expanse even when its subject is misperceiving or hallucinating because the experience represents the presence of a blue expanse of water in the subject's environment and does so whether or not that state of affairs obtains. Moreover, according to the representational account, the phenomenological character of a conscious experience is determined by how it represents the environment to be. So, a conscious experience can have the same phenomenological character in a case of illusion as in a case of veridical perception, and in both cases that character involves an actual or possible state of affairs in the mind-independent environment.

In this way, the representational account uses an analogy with belief or judgement to explain how public, mind-independent, objects and properties can figure in an account of the what it is like of conscious experience. It is fairly easy to see how this strategy will be compromised should the representationist maintain that the representational properties of experiences are items of which we are aware in the having of those experiences. When I look at a public sign, say one that tells me to beware of the dog, then, one might suppose, I become aware of the representational properties of the sign. Or, in looking at a photograph of the dog, one might suppose, I become aware of the representational properties of the photograph. In both cases, *if* I indeed become aware of the representational properties of the signs, *then* I do in virtue of becoming aware of some of the intrinsic properties of those signs, and understanding the connection between these intrinsic properties and the public entities the signs are about. However, if this sort of model is applied to awareness of one's own conscious experiences, then we immediately find ourselves back with an account that the representationist should reject: a model on which awareness of how one's experience represents the environment is mediated through awareness of some of the properties in virtue of which it represents them. And then the representationist will be back with the problem of explaining how mind-independent objects can figure in an account of what experience is like.

In other words, if the representationist claims that the representational properties, or the content constituted by those properties, of any given experience are items of which we are aware in the having of that experience, then he is going to be committed to the kind of mediational conception of the relation between experience and the world that ultimately undermined empiricist or sense-datum accounts. To regard the representational properties of experience as objects of consciousness is to leave the representationist account open to essentially the same objections as those facing the sense-datum account.

There is, in fact, nothing in the representationist account which requires that the representational properties of experiences are among the objects of consciousness. Recall the analogy with belief or judgement that is central to the representationist position. If I believe that the cat is on the mat when the cat is, in fact, not on the mat, then it does not follow that my belief is one about a non-actual state-of-affairs: one in which the cat is on the mat. The entire point of the analogy with belief is to resist this sort of inference. My non-veridical belief does not have to be explained mediationally. It is not as if my non-veridical belief must be explained in terms of its, first, standing in a relation to a non-actual state-of-affairs – one with respect to which it is veridical – and then, in virtue of this, standing in relation to the world. Mediational views of experience are anathema to representationism. But to adopt the view that the representational properties, or the content constituted by such properties, of an experience are objects of consciousness is, in effect, to adopt a mediational view. Therefore, this objectualist gloss on representationism should be rejected.

The most natural, and certainly the best, way of understanding representationism is, I think, *not* in terms of the idea that the representational properties of an experience are items of which we are aware in the having that experience. Rather, it is in terms of the idea that, in having an experience, the immediate objects of which we are aware are public objects and properties *and* that in having experiences we are aware of such things *in virtue of* the representational properties of those experiences. The representational properties are not items *of* which we are aware in the having of an experience but items *with* which we are aware; items in virtue of which we are, in the having of an experience, aware of public objects and properties which that experience is about.

We might garner additional support for this claim by way of the following considerations. Consider again a public sign, say 'Beware of the dog!' Earlier, I said that it *might be supposed* that in seeing and understanding this sign we become aware of the representational properties of the sign. In fact, I do not think this supposition survives careful scrutiny, at least not if 'become aware' is intended to mean 'make them into objects of conscious awareness'. I see the sign, and, assuming I understand the language, I become aware of what the sign is *about*; i.e. of the dog and the relational properties it bears to the vicinity. But this is to become aware of the content of the sign only in the Russellian sense. What of the representational properties of the sign? Such properties are, presumably, to be understood as types of function relating – via use, history, or whatever – the intrinsic properties of the sign to public objects and properties which the sign represents. But is there any reason for supposing that we are aware *of* these functions? Well, in the required sense of being made an object of conscious awareness, there is no reason for supposing that such functions are things of which we are aware. It is one thing to claim that we tacitly know or understand these functions. Clearly we do. It is quite another to say that these functions are among the objects of our conscious experience; items with which we are consciously acquainted when we understand the sign. Almost as clearly, they are not. Rather, these functions, of which our induction into the linguistic community has made us tacitly aware, are items *in virtue of* which we are made, consciously, aware of the public objects and properties the sign is about.

Therefore, on analysis, there is, I think, little plausibility in the claim that we are aware of – in the relevant sense of making into objects of conscious awareness – the representational properties of public signs. Therefore, what plausibility is there in the claim that we are aware, in the relevant sense, of the representational properties of private signs; of representations? Moreover, to claim that we are aware of the representational properties, or the content constituted by these properties, of such signs, is to commit representationism to the sort of mediational conception of the relation between experience and the world that did for sense-datum accounts. The representationist should avoid this claim like the plague.

This section has not tried to assess the validity of the representationist account of what it is like. A more detailed evaluation of representationism will be attempted in chapter 9. Rather, this section has simply been concerned with whether representationism entails, or in any way supports, the claim that the what it is like of conscious experience is an object of conscious acquaintance. I have argued that it does not. Not only is there no reason for thinking that representationism requires the claim that the representational properties of experience are objects of consciousness, there are very good reasons for thinking that representationism is committed to denying this claim. Representational properties are better understood as items in virtue of which our experiences make us aware of the world, not items of which we are aware. Thus, if what it is like is to be reduced to representational content, this means, again, that what it is like is not an object of consciousness.

5   For actualism

The previous three sections have tried to refute the idea that the what it is like of conscious experience is an object of consciousness, something of which we are aware in the having of experience. It has, that is, tried to refute the objectualist interpretation of what it is like. If we combine objectualism with the claim that what it is like is a phenomenal particular, we are committed to abandoning materialism. On the other hand, both the understanding of what it is like as a phenomenal property and the understanding of it as a representational property are incompatible with the objectualist interpretation of what it is like, since neither phenomenal properties nor representational properties can plausibly be thought of as objects of consciousness. Thus, we can have a consistent objectualist interpretation of what it is like only at the cost of abandoning materialism. And this, I assume, is too high a price to pay.

The alternative is to adopt an actualist interpretation of what it is like. The what it is like of conscious experience is not an object of consciousness; it is not something upon which consciousness can be directed. Rather, it is a feature of conscious experience that exists only in the directing of that experience towards a quite distinct, and non-phenomenal, object. What it is like is that in virtue of which we experience objects in a certain way, a phenomenological way. It is not an object we experience. This section defends, by more direct means, the actualist interpretation. In this section, I argue that the actualist interpretation brings with it other benefits; specifically, it allows us to account for a certain central and well-known feature of what it is like, a feature that the objectualist interpretation would seem to render mysterious.

Firstly, as was remarked upon at the beginning of the previous chapter, it is seemingly impossible to supply an adequate definition of the notion of phenomenal consciousness. Indeed, there seems to be no perspicuous and non-circular way of explaining what phenomenal consciousness is. Thus, as we saw, attempts to explain its content tend to rely on a number of devices, linguistic and otherwise.

This feature of consciousness, its *ineffability*, can readily be explained if we assume that (i) phenomenal consciousness is constituted by the what it is like of experience, and (ii) what it is like is not an object of consciousness. If what it is like is constitutive of phenomenal consciousness, and if what it is like could become an object of consciousness, it would be a mystery as to why there should be this trouble in providing a description or definition of it. Objects of consciousness can typically be described. Snow is white, and when I am conscious of snow, I am conscious of something that can be described as white. However, if we suppose that what it is like cannot become an object of consciousness, the seeming ineffability of phenomenal consciousness becomes readily understandable. We cannot describe the what it is like of conscious experience, hence we cannot define or explain the notion of phenomenal consciousness, because it is not an object that lies before our conscious gaze, hence not an object that this gaze can permit us to describe.

Even more significant than the ineffability itself of phenomenal consciousness is what underlies this ineffability. All attempts to describe what it is like to undergo a conscious experience seem to have a peculiarly *regressive* character (Malcolm and Armstrong 1984). If what it is like could become an object of consciousness then it should, it seems, be possible to describe it, at least in principle. Objects of consciousness are typically describable. But what is most instructive here is not simply that all such attempted descriptions fall short of the mark, but the reason they do so. Suppose, for example, we have to describe what it is like to have cold feet (in the literal sense). Then we might say things like 'My feet feel like blocks of ice'. This description, however, simply invites the further question, 'What is it like to have feet that feel like blocks of ice?' And, if I say my stomach feels like it is tied in knots, then this simply invites the further question of what it is like to have a stomach that feels as if it is tied in knots. In fact, no matter what description we supply in attempt to answer a 'What is it like?' question, it seems that it will simply invite the further question of what it is like to satisfy that description. Attempts to answer a 'What is it like?' question thus have, in this sense, a peculiarly regressive character. This regressive nature of attempts to describe what it is like to undergo a conscious experience can be explained if we assume that what it is like can never be made an object of consciousness. Objects of consciousness should be describable, at least in principle: all one would have to do, it seems, is focus one's attention on the object and list its features. What it is like, it seems, is not describable. And this suggests that what it is like is not an object of consciousness. And, therefore, any attempt to focus our attention on the what it is like of conscious experience simply results in its slipping away from our conscious grasp, evading, as Sartre would say, our conscious gaze in a perpetual *play of mirrors*.

If we think of what it is like as an object of consciousness, then the only way of accounting for the above problems is to regard it as what Wittgenstein would have called a *queer* object, an object with magical properties. It is an object of consciousness but, somehow, different from those other (non-phenomenal) objects of consciousness that are patently describable. It is the queerness of what it is like as an object of consciousness that 'explains' why it is not, in principle, describable. This strategy, of course, involves our going down a road against which Wittgenstein has sternly cautioned us. And I assume its bankruptcy is evident to all.

6   Phenomenology by proxy

If the arguments developed in the previous two sections are correct, we should reject an objectualist interpretation of the what it is like of conscious experience and endorse, instead, the actualist alternative. What it is like is not an object of conscious acquaintance but, rather, a feature of conscious experience that exists in the directing of such experience towards a quite distinct object.

However, even if this is true, it cannot be the whole story. Something remains in need of explanation. For it certainly *seems* to us, or has seemed to many people, that the what it is like of conscious experience is an object of conscious acquaintance. It certainly *seems* as if what it is like is an object upon which our conscious gaze might, and frequently does, fall. And it is this intuition which surely underlies the ubiquity of the objectualist interpretation of what it is like identified in the previous chapter. Therefore, any defence of the actualist interpretation of what it is like cannot rest simply on the arguments it presents for that interpretation. The defence is also under an obligation to explain why what it is like seems to be an object of consciousness; why it seems to be something of which we are aware in the having of an experience. What is required, that is, is an explanation of why the objectualist interpretation seems so intuitively natural. This section attempts to provide such an explanation.

At this point, one might be tempted to list a series of linguistic and/or conceptual confusions that might underwrite the objectualist interpretation. Some of these will be dealt with, for slightly different reasons, in the next section. However, while such confusions might, in part, be helpful in identifying some of the philosophical reasons for adherence to the objectualist interpretation, they do not, I think, take us to the heart of the issue. They might explain some part of the philosophical attractiveness of the view but they cannot, I think, explain its intuitive attractiveness. To explain this, we need to focus on the nature of experience itself. The intuitive naturalness, though not, of course, the veracity, of the objectualist interpretation of what it is like derives from the nature of experience itself, specifically from a feature of introspective experience: such experience has no *specific* phenomenology.

In the earlier discussion of representationism, the idea of experiential *transparency* was introduced. As I look out of my study window, across the field and down to the ocean, I may attend to the mist, the trees, the seagulls, or the droplets of dew clinging to the grass outside my window. I can also reflect on what it is like for me to be staring at the mist and the seagulls and the dew. That is, I can direct my attention on my experience of these items. However, when my attention is thus directed inwards, the mist and seagulls and dewdrops are not replaced by some other entities, ones belonging to the inner realm of the mind. Rather, I focus on my experience by perceptually attending to the external items themselves, and reflecting on this while I do it. Experience is, in this sense *diaphanous* (Moore 1903), or *transparent*. The idea is expressed quite beautifully by G. E. Moore:

[T]he moment we try to fix our attention upon consciousness and to see *what*, distinctively, it is, it seems to vanish: it seems as if we had before us a mere emptiness. When we try to introspect the sensation of blue, all we can see is the blue: the other element is as if it were diaphanous. (1903: 450)

When we try to focus on the distinctively phenomenal characteristics of our experience, these, so to speak, slip from our conscious gaze; all we are left with are the public objects and properties our experience is of, or as of.

Now, it seems a reasonable assumption, although one that will not be properly defended until chapters 9 and 10, that, even if the what it is like of an experience cannot be *reduced* to that experience's representational content, there is, nonetheless, an essential connection between the former and the latter. The phenomenal character of an experience seems constitutively connected with the way that experience represents the world in that while it may be possible for experiences to vary in the objects they represent without a corresponding variation in their phenomenal character,[4] it is far less clear that they can vary in the *way* in which they represent those objects without a corresponding change in their phenomenal character.

---

[4] Ned Block's classic inverted earth thought experiment is a graphic way of illustrating the possibility of variation in objects represented by experience-tokens without corresponding variation in their phenomenal character. Inverted earth will be discussed in chapter 9.

Let us clarify this by distinguishing between the representational *content* and the representational *character* of an experience.[5] The representational content of any given experience is constituted by the property, possessed by that experience, of representing a particular object, event, process, situation, state of affairs, etc. The representational character of any given experience, on the other hand, is constituted by the property of representing that experience's object under a given *mode of presentation*.[6] With this distinction, we can state what I think amounts to a plausible supervenience principle for the phenomenal character, or what it is like, of experience:

There can be no variation in the representational *character* of an experience without a corresponding change in the phenomenal character (the what it is like) of that experience.

Equivalently:

Any two experience tokens that are identical with respect to their phenomenal character must be identical with respect to their representational character.

I do not pretend to have defended this supervenience claim yet. However, I will do so in chapter 9, where there will be a proper discussion of the forms, merits and shortcomings of representationism. Here, I simply propose to use the supervenience principle to create a plausible *prima facie* case for the claim that introspection has no specific phenomenology. To those who find this case less than compelling in the absence of a proper defence of the supervenience claim, I (i) understand, but (ii) beg your indulgence until chapter 9.

With this in mind, let us focus again on the status of the phenomenal character of introspection. Suppose I have a visual experience of, say, a seagull. Then, given the above supervenience claim, the phenomenal character of this visual experience is dependent on its representational character. It depends on the *way in which* the seagull is represented in that if this changes then the phenomenal character must also change. It is this phenomenal character which is, let us suppose, my introspective target; it is upon this that I wish to focus. But my introspective act, if Moore is correct, passes all the way through to the seagull, and to the properties in terms of which it is presented to me, and does not stop at some private intermediary. However, and this is the force of the supervenience claim,

---

[5] The distinction is, of course, closely modelled on Kaplan's (1989) distinction between the content and character of representational states.

[6] This distinction will be more fully worked out in chapter 9. There it provides the basis of the distinction between what I call *object* and *mode* representationism. While not fully endorsing either form, I shall argue that mode representationism is far more plausible than its object cousin.

the act of introspection cannot change the way in which the seagull is presented. If it changes the mode of presentation of the seagull, then it also changes the phenomenal character. And, if this is the case, introspection will necessarily fail in hitting its target: the phenomenal character, or what it is like, of experience. Thus, there can be no change in the way the act of introspection represents the object of the original experience. But, because of the transparency of experience, there is no other object towards which the introspective act can be directed. Therefore, if the introspective act is to be successful it must be directed towards the same object as the original experience and it must present this object in the same way, that is, under the same mode of presentation.

The result is that every act of introspection must have the same phenomenal character as the experiential act that it introspects. This, ultimately, is the force of the combination of the supervenience principle and the principle of experiential transparency. And this entails, in effect, that introspective experience, unlike sense experience, *has no specific phenomenology*. Whatever phenomenal character an act of introspection has, it necessarily inherits this from the experience that is its object.

The claim that introspection has no specific phenomenology is by no means a non-standard one. Without too much, or indeed any, air of controversy, McGinn, for example, writes:

One thing that seems clear is that introspective awareness is not itself a kind of *experience*: you do not have an experience as of your experience as of the sun setting. This is because the act of inner awareness does not have the phenomenology characteristic of a sense-modality. The only phenomenology attending such awareness comes from the *object* of the awareness. (1997: 64)

We should, perhaps, take care to distinguish two interpretations of this claim, since these are often run together. Firstly, there is what we can call the *modality* interpretation. Introspection, as a modality, has no specific phenomenology: the act of inner awareness does not have the phenomenology that is characteristic of a sense modality. While there may be something that it is like to see, something that is quite different from the what it is like to hear or smell, there is nothing that it is like to introspect. This is an interesting claim, but not one upon which I shall rely here: the modality interpretation is not what I mean by denying that introspection has a specific phenomenology.

The claim concerns, rather, specific acts of introspection rather than introspection as a modality. I shall refer to this as the *episode* interpretation. It is no part of the episode interpretation to deny that introspection tokens possess a phenomenological character. They clearly do (if in doubt, just try reading Proust). Rather, the claim is that introspection tokens have no *specific* phenomenology; they have no phenomenology that defines them, or otherwise marks them out, precisely as the individual introspective tokens they are. Rather, the phenomenological features possessed by any token introspective act are essentially connected with those of the experience that is the object of the act. The phenomenological features of any token introspective episode are acquired, or inherited, from the experience that is its object. Introspective phenomenology is *phenomenology by proxy*.

Thus, suppose one attempts to introspectively focus one's attention on the what it is like of one's experience. The what it is like that one attempts to thus focus on, because of the transparency of experience, slips away, and one is left with the worldly objects and properties that one's experience is about. However, when one does this, one ends up with an introspective experience that has precisely the same phenomenology as that of the original experience. This is because introspective experience has no phenomenology that is *specific* to it, but, rather, inherits whatever phenomenology it has from the experiences upon which it is directed. The what it is like of the introspective experience, on the actualist interpretation of what it is like, exists in the directing of the introspective experience towards the experience that is its object; it is not itself an object of the introspective experience. However, the what it is like of the introspective experience that exists in the directing of the introspective experience is the same as the what it is like of the original experience, a what it is like that itself existed in the directing of that experience towards its (non-phenomenal) objects. We thus have a type-identity of phenomenologies, *neither of which were ever objects of conscious experience.*

The type-identity of the phenomenologies possessed by the introspective experience and the experience towards which it is directed will, I suggest, tempt us into supposing that in introspective experience one has succeeded in objectifying – making into an object of one's conscious gaze – the what it is like of the original experience. But one has not. Instead, one ends up with a new experience – an introspective one – which has precisely the same phenomenology – precisely the same what it is like – as the original experience. But this what it is like belongs now to the act of introspecting, to the directing of the introspection towards its object, and not to the experience upon which one is introspecting. The what it is like, that is, is still part of the act of conscious awareness, it is not part of the object. The type-identity of the two phenomenologies, however – the fact that the phenomenology of the original directing of awareness is type-identical with the new introspective directing of awareness – tempts us into thinking that in introspection we have objectified the original phenomenology. But, in fact, we have not.

Therefore, I suggest, it is the fact that introspection has no *specific* phe-nomenology, a fact entailed, ultimately, by the phenomenon of experien-tial transparency, that, in part, creates the illusion that we can objectify the what it is like of conscious experience. The intuitive naturalness of the objectualist interpretation of what it is like derives from the fact that introspection has no specific phenomenology, that its phenomenology is *phenomenology by proxy*.

7   Objections and replies

By far the most obvious and pressing objection to the position developed in this chapter is this. Can we not make the act of conscious awareness – consciousness conceived of from the actualist perspective – into an object of consciousness? Can we not, that is, make the functioning of conscious-ness as directing of awareness an object of consciousness? Can we not, that is, direct our attention to the act of directing attention? And if we can do this, then it seems we should be able to make the properties associated with the act of consciousness into objects of consciousness.

Nothing in the argument developed here, in fact, rules out the possibil-ity of making the functioning of consciousness as directing of awareness into an object of awareness. Nothing said here, that is, precludes the possibility of directing one's attention towards consciousness functioning as the directing of awareness. In part, of course, this is precisely what this chapter has been doing. What the argument developed here does entail, however, is that it is not possible to make the functioning of con-sciousness as directing of awareness into an object of awareness without losing, abstracting away from, certain features that are associated with the functioning of consciousness as directing. These features are those that constitute the what it is like of conscious experience. The what it is like of conscious experience is lost when we direct our attention towards it. The phenomenal character of experience cannot be made an object of consciousness, even though the functioning of consciousness as directing of awareness, to some extent, can. And the what it is like of conscious experience cannot be made into an object of such experience because it can exist only as part of the functioning of consciousness as directing of awareness, rather than as that upon which consciousness is directed.

This point can be obscured by a failure to distinguish two very dif-ferent explanatory projects. On the one hand, there is the attempt to explain what it is about the brain that allows consciousness to function as directing of awareness. This project is *not* jeopardised by the argument developed in this chapter. Consider, for example, the case of pain. Be-ing in pain involves not just the taking of bodily damage as the object of consciousness. Compare, for example, being in pain with viewing one's bodily damage while in an anaesthetised state. Rather, it involves apprehending the bodily damage from, so to speak, *the inside*. Being in pain is constituted by the functioning of consciousness as an act directed towards the bodily damage. Our *capacity* to apprehend bodily damage in this way, from the inside, is, presumably, simply a matter of our brain, and central and peripheral nervous systems, being hooked up to the damage in the appropriate way. This much is not in dispute. There is no problem here, still less is there any mystery. We already possess much of the relevant knowledge about how this hook-up is effected.

On the other hand, there is the very different explanatory project of accounting for how the brain produces the properties associated with, and constitutive of, the directing of consciousness towards its objects; the properties that constitute the what it is like of conscious experience. The former project was one of explaining how the brain produces the capacity for consciousness to be directed towards objects. The latter project is one of explaining how the brain produces the various features associated with the directing of consciousness towards its objects, specifically the feature of its being like something to undergo a conscious experience. It is this project that, I shall argue in chapter 10, will be undermined if the arguments developed in this chapter are correct. It is one thing to show how acts of consciousness are effected. It is quite another to show how these acts have the properties they have.

It is, of course, open to anyone to claim that unless one is able to show how acts of consciousness have the properties they have one has not really explained how the brain gives us the capacity for such acts either. This issue is largely terminological. The important point is that these two explanatory projects are clearly distinct. To succeed or fail in either one of these projects is not, necessarily, to succeed or fail in the other.

Nothing in the arguments developed in this chapter, then, shows that it will not be possible to give an account of how consciousness as a directing of awareness is effected. I assume that such an explanation is not only possible but, moreover, not particularly distant. Furthermore, I assume that such an explanation will appeal only to physical properties, concepts, and laws. This is what makes the view I advocate a form of naturalism.[7] Whatever events, states, or processes turn out to be responsible for our being phenomenally conscious, and being subjects of consciousness, they will be natural, physical events, states, or processes. However, I shall argue in chapter 10 that consistent adoption of the actualist interpretation rules out the possibility of a reductive explanation of the what it is like

---

[7] The issue of naturalism, and its relation to actualism, will be discussed in more detail in chapter 10.

of conscious experience. This is what makes the naturalism defended here anticonstructive. This is not because these features are supernatural. If they were supernatural features, they would be incorporated into a supernatural metaphysic, and would possess a supernatural explanation. Such a view is, I think, dubiously coherent and, in any event, almost certainly false. But, as I shall also argue later, the actualist interpretation rules out the possibility of *any* reductive explanation of the phenomenal character of conscious experience; whether this explanation is cast in terms of physical substance *or* in terms of spiritual substance. The what it is like of conscious experience has no explanation, either natural or supernatural, or any other imagined form. And this, ultimately, is because the what it is like of conscious experience cannot be made into an object of experience.

A second objection to the position developed here runs as follows. If what it is like cannot be an object of consciousness then we would be unable to know anything about it, including the sorts of claims made by this book and others. The problem with this objection, however, is that it presupposes a model of knowledge that is inappropriate to the case of the what it is like of conscious experience. What it is like belongs to the act of conscious experience. To the extent that we are subjects of consciousness, we are aware of our experiences. But it would be a serious mistake, I have argued, to think that this means we know what it is like to have an experience, at least if this knowledge is conceived along traditional dyadic lines (and it is difficult to imagine upon what other lines it might be conceived). Knowing what it is like to undergo a conscious experience is not the same thing at all as knowledge of objects and their properties. We do not know what it is like to be a subject of consciousness because we can make the what it is like to be a subject of consciousness into an object of consciousness. To claim that we know what it is like to be subjects of consciousness means nothing more than this: we are subjects of consciousness capable of directing our consciousness towards its objects. We should remember Wittgenstein's claim of the previous chapter: 'It can't be said of me at all (except perhaps as a joke) that I *know* I'm in pain.' Knowledge, and the associated idea of giving reasons justifying one's claim, is appropriate to objects of consciousness, but not to features existing in the directing of consciousness towards its objects. Such features are too 'close' to us, and do not belong to the domain of giving reasons. This is where our spade is turned. Once again our language sets us traps. We are tempted to move from the claim that 'I know what it is like to undergo a conscious experience' to the claim 'There is something that I know when I undergo a conscious experience'. The pitfalls of this sort of inference, and of the temptations underlying it, have been well documented by Moore, Wittgenstein, and others. I suggest we firmly resist this temptation in the case of the what it is like of conscious experience.

A third objection is based on the idea that if the what it is like of conscious experience cannot be made into an object of consciousness then neither can it be made into an object of linguistic reference. And if it cannot be made into an object of reference, then, it might be thought, we cannot meaningfully talk about it. However, in order to be swayed by this argument, one has to fall victim to a linguistic version of the temptation described above. The response, I think, is to allow that what it is like is *not* an object of reference, linguistic or otherwise. Our talk of about the what it is like of conscious experience is meaningful, but not because it derives its meaning from reference to the what it is like of conscious experience. This sort of claim, of course, is familiar from Wittgenstein's ruminations about private languages, and the like. The general idea, here, would be that talk of what it is like gets its meaning, perhaps, because it is uttered by conscious subjects for whom there is something that it is like to undergo an experience, and who, partly in virtue of this, engage in various social practices and customs, including practices of expressing their experiences, and who adhere to various community-authorised linguistic norms in doing so. Its meaning, however, does not derive, in any straightforward way, from reference to this what it is like. Within this general framework, there are several well-known possible alternative accounts of how talk about what it is like acquires its meaning, and I am not, I think, forced to choose one here.

8   Summary

The what it is like of conscious experience is not an object of conscious acquaintance. It is not one of the objects of one's consciousness, one of the items towards which one's consciousness can be directed. Rather, it is a feature that exists in, and only in, the directing of one's consciousness towards other, non-phenomenal, objects. The objectualist interpretation of what it is like, that is, should be rejected. If what it is like is an object of consciousness, then it must be either a phenomenal particular, a phenomenal property or an intentional property. But the latter two proposals, upon examination, prove to be incompatible with objectualism. Phenomenal properties and representational properties cannot, plausibly, be regarded as objects of consciousness. But the claim that what it is like is a phenomenal particular entails the rejection of materialism. Therefore, what it is like is best understood in actualist terms. This allows us to understand the ineffability of phenomenal consciousness and the regressive character of all attempts to describe what it is like upon which this ineffability seems to be based. And we can also explain away the intuitive naturalness of the objectualist interpretation by way of the fact that introspective experience has no specific phenomenology. Finally, there do not seem to be any obviously insurmountable or otherwise compelling objections to the actualist interpretation. All this, I suggest, adds up to a legitimate case for actualism about the phenomenal character of experience.

8　Against objectualism II: mistakes about the way things seem

1　Introduction

The objectualist interpretation of what it is like has, undeniably, a powerful intuitive appeal. If a given experience *seems* or *feels* a certain way, what could be more natural than supposing that in having that experience we are aware of the way it seems or feels? The previous chapter supplied (i) arguments against the objectualist interpretation, (ii) arguments for the actualist interpretation, (iii) a diagnosis of why the objectualist interpretation should be so intuitively natural even if false, and (iv) responses to objections to the abandoning the objectualist interpretation. However, such is the appeal of the objectualist account of what it is like, that it is difficult to shake the suspicion that even all this is not enough. Accordingly, this chapter develops further the case against objectualism.

In developing this case, I shall adopt the common assumption that the phenomenal constituents of the what it is like of experience are phenomenal properties or, as they are sometimes called, *qualia*. I shall use these terms interchangeably. Roughly, then, the idea is that if, for example, there is something that it is like to visually experience a red square, then this what it is like will be made up of a red quale, or phenomenal property, and a square quale, or phenomenal property. For those who believe that experiences are constituted by the what it is like to have them, this assumption about their relation to qualia is uncontroversial.

Adopting this terminology, then, the principal claims for which I shall argue in this chapter are as follows:

The weak thesis. That an experience seems or feels a certain way does not require that we be aware of the phenomenal properties, or qualia, of that experience.

The strong thesis. The way an experience seems or feels is not something to be explained in terms of awareness of the phenomenal properties, or qualia, of that experience.

I shall try to show that both theses can be established on the basis of essentially the same arguments. In more detail, I shall develop the following argument in support of both the weak and strong theses. If the way an experience seems or feels to a subject is explained in terms of the subject's awareness of the phenomenal properties or qualia of that experience, then a certain sort of mistake is possible about this experience: it is possible for the subject to be mistaken about how the experience seems to her. However, this sort of mistake is, in fact, not possible. Therefore, not only are we not required to explain the way an experience seems or feels to its subject in terms of awareness of phenomenal properties or qualia, we, in fact, cannot explain it in this way.

2   Three mistakes about experience

This much, of course, is post-Nagelian orthodoxy: there is *something that it is like* to have an experience. (Or, if some experiences are unconscious (or sub- or pre-conscious) then the qualifier 'conscious' should be inserted before 'experience'.) Indeed, experiences are typically regarded as defined by this what it is like. Since the category of experiences incorporates both perceptual episodes and bodily sensations, epithets such as 'seems' (appropriate more to perception) and 'feels' (appropriate more to sensation) are often used to characterise this idea that there is something that it is like to have an experience. Thus, part of the orthodoxy is that experiences seem a certain way, or that experiences feel a certain way, and this seeming or feeling is an essential feature of the experience.

Actually, the idea that experiences seem or feel a certain way is misleading, in certain contexts dangerously so.[1] I take it that talk of experiences seeming a certain way is elliptical for the following: *in having an experience the world seems a certain way*. That is, it is not an experience that seems a certain way, but the having of an experience that seems or feels a certain way. And all this means is that in the having of an experience the world seems, or is presented in, a certain way. I shall go on speaking of 'the way an experience seems', but one should take this as elliptical for the above sort of account.

---

[1] The idea that experiences seem a certain way is one of Carruthers' principal avowed motivations for adopting a higher-order representation account of consciousness (see chapter 4, note 1). The idea is that we must be able to account not only for how the world seems to a conscious subject, but also how their experiences seem, and this latter is explained in terms of a higher-order representation. I reject the assumption. To have an experience is for the world – external or internal – to seem a certain way to one. In other words, experiences do not seem a certain way, the world seems a certain way in the having of experience. This is, arguably, entailed by the transparency of experience. When we focus on the way an experience seems, we find only environmental objects and properties (where 'environmental' is broadly construed).

Given that experiences, in the sense qualified above, seem or feel a certain way to their subjects, it is possible to distinguish three different kinds of mistake associated with the idea that in having an experience things seem a certain way to one. The first is very familiar.

(1) How things seem to a subject in the having of an experience does not reflect how the world really is.

Embodied in this type of mistake are traditional philosophical preoccupations with our knowledge of the external world, and how this knowledge is or is not impugned by the existence of perceptual illusions, hallucinations, etc. Mistakes of category (1) will not be discussed in this chapter.

Mistakes of category (1) should be clearly distinguished from what I shall call mistakes of category (2):

(2) How things seem to a subject in the having of an experience does not reflect how the experience really is.

Daniel Dennett (1991) has recently drawn our attention to mistakes, or alleged mistakes, of category (2). In one of the cases to be discussed later, Dennett argues that the apparent richness, detail, and completeness of an experience (e.g. of a wall of pictures of Marilyn Monroe) does not reflect richness, detail and completeness that is actually in the experience itself. Thus, we have a clash between the way an experience seems and the way it really is. Mistakes of category (2) will be discussed in this chapter only to the extent that it is necessary to distinguish them from a distinct mistake, one that is the proper subject of this chapter (indeed, I shall argue that mistakes of category (2) are, probably, not really mistakes at all).

The principal subject of this chapter is a distinct type of mistake, one that does not seem possible:

(3) How things seem to a subject in the having of an experience does not reflect how things really seem in the having of that experience.

This seems nonsensical. To allow the possibility of a mistake of category (3) would force us to admit an appearance/reality distinction for seemings. However, seemings are supposed to be appearances: to say that things seem a certain way to a subject in the having of an experience is precisely to say that the world appears to that subject in a certain way in the having of that experience. To admit an appearance/reality distinction for seemings, then, is to admit a logical contradiction. Category (3) mistakes, therefore, are impossible mistakes.

However, I shall argue that if we endorse the objectualist account of the way an experience seems or feels to a subject, according to which this is a matter of the subject's being aware of the phenomenal properties or qualia of that experience, then we will be committed to the possibility of mistakes of category (3). The objectualist gloss, that is, commits us to the possibility of an impossibility, and should be rejected on these grounds.

3   The objectualist gloss: qualia

The objectualist gloss should by now be familiar. In having an experience, we are aware of certain items, usually referred to as *qualia* or *phenomenal properties*, and our having an experience that seems or feels a certain way consists in our being aware of the relevant qualia or phenomenal properties instantiated by that experience. So pervasive and tenacious is the gloss that it is almost, at least in some circles, regarded as synonymous with what it glosses. That is, it is often supposed that for an experience to seem or feel a certain way to its subject just *is* for the subject to be, or even just *means* that the subject is, aware of the appropriate qualia.

I wish, of course, to maintain the distinctness of gloss and glossed. The objectualist gloss is a theoretical interpretation of the experiential data and not something mandated by that data. That an experience seems or feels a certain way to the subject that has it does not entail that the subject is aware of certain qualia or phenomenal properties of that experience. Indeed, it is false that the subject is aware of these items.

Qualia, or phenomenal properties, it is commonly supposed, are the phenomenal constituents of the what it is like of experience. The term 'qualia' has, perhaps, so far been conspicuously absent in a book that purports to be concerned with the what it is like of experience. I have, of course, effectively discussed qualia at some length in the previous chapter, it is just that I chose to refer to them as phenomenal properties. This is no accident. Talk of qualia tends to bring with it a lot of theoretical baggage, most of it distinctly unhelpful. That is, qualia, understood as the apprehended phenomenal properties of experience, are often loaded down with various other properties, of varying degrees of implausibility, and then attacked from this standpoint. Thus, we are often told that qualia are *intrinsic* properties of experiences, that our access to them is *privileged*, that we can know *incorrigibly* of their presence, perhaps because we are *directly aware* of them, and so on. But to attack qualia because of their possession of a series of improbable properties that one has oneself foisted on them smacks of cheating.

In any event, I shall liberate qualia from most of this theoretical baggage. The conception of qualia employed here is, accordingly, pretty minimalist, consisting of only two central claims. Firstly, qualia are things of which we are aware. They are objects of awareness. Thus, when one has an experience that seems or feels a certain way this is because one is aware of, conscious of, the qualia instantiated by that experience. This condition is, of course, a requirement of the objectualist gloss that is to be attacked.[2]

Secondly, if one is aware of the qualia possessed by one's experience, and thus aware of how one's experience seems to one, this is so because of events, processes and properties that are occurring or instantiated inside one's skin. That is, I shall assume an *individualist* conception of qualia. The qualia of experience are constituted by activities internal to the subject of experience. Individualism of this sort goes hand in hand with a working assumption of this book: naturalism. Qualia, whatever they are, are not supernatural items; they are constituted by, or supervene upon, physical processes. Individualism about qualia merely circumscribes the type of physical processes involved: the qualia of experience are constituted by brain, and perhaps wider neural, activity. In any event, they are constituted exclusively by physical processes internal to the experiencing subject. Individualism about qualia is almost universally accepted.[3]

The view to be attacked in the remainder of this chapter is the idea that the way an experience seems or feels to its subject can be explained in terms of her awareness of qualia or phenomenal properties. The idea, broadly speaking, is that (i) in certain circumstances the way an experience seems or feels to a subject and that subject's awareness of the qualia of that experience can, quite clearly, come apart, and (ii) they do so in such a way that makes it implausible to suppose that it is possible to explain the former in terms of the latter. The circumstances in which the objectualist gloss can come apart from the idea that an experience seems or feels a certain way to a subject are identified most clearly by way of recent work in visual science; in particular by way of work on *perceptual completion* and *neural filling in*.

---

[2] Thus, nothing I say here rules out an actualist construal of qualia. Indeed, such a construal is, in effect, precisely what this chapter is trying to defend.

[3] Individualism about qualia is presupposed, for example, by Block's famous *inverted earth* thought experiment. Conversely, individualism about qualia will be rejected by those who adopt one or another form of *representationism* about phenomenal character: the view that phenomenal differences between experiences do not outrun intentional differences (cf. Lycan 1996). My own view is, actually, much closer to representationism. So, it is possible, if one is so inclined, to understand the arguments developed in this chapter as an attack on the individualist conception of qualia. In any event, I shall argue that if qualia are understood as (i) things of which we are aware, (ii) locally supervenient on the subjects of experience, then they cannot account for the way an experience seems. If this is correct, (i) or (ii) or perhaps both must go.

4 Perceptual completion and neural filling in

The concepts of perceptual *completion* and neural *filling in* are often run together but are, nevertheless, quite distinct. The confusion in this regard is a symptom of a more general confusion that we shall have cause to discuss later: the distinction between *organismic* and *algorithmic* levels of description, explanation and task specification. This section surveys and contrasts completion and filling in phenomena.

The concept of perceptual completion applies to situations where subjects report that a certain item is present in a particular region of their field of vision when it is actually absent from that region, either because it is not present anywhere or because it is present in some other region. The most obvious example is provided by the *blind spot*. In each eye, there is a region where the optic nerve leaves the retina. In this region there are no photoreceptors, with the result that it can receive no visual information; it is blind. In ordinary perceptual situations, we are never aware of the blind spot; since the blind spots of the two eyes do not overlap an item that falls on the blind spot of one retina will fall outside that of the other. Even under monocular viewing, the blind spot is not easily revealed. Close one eye and fixate on the mid point between two dots on a uniformly coloured piece of paper. There is no experience of a gap or discontinuity in the visual field. Now move the paper slowly towards your face. At some point, the left dot disappears as it enters the blind spot. What is noticeable, however, is that one continues to perceive a uniform expanse of brightness and colour This is an example of perceptual completion: the colour and brightness surrounding the area corresponding to the blind spot are used to complete the blind area, so that one has an experience as of a uniform expanse.

This is a very simple example of perceptual completion, but the category covers a wide-ranging array of almost certainly heterogeneous cases. Pessoa, Thompson and Noe (1998) provide a useful classificatory system for perceptual completion, identifying four main categories composed of two central divisions that cross-classify each other.

The first division is between *amodal* and *modal* completion. Amodal completion is the completion of an object that is not entirely visible because it is covered or occluded by something else (Kanizsa and Gerbino 1982). Modal completion, on the other hand, occurs where the completed parts of an object display the same type of attributes or 'modes' as the rest of the figure. That is, whereas amodal completion is completion of occluded objects, modal completion is perceptual completion of objects in the foreground. The second division is between *boundary* and *featural* completion. Boundary completion, as the name suggests, is the completion of the edges or boundaries of objects. Feature completion is the completion of features or characteristics that fall within a given region or boundary.

Perceptual completion is a phenomenon best described at the level of persons. That is, perceptual completion is, in the first instance, something that persons or organisms do, something they do in virtue of their underlying cognitive architecture. Evidence for its existence is, accordingly, derived from the reports of persons or, alternatively, from first-person experience. Evidence for the perceptual completion of the blind region, for example, is simply our first-person awareness of the continuity of our visual field, or the reports of the awareness of such continuity in others. The existence of perceptual completion phenomena, in this sense, is uncontroversial. However, it is often confused with a much more controversial idea, that of *neural* filling in. This is, allegedly, something that neurons do. In this controversial sense of filling in, the brain is supposed to actively fill in information that would otherwise be absent. For example, the reason why we do not perceive the blind spot, a region of our visual field bereft of visual information, even under monocular viewing conditions, is that the brain somehow *fills in* the missing information. The brain, on this view, actively makes up for an absence; it provides information that otherwise would not be there.

The distinction between perceptual completion and neural filling in may appear tenuous. If perceptual completion occurs, and it clearly does, then this is presumably because, ultimately, of various neural mechanisms performing various operations. This is true, but the distinction is still valid because the existence of perceptual completion is compatible with a variety of hypotheses about the brain activity that underlies it. The existence of perceptual completion, that is, does not *require* neural filling in. To see this, however, we must first properly grasp the distinction between *personal* and *sub-personal* levels of description; or, as I prefer it, the distinction between *organismic* and *algorithmic* attributions of content (Rowlands 1997, 1999, ch. 10).

The algorithmic proper function of an ensemble of neurons is, roughly, what they are supposed to do, what operations they are supposed to perform. If the function of this ensemble is proto-representational – for example, they are designed to fire in the presence, and only in the presence, of a certain stimulus – then it might, on the basis of this, be possible to attribute the content C_a to this ensemble. This is algorithmic content, sub-personal content: content attributable to mechanisms of an organism rather than an organism itself. The same neuronal ensemble, however, may have a distinct proper function: it may have the function of *enabling the organism* that possesses it to achieve a certain environmentally specified goal: i.e. detecting a certain environmentally salient feature. On the basis of this, it may be possible to attribute the content C_o to the organism itself. Such content is organismic content.

It is important to realise that organismic and algorithmic attributions of content do not, generally, coincide, even when it is the functioning of the same mechanism that underwrites both attributions of content. Suppose the mechanism in question is a visual one whose function is to detect the presence of a horizontal ground receding into the distance. Then, the algorithmic function of the mechanism might be, for example, to detect the presence of a texture density gradient in the optic array. Then, the content 'detects density gradient d' would be attributable to the mechanism itself, and this is content attributed on the basis of the algorithmic proper function of the mechanism. However, in addition to this function, the mechanism also has an organismic function, namely to *enable the organism* to detect the presence of a horizontal ground (or perhaps, in a more Gibsonian vein, a walk-on-able ground, the possibility of locomotion, etc.). And on the basis of this function, it is possible to attribute the content 'detects ground g' to the organism, rather than the mechanism. This is content attributed on the basis of the organismic proper function of the mechanism. The two contents are clearly different, even though it is the functioning of the same mechanism that underwrites both.

In general, the content underwritten by the organismic function of a mechanism is not identical to the content underwritten by the algorithmic function of that mechanism, and the content is, moreover, attributable to different individuals: the former to the organism, the latter to the mechanism. And both these claims are true even though it is the same mechanism that underwrites both attributions of content. What is crucial is that it is *different* functions of the same mechanism that are responsible for the two attributions of content.

The relevance of this to the distinction between perceptual completion and neural filling in is as follows. Let us suppose that perceptual completion is, in any given case, underwritten or realised by certain neuronal mechanisms performing certain operations. Then, in virtue of these operations, we might attribute to the person or organism the content 'completes region R of visual field'. Then, given the distinction between organismic and algorithmic attributions of content, we would not need to attribute content of the same type to the neuronal mechanisms that underwrite this completion, even though it is these mechanisms that underwrite this attribution of content to the organism. We would not, that is, have to regard what the mechanisms do as completing or filling in at all. Just because the person can be said to be completing a portion of the visual field does not require that the underlying mechanisms have to be functioning in this way at all, even though it is the mechanisms that enable the person to complete the field.

The phenomenon of perceptual completion, understood as something that an organism or person does, is, in fact, compatible with a variety of hypotheses about the algorithms performed by those neuronal mechanisms which enable the organism to perceptually complete. This follows from the general distinction between organismic and algorithmic attributions of content. The most impressive concrete application of this distinction is, in fact, found in Dennett's criticism of the idea of neural filling in. It is to this that we now turn.

5   Dennett's criticism of filling in

Dennett's criticism of neural filling in turns on the distinction between the *presence* of a representation and *ignoring the absence* of a representation. Consider, again, the blind spot. The fact that no one has awareness of a gap in their visual field is evidence of perceptual completion. That is uncontroversial. The hypothesis of neural filling in is that this completion is underwritten by a neural representation of a gapless visual field; that the brain supplements or embellishes the distinctly gappy information received from the retina with information of its own, information that fills in the gaps. Dennett points out that this hypothesis does not follow. The lack of a perceived gap in one's visual field can be explained simply in terms of the brain ignoring the absence of information (i.e. receptor signals) from the blind part of the retina. The visual cortex, after all, has no precedent of getting information from that region of the retina, so why should it not simply ignore the absence of signals from that area?

Often Dennett develops this argument by claiming that in this sort of case, the brain simply 'jumps to a conclusion'. Since the visual cortex never receives information from the blind retinal region, it never 'expects' such information, consequently ignores its absence, and as a result simply 'jumps to a conclusion' about the character of the perceived visual field. While it is not entirely clear what he means by this, a reasonable guess would be that the brain supplements the entirely predictable lack of received information with a symbol, one which has, roughly, the content *same again*. While this is certainly a matter of supplying content, there is no representational vehicle specifically devoted to the blind spot, and, crucially, there is no attempt by the brain to supplement and embellish the information received from the retina.

Dennett's argument is plausible. Underlying it is a principle of brain function he calls the 'thrifty producer principle': 'If no one is going to look at it, don't waste effort producing it'. For example, to see a region as uniformly coloured, all the brain has to do is arrive at the judgement that the region is uniformly coloured. And it can do this either by supplying a representation of uniform colour, or by ignoring the ('expected') absence of a representation and using the representational rule 'same again'. In any event, Dennett is surely correct that filling in the colour of each sub-area is not the thriftiest way to do it.

However, although he is almost certainly correct about particular cases, it is too early to endorse Dennett's account as a general model. Part of the problem is that the category of perceptual completion is such a broad and apparently heterogeneous one that it would be dangerous, and, quite probably, unrealistic to suppose that there is a uniform answer to the question of the relation between perceptual completion and neural filling in. Moreover, as Pessoa, Thompson and Noe (1998) have pointed out, there is, in the case of certain types of completion, *some* evidence for neural filling in. So, in the development of the arguments of the remainder of this chapter, I shall not assume that there is no such thing as neural filling in. Happily, those arguments require no such assumption.

6   Change blindness and the richness of experience

With respect to the arguments to be developed in the remainder of this chapter, a certain type of perceptual completion operation will assume particular importance. This operation pertains to the richness, detail, and completeness of experience. Dennett himself provides one well-known example of this.

Suppose you walk into a room and notice that the wallpaper is a regular array of hundreds of identical Marilyn Monroes (*à la* Andy Warhol). In order to identify a picture as one of Marilyn Monroe, you must foveate it, since your parafoveal vision does not have good resolution, not good enough to discriminate between Marilyns and coloured shapes. You are, however, able to foveate only two, perhaps three, of the pictures at any one time. Nevertheless, if you were to enter the room, you would instantly see that the wall was covered with identical Marilyns. One can conclude, Dennett argues, that the brain represents *that* there are hundreds of identical Marilyns, but not that there is a spatial or pictorial representation of each identical Marilyn. This example is analogous to the case of the blind spot discussed earlier. Just as the experience of a gapless visual field does not entail neural filling in of the blind spot, so seeing that the wall is covered with identical Marilyns entails neither a neural representation of each individual Marilyn nor a detailed neural representation of the wall as a whole. The brain, Dennett suggests, does not bother to fill in the Marilyns, in the sense of propagating a high-resolution Marilyn image across an internal mapping of an expanse of the wall. Rather, it just 'jumps to the conclusion that the rest are Marilyns, and labels the whole region "more Marilyns" without any further rendering of Marilyns at all' (1991: 355). In other words, as in the case of the blind spot, the brain, roughly speaking, simply employs the symbol: 'same again'.

Similar conclusions emerge from recent studies of *change blindness*: the inability of subjects to perceive changes, often apparently obvious changes, in a visual scene. Building on Dennett's discussion, Blackmore et al. (1995) investigated the ability to register changes in visual scenes across saccadic eye movement. In the first experiment, they compared changes where the image altered (or did not alter) and, at the same time, moved in an unpredictable direction – forcing a saccadic eye movement – with cases where the image altered (or did not alter) while staying in the same place. Blackmore et al. found that when the image did not move, subjects reliably detected the changes, but when the image did move their performance fell to chance. In the second experiment, they compared cases where the image changed and moved with cases where the image changed, stayed in the same place, but where a mid-grey interstimulus separated two images in time. This 'grey-out' condition was designed to mimic what happens during a saccade. In the grey-out condition, the subjects' performance was considerably reduced, although not to chance levels.

O'Regan, Rensink and colleagues have also provided important studies on the ability to perceive changes in scenes (O'Regan 1992; O'Regan et al. 1996; Rensink et al. 1996). In one study (Rensink et al. 1996), an image of a natural scene was continually alternated with a modified image, with a blank field inserted between each display. The duration of each image was 240 milliseconds; the blank field lasted 80 milliseconds. The modified image was the same as the original except for one change that involved either the removal of an object present in the original scene, or a change in the colour or relative position of an object. Subjects found the changes very difficult to notice under these 'flicker conditions', even though the changes were large and easily observable under normal conditions.

These are interesting and important experiments. The question is: what do they show?

7		**Category (2) mistakes: how an experience seems and how it really is**

Dennett, Blackmore et al., O'Regan et al. and Rensink et al. all seem to converge on the same conclusion: there is a clear distinction between how an experience seems and how it really is. Dennett writes:

> It seems to you as if you are seeing hundreds of identical Marilyns. And in one sense you are: there are, indeed, hundreds of identical Marilyns out there on the wall, and you're seeing them. What is not the case, however, is that there are hundreds of identical Marilyns represented in your brain. Your brain just somehow represents that there are hundreds of identical Marilyns, and no matter how vivid your impression is that you see all that detail, the detail is in the world not in your head. (1991: 355)

The implication here seems to be that there is a clash between the way having the visual experience of the wall *seems* and the way that experience really *is*. The experience seems detailed, seems composed of hundreds of Marilyns extended in space, but it really is not that way at all. The apparent richness, detail and completeness of the experience is just that: apparent. Blackmore et al. are less circumspect:

> We believe that we see a complete, dynamic picture of a stable, uniformly detailed, and colourful world. [But our] stable world may be constructed out of a brief retinal image and a very sketchy, higher-level representation along with a pop-out mechanism to redirect attention. The richness of the visual world is, to this extent, an illusion. (1995: 1075)

Similar sentiments are echoed by O'Regan et al. They write:

> Essentially only the 'center of interest' of a picture is encoded in memory. The impression of continuously seeing 'all' of a visual scene may be an illusion deriving from the fact that any change creates a visual transient that attracts attention to the changing location. (1996: 7)

What seems to underlie all of these interpretations of the experimental results is the idea that there is a distinction between (i) the way an experience seems to its subject and (ii) the way an experience really is. That is, the interpretation of the results advocated by the experimenters is that we are all prone to make mistakes of what I have called category (2): confusing the way an experience seems with the way it really is.

Let me make it clear that I in no way wish to denigrate the experiments. On the contrary, I think they are among the most interesting and important empirical work done on the nature of visual experience in many years. However, I do think there is a serious problem with this way of interpreting them. The basic problem is that to understand the significance of the experiments as indicating a distinction between the way experiences seem and the way they really are involves failing to properly observe the distinction between personal or organismic and sub-personal or algorithmic specifications of content, ironically the very distinction that allows us to properly distinguish between perceptual completion and neural filling in.

To talk of the way an experience seems is to make an organismic attribution of content: it is to attribute content to the person or organism. To talk of the way an experience really is is to make an algorithmic attribution of content; it is to attribute content to the sub-personal mechanisms that (in part) underwrite content attribution to the organism. The point is that organismic and algorithmic attributions are attributions to different things. When we talk of the way an experience seems, we are simply not talking about the same item as when we talk about the way an experience really is. That is, although the way an experience seems is undoubtedly the result of various sub-personal mechanisms performing certain operations, when we attribute the content 'seems that p' we are attributing this to an item distinct from that to which we attribute the content 'is really q'. The former is an attribution to an organism or person. We are saying, in effect, that in the having of an experience, the world seems a certain way to the subject of that experience. The latter, on the other hand, is an attribution of content not to a person or organism but to various sub-personal mechanisms. We are saying, in effect, that these mechanisms are performing in a certain way; that they are, for example, ignoring an absence of a representation as opposed to filling in, or employing the algorithm 'same again' as opposed to remedying informational poverty, and so on.

If this is correct, then there can simply be no dispute over whether the way an experience seems is the same as the way it really is. We are not talking about the same items, so there can be incompatibility here. When we talk about the way an experience seems, we are talking about the way in which the world appears to a subject in the having of an experience. And we are making an attribution of content to an organism or person. When we talk about the way an experience really is, we are talking about the various types of operations performed by sub-personal mechanisms, and we are making an attribution of content to these mechanisms in virtue of the operations they perform.

With this in mind, consider Dennett's claims that: 'One of the most striking features of consciousness is its discontinuity. Another is its apparent continuity.' But for this to be true requires that we equivocate on 'consciousness'. Talk of the discontinuity of consciousness is talk of the facts (or supposed facts) that (i) the input to the brain is severely informationally impoverished, as a result of the blind spot, other scotomata, narrow range of foveation, and so on, and (ii) that the brain deals with this informational poverty in certain ways rather than others, for example, by ignoring the absence of information and/or employing algorithms such as 'same again' rather than filling in, and so on. Talk of the discontinuity of consciousness, then, is talk of the character of input to, and operations of, various neural or otherwise sub-personal ensembles. Talk of the continuity of consciousness, on the other hand, is not talk of these sorts of things at all. It is talk of the way the world appears to the subject in virtue of having a certain sort of experience.

In short, 'discontinuity' is an abstract singular term that, in this instance, refers to processes undergone by sub-personal mechanisms, whereas 'continuity' is, in this instance, an abstract singular term that refers to processes undergone by a person. We are simply talking about different things when we talk about continuity and discontinuity in this regard. Therefore, and similarly, there can be no question of the experimental results outlined above showing that the richness of our visual world is an 'illusion', or in other ways questionable. 'Richness' in this case is an adjective that applies to the way the having of experience seems to its subject, and not to the underlying sub-personal mechanisms and processes that, in part, underwrite the application of this locution to the subject's experience.

Therefore, I do not think these experiments indicate the possibility of mistakes of category (2): confusing how an experience seems with how it really is. To suppose that they do is to oneself fall victim to a confusion of personal or organismic levels of description, explanation and content attribution with sub-personal or algorithmic levels. When we talk of the way an experience seems, we are not at all talking about the same item as when we talk about the way an experience really is. Therefore, there can be incompatibility. Hence, no confusion.

8   Mistakes of category (3)

Mistakes of category (3) are impossible mistakes. To commit a mistake of category (3) would be to confuse how an experience seems to one with how that experience really seems to one. As such, the mistake involves commitment to an appearance/reality distinction for the way an experience seems to its subject, and such a distinction is nonsensical. In the remainder of this chapter, I shall attempt to show that the real significance of the cases outlined above is that, in conjunction with the objectualist gloss on the way experiences seem or feel, they indicate the possibility of a category (3) mistake. If we regard the way an experience seems or feels to its subject as consisting in that subject's awareness of the qualia or phenomenal properties of that experience, then the cases outlined above indicate the possibility of mistaking the way an experience seems with the way it really seems. The perceptual completion and change blindness cases, that is, commit the objectualist gloss to the possibility of an impossible mistake. And, therefore, I suggest we reject the gloss.

Let us return to the wall of Marilyns. Dennett's explanation of why we seem to experience an entire wall of Marilyns in the absence of a pictorial or neural representation of each Marilyn is that the brain 'jumps to a conclusion'. That is, it employs, very roughly, a policy of (i) ignoring the absence of 'unexpected' information, and (ii) combining this with a 'same again' algorithm, understood as a symbolic, rather than pictorial, representation. It is by no means guaranteed, of course, that Dennett is correct about this, and whether he is or is not is, of course, an empirical matter. But we can be pretty sure that either he is right (or that an account that is, for our purposes, relevantly similar is right) or he is wrong.

So let us imagine two possible worlds, one in which Dennett is right, and one in which Dennett is wrong.

World 1: Dennett correct

Brain works by:	Experience seems as of:
Ignoring absence of information	Wall of Marilyns
Employing 'same again' algorithm	

World 2: Dennett incorrect

Brain works by:	Experience seems as of:
Filling in absent information	Wall of Marilyns
Forming detailed pictorial representation	

One's experience *as of* a wall of Marilyns is, if Dennett is correct, phenomenologically identical in both worlds. The same phenomenological facts are compatible with these two distinct models of how the brain underwrites or subserves these facts. This, of course, is the basis of the claim that we can explain perceptual completion without recourse to neural filling in. So, that the way one's experience seems or feels remains constant across worlds is a given. The question is: how plausible is it to suppose that the qualia or phenomenal properties of the experience remain the same across worlds? I shall argue that it is not very plausible at all.

The first potential source of difficulty for the claim that qualia are constant across worlds 1 and 2 lies in the fact that very different neural processes are involved, in each world, in the production of the way the experience of the Marilyns seems. In world 1, the brain produces the way the experience seems by ignoring the absence of information and employing a, symbolic rather than pictorial, 'same again' algorithm. In world 2, on the other hand, the brain produces the way the experience seems by filling in absent information and producing a detailed, pictorial rather than symbolic, representation of the wall. It might be thought unlikely that neural processes which involve (i) foveating on two or three Marilyns, (ii) ignoring the absence of information, and (iii) employing a symbolic algorithm could produce the same qualia as ones which involve (i) foveating on two or three Marilyns, (ii) filling in absent information and thus, (iii) constructing a detailed pictorial representation of the wall.

However, the fact that very different brain processes are involved in each case need not, in itself, trouble the objectualist. The objectualist, of course, is likely to construe the relation between qualia and underlying neural properties as one of *supervenience*: sameness of neural properties (necessarily) implies sameness of qualia, *but not vice versa*. The supervenience of qualia on neural processes is, therefore, compatible with the former having distinct, and perhaps quite different, neural realisations. And in response to the question of how so very different neural processes can produce the same qualia, the answer open to the objectualist is quite simple: *they just do*! If very different types of neural process can produce experiences that seem or feel the same way to their subjects, then they can also produce the same qualia. So, the objectualist can, I think, remain unperturbed by the significant difference in neural processes in each world.

The real problem for the objectualist, however, is not simply that the neural processes differ radically between each world but, rather, that in world 1, the world where Dennett is correct, the way an experience seems does not depend just on the neural processes occurring inside the head of the experiencing subject but also, crucially, on the world in which that head is located. And, if this is true, then one of the constitutive features of qualia must be abandoned. If the way an experience seems or feels depends not just on properties occurring inside the head but also on ones in the world, then individualism about qualia must be rejected.

Dennett, Blackmore et al., O'Regan et al., and Rensink et al., are all very clear on the role that *attention*, specifically the *directing* of attention, plays in producing the way an experience seems or feels. As we have seen, Blackmore et al. emphasise the role played by a 'pop-out mechanism to redirect attention' in creating the rich, detailed, and stable character of the way an experience seems. And O'Regan et al. accord a significant role in their account to 'visual transient[s] that attracts attention to the changing location'. What underlies this emphasis is, in outline, the following sort of account. When we look at the wall of Marilyns, our experience seems rich, detailed, complete, and stable. Why is this so, given the nature of the neural activity involved? Well, at least in part, it is because we have, at any moment, the ability to redirect our attention to any part of a rich, detailed, complete, and stable environment. Dennett makes much the same point. When you look at the wall, 'no matter how vivid your impression is that you see all that detail, the detail is in the world, not in your head' (1991: 355).

An experience seems or feels rich, detailed, complete and stable, not just because of what is going on inside your head but also because of what is going on in the world which your head is inside. If the way your experience seems or feels, then, consists in your being aware of the appropriate qualia, then individualism about qualia is false. Therefore, objectualism about the what it is like of experience requires abandoning individualism about qualia.

Why can the objectualist not simply accept this? The problem is that it seems to leave the notion of qualia with very little content. Indeed, once individualism falls, it seems objectualism must soon follow. Once we allow that the way an experience seems or feels to us consists, in part, in our ability to direct our attention to relevant parts of the environment, an environment whose features are then incorporated into the way the experience seems, what is left of the idea that we are aware of the qualia of our experience? Apparently, nothing more than this. We are aware of the world and its features. My having an experience that seems rich and detailed consists in nothing more than my ability to direct my attention to a rich and detailed world. I am not aware of the richness and detail of my experience, I am aware of the richness and detail of the world. This is no longer awareness of qualia; it is awareness of the world as being a certain way. Hence it is no longer an objectualist account of what it is like. Indeed, it is an actualist account. My having an experience that seems rich and detailed is my being aware, via the relevant attentional mechanisms, of the world as being a certain way. The phenomenal character of my experience consists in my being aware of the world as being thus-and-so. Thus, we are driven back to an actualist account of what it is like.

9   Why the way an experience seems cannot be explained as awareness of qualia

In this chapter, I have argued that the way an experience seems or feels to a subject cannot be explained in terms of awareness, by that subject, of the qualia, or phenomenal properties, of that experience. To many, this will seem an outlandish conclusion. I, on the other hand, suspect that it is an utterly expected one; indeed, one that can be established without recourse to perceptual completion phenomena, and the like.

The reason why the way an experience seems or feels cannot be explained in terms of awareness of qualia is, in a nutshell, this. It is not possible to make mistakes about the way experience seems to one. However, it is possible to make mistakes about whether or not one is experiencing any given qualia. Therefore, it is not possible to explain the former in terms of the latter. The analysis of perceptual completion phenomena simply provides a graphic way of illustrating this more general point. This general point can be developed by way of a comparison between the way in which qualia are supposed to explain the way an experience seems to a subject and the way in which *sense-data* are supposed to do so. There is, in fact, a close parallel between the failure of each to fulfil their allotted role.

As we saw in the previous chapter, the idea that, in having an experience, we are aware of sense-data seems to be incompatible with the phenomenon of experiential transparency. In reflecting on my perceptual experience of a seagull, for example, the seagull is not replaced by some private, mind-dependent, entity. My experience is transparent; in reflection on it, my experience does not stop short of its public, mind-independent, intentional objects. One implication of experiential transparency, an implication not emphasised in the previous chapter, is that the way an experience seems to its subject cannot be explained in terms of awareness of sense-data.

To see this, consider the attempts of sense-datum theorists to accommodate the transparency of experience. The major proponents of sense-datum accounts were well aware of the problem (Hume 1975; Price 1932; Prichard 1950; Broad 1956). What is of interest to us is their response. Typically, sense-datum theorists would attempt to draw a distinction between our initial, naive, reaction to introspection on experience and our corrected judgement when we think about how experience must, in fact, be.[4] And this, in turn, typically required a distinction between the sensory core of an experience and the interpretation we give of that core: that is, the phenomenal transparency objection, it was argued, rests on a confusion of the interpretation of sensory experience with such experience in uninterpreted form.

This strategy, pretty clearly, involves abandoning the idea that sense-data provide an explanation for the way an experience seems to its subject. The response acknowledges that it does not seem to the subject of an experience that she is immediately aware of sense-data. Rather, the awareness of sense-data by the subject is, partly but essentially, the result of certain cognitive operations; of theoretical construction broadly construed.

---

[4] See, for example, Broad's (1925) distinction between the material and epistemological objects of sense. Also, see Price's (1932) distinction between the sensory given and perceptual acceptance.

The subject becomes aware of sense-data not in the sense that they are immediately presented to her in experience but because of her reflections on the way what is immediately presented must, in fact, be.

Therefore, what this response to the problem of experiential transparency does, in effect, is to make explicit something that is already implicit in that problem: the idea that sense-data are not things given in experience, but, rather, are items hypothesised on the basis of what is given in experience. As such, it is possible for a subject to make mistakes about the presence of particular sense-data in her experience. This could occur, for example, if her relevant theorising about what is presented in experience was faulty. And, if it is possible for her to make mistakes about whether or not her experience contains particular sense-data, but not possible for her to make mistakes about the way her experience seems, then the latter is not equivalent to, and cannot be explained in terms of, the former.

Ultimately, I think, essentially the same problem afflicts the objectualist interpretation of qualia. Qualia are not items given in experience, they are not things of which we are aware in the having of an experience. World 1 and world 2 are identical with respect to the way experiences seem to their subjects but, at the same time, cannot be identical with respect to the qualia possessed by those experiences. Therefore, if one did not know which world one inhabits – and, as a matter of fact, we do not know – then one could also not know which qualia, if any, one's experience instantiates. Qualia, therefore, are things about which it is possible to be mistaken. The way an experience seems or feels to one, almost certainly, is not something about which it is possible to be mistaken. Therefore, having an experience that seems or feels a certain way does not consist in being aware of certain qualia. And, therefore, the objectualist account of the way an experience seems or feels should be rejected.

9 Consciousness and representation

I have argued that consciousness is characterised by what is essentially a structural rift; consciousness is both act and (in certain cases) object of experience. Consequently, there are two, essentially disparate, conceptions of phenomenal consciousness, an actualist conception and an objectualist one. Consequently, there are two, essentially disparate, conceptions of the what it is like of conscious experience. According to the objectualist conception, the what it is like of conscious experience is an object of conscious acquaintance; it is one of the things of which one is aware when one undergoes a conscious experience. According to the actualist conception, the what it is like of conscious experience is a property that exists in the directing of consciousness towards a distinct, and presumably non-phenomenal, object. The burden of the previous chapter was, then, in effect, to argue that the what it is like of conscious experience not only exists in the directing of consciousness towards a distinct and non-phenomenal object, but exists *only* in this directing of consciousness. What it is like, that is, cannot become an object of conscious acquaintance.

The model of consciousness defended in the previous chapters has obvious affinities with what are known as *representationist* accounts of phenomenal character, understood, roughly, as the view that the phenomenal character of an experience reduces to its representational, or intentional, content. This chapter compares and contrasts the present model with representationist accounts. I shall argue that if the actualist model of phenomenal character defended in the previous chapters is correct, then representationism must be false.

Nevertheless, there are certain important affinities between the account of consciousness defended here and representationist models. We shall begin by examining the principal one of these.

1   Brentano's thesis

The preceding chapters have defended a view of conscious states as essentially involving (i) an act of directing of consciousness towards an object, and (ii) an object upon which consciousness is directed. This entails that all conscious states are directed towards objects, objects which they *intend* or *represent*. This, then, is the most obvious sense in which the account of consciousness developed here is tied to the notion of representation: *all conscious states are representational states*. This claim we can refer to as *Brentano's thesis*.

That at least some conscious states are representational ones will presumably be granted by everyone. The most obvious examples are visual experiences of the environment; and experiences associated with the other sensory modalities are only slightly less obvious. However, it has seemed to many that at least some types of conscious experience are not essentially representational, and thus provide counterexamples to Brentano's thesis. Colin McGinn, for example, writes:

Bodily sensations do not have an intentional object in the way perceptual experiences do. We distinguish between a visual experience and what it is an experience of, but we do not make this distinction in respect of pains. Or again, visual experiences represent the world as being a certain way, but pains have no such representational content. (1997: 8)

This passage expresses what was, until very recently, pretty much received wisdom. The grip of this wisdom has, however, recently relaxed. In particular, Tye (1990, 1995) has developed a representational account of bodily sensations such as pain. Here is, in all essentials, the bare bones of Tye's account, adulterated with an emphasis on teleology that reflects my own tastes.

Let us suppose that there are various bodily mechanisms that have evolved in order to detect bodily damage. Such mechanisms, in virtue of their evolutionary history, have what Millikan (1984, 1993) calls a *proper function*, the proper function of detecting bodily damage. The proper function of some mechanism, trait, or process is what it is *supposed* to do, what it has been *designed* to do, what it *ought* to do. More precisely, consider the following simplified version of Millikan's already simplified version of her definition of proper function given in *Language, Thought, and other Biological Categories*.

An item X has proper function F only if: (i) X is a reproduction of some prior item that, because of the possession of certain reproduced properties, actually performed F in the past, and X exists because of this performance; or (ii) X is the product of a device that had the performance of F as a proper function and normally performs F by way of producing an item like X.

This definition, simplified though it is, takes some unpacking. Firstly, the concept of a proper function is a normative concept. The proper function of an item is defined in terms of what an item *should* do, not what it normally does or is disposed to do. The concept of proper function, being normative, cannot be defined in causal or dispositional terms. What something does, or is disposed to do, is not always what it is supposed to do. This is for three reasons. Firstly, any mechanism, trait or process will do many things, not all of which are part of its proper function. A heart pumps blood; it also makes a thumping noise and produces wiggly lines on an electrocardiogram. But only the first of these is its proper function since only pumping blood is something performed by hearts in the past that explains the existence of hearts in the present. Secondly, a process, trait or mechanism can have a proper function even if it never, or hardly ever, performs it. To use a flagship example of Millikan's, the proper function of the tail of a sperm cell is to propel the cell to the ovum. The vast majority of sperm cells, however, do not accomplish this task. Third, a process, trait or mechanism may have a proper function and yet not be able to perform it properly. A person's heart may be malformed and, thus, not be able to pump blood properly. Nevertheless, pumping blood is its proper function because ancestors of the person whose heart it is had hearts which pumped blood and this (in part) explains why they survived and proliferated and, thus, why the person in question possesses a heart. The concept of proper function is, thus, a normative concept. The proper function of an item is its *Normal* function where, following Millikan, the capitalised 'N' indicates that this is a normative sense of normal and not a causal or dispositional sense.

The core idea of the teleofunctional account of representation predicated on Millikan's notion of proper function is that the mechanisms responsible for mental representation are evolutionary products also. As such they will have proper functions. The idea, then, is that the representational capacities of a given cognitive mechanism are specified in terms of the environmental objects or features that are incorporated into that mechanism's proper function. That is, if a cognitive mechanism M has evolved in order to detect environmental feature E, then this is what makes an appropriate state S of M about E; this is what gives the state S the content that E. In this way, the representational content of cognitive state S derives from the proper function of the mechanism M that produces S, and S itself has the derived proper function of representing E.

Applying this general idea to the case of pains, we arrive at the following account. There are, let us suppose, various mechanisms whose proper function is to detect tokens of relevant types of bodily damage. Thus, according to the representational account, when a particular mechanism

M has the proper function of representing bodily damage D and fulfils this function by going into state S, then state S of M represents D. S is, of course, a pain state, D is appropriate bodily damage. S, therefore, represents D.

This, in essence, is a representational account of pains. And as Tye points out (1990: 333), this model can be extended to pains of more specific sorts. A twinge of pain, for example, can be thought of as a pain that represents a bodily disturbance that is mild and brief. A stabbing pain is one that represents abrupt damage to a particular, well-defined, bodily area. Aches represent damage that occurs inside the body, rather than on the surface, and so on.

Being a representational view, this is also a relational view of pains. To be in a token pain state is to stand in a certain relation to a token of bodily damage. However, the view has a definite advantage over earlier relational views (as in, for example, Aune 1967: 130). Such views were thought to be fatally damaged by such things as phantom limb phenomena. Pain, it was commonly thought, could not be a relation between a person and bodily damage at a particular location since it is, as in the case of phantom limb pains, possible to have pain without there being any such location. The representational view of pain mooted here, however, can regard this as simply a case of misrepresentation, and can handle this in the same sort of way that the teleofunctional account handles misrepresentation generally. In this case, the idea, very roughly, would be that the relevant mechanism M that has evolved for detecting bodily damage is malfunctioning (or, alternatively, that the context is not proper or Normal), but it still represents D on the basis of its proper function.

According to this form of representational view, the representation of bodily damage is *non-conceptual* (Tye 1990: 333). On this model, a subject is, in any particular case, conscious *of* a tokening of bodily damage, and is aware of this tokening in virtue of possessing a mechanism with a certain proper function. However, the subject is not conscious *that* it is a tokening of bodily damage. That is, the relevant type of consciousness is what Dretske (1993) has called *thing* consciousness as opposed to *fact* consciousness.

One does not, of course, have to buy into the teleological account of representation favoured by Millikan in order to accept this sort of general account of the representational character of pain.[1] If other sorts of relation constitute the basis of representation quite generally, so be it. The point is that a coherent and, I think, convincing case can be made out

---

[1] Tye (1995), for example, endorses a causal covariation account rather than a teleological one.

for the claim that pains and other bodily sensations are representational states. Thus, the fact that the account of consciousness developed in preceding chapters is committed to the claim that all conscious states are representational ones is not, in itself, an objection to that account.

It is one thing to claim that all conscious states are representational, but quite another to claim that all the characteristic properties of conscious states can be reduced to representational properties. This, in effect, is the claim of representationism. The characteristic properties of conscious states are, apparently, phenomenal ones. And representationism is the view that phenomenal properties reduce to, or are constituted by, representational properties. While the model of consciousness developed in chapters 6 and 7 entails that all conscious states are representational ones, it is, I shall argue, incompatible with the view that phenomenal properties are constituted by representational ones. Before properly examining this issue, however, we shall first have to look more closely at the sense in which conscious states are representational.

2   Consciousness as revealing and as revealed

There is a pair of related concepts that can be used to provide a very general way of characterising the structural rift in consciousness that has been defended and developed in the previous two chapters. The concepts are those of *revealing* and being *revealed*. Infused with Heideggerian associations these concepts may be, but the idea underlying them is, nonetheless, simple.

Suppose I see a red object. Then a portion of the world is revealed (to me) as red. I uncover (that part of) the world as red. What is revealed is a part of the world, and it is revealed in a certain way: as red. Similarly, we hear a certain kind of compression wave in the air as the sound of a tree falling. We feel a certain kind of molecular activity as hot. All these are cases of revealing. The object, in virtue of the type of molecular structure it has, is revealed as red; the compression wave is revealed as the sound of a tree falling; the molecular motion (or object undergoing it) is revealed as hot. That is all revealing, in this sense, is. Revealing is seeing as, hearing as, feeling as, smelling as, tasting as, and the like. Revealing the world is simply representing it to be a certain way.

Revealing, however, need not involve just perceiving. When we *conceive*, as opposed to perceive, of something in a particular way – say as a resource, an obstacle, as danger, as food, as a friend, as a source of sexual gratification, and the like – then we reveal the object to be thus-and-so. Indeed, some objects – some theoretical entities, for example – can be revealed only through conception rather than perception.

Less obviously, but in other contexts, I think, very significantly, activity, in particular intentional action, can be a form of revealing. The competent surfer, through his activity, is able to reveal characteristics of the wave that would otherwise have remained hidden. In moving, and thus transforming the structure of the ambient optic array, a creature with suitable visual apparatus is able to reveal transformationally invariant optical information that would otherwise have remained hidden. Moreover, the interaction between perception and action is, in any given case, often significant. Most obviously, the mode of revealing of an object depends not just on basic sensory or motor capacities, but also on the various acquired skills of the organism that possesses those capacities. To use a familiar example, the experienced wine taster is able to reveal a particular wine in ways that an enthusiastic amateur could not.

Moreover, not only can we reveal – through perception, conception or intentional action – external objects, events, and processes as being a certain way, we can do the same to internal objects, events, and processes. For example, one can reveal, if the representational account is true also of bodily sensations, certain types of bodily damage as painful. That is, when one experiences pain, one reveals bodily damage as being a certain way; as being hurtful or painful. Similarly, various bodily occurrences and disturbances are revealed in various ways: as stinging, as throbbing, as aching, as tickling, as orgasmic, and so on.

That perception, conception, and intentional action can all be means of revealing is precisely what we should expect: all three types of state possess intentional or representational content. And revealing the world to be P is simply representing it as P. States with intentional content, whether perceptual, conceptual or motor, are states that reveal the world, external or internal, as being thus-and-so. That, from a somewhat abstract vantage point, is precisely what representing is. To talk of acts of consciousness as acts of revealing is simply a way of expressing the intentionality or representationality of conscious states. To talk of acts of consciousness as acts of revealing, then, is just to express in a somewhat unfamiliar, but for our purposes suitably abstract, way, a very familiar idea.

Implicit in the foregoing is the claim that any instance of revealing or representation has a tripartite structure. We can distinguish:

(i) That which is revealed: the object of consciousness.
(ii) The way in which it is revealed: the mode of presentation of the object of consciousness.
(iii) The revealing of that which is revealed in the way in which it is revealed: the act of consciousness that represents the object under a particular mode of presentation.

That is, we must distinguish the object represented in an experience, the way in which it is represented, and the properties of the experience in virtue of which the object is represented in this way. The expression *in virtue of* in this context is a dangerous one, and in turn requires a further distinction. We must distinguish between *causal* and *constitutive* interpretations of this phrase. We must distinguish, that is, between the properties of an experience that cause that experience's object to fall under a given mode of presentation and the properties of the experience that constitute its object falling under a given mode of presentation. In later sections, I shall argue that the phenomenal properties of any given experience are those which *constitute* the object of that experience falling under a given mode of presentation.

Understanding the tripartite structure of revealing allows us to appreciate more fully the difference between, on the one hand, the distinction between actualist and objectualist conceptions of consciousness and, on the other, that between first- and third-person conceptions. These distinctions are far from equivalent, and grasping the tripartite structure of revealing allows us to avoid what might otherwise be a tempting conflation. The distinction between actualist and objectualist conceptions of consciousness cuts across that between first- and third-person conceptions for two reasons.

Firstly, at least some items can be revealed both from a first- and a third-person perspective. I can adopt both a first-person and a third-person perspective towards bodily damage, whether this damage is to my own body or that of another. I can, for example, adopt a third-person perspective to damage to my own body by, say, looking at it, noticing the pattern of tissue damage, assessing its likely long-term effects on my well-being, and so on. This itself is a mode of revealing. The bodily damage is revealed as disturbing or insignificant, completely gross, or just a scratch. When bodily damage is revealed in this way, revealed from the third-person perspective, there is a corresponding act of consciousness which reveals it in this way. The act of consciousness, that is, is the adopting of the perspective according to which bodily damage can be revealed in this way. However, I can also adopt a first-person perspective towards this bodily damage. When I do so, what is revealed by the adopting of this perspective is the bodily damage as painful. However, the phenomenal character, the what it is like, of my experience is not, if the actualist model is correct, something thus revealed. What is revealed is the bodily damage as painful. But the revealing of the bodily damage as painful consists in having an act of consciousness with a specific phenomenal character. The phenomenal character of the act, I shall argue in the next section, is not something revealed by the act, but it is in what the revealing activity of the act – the revealing of the bodily damage as painful – consists.

Secondly, as we have seen, any instance of revealing has a tripartite structure. We can distinguish the object revealed, the way it is revealed, and the act in virtue of which it is revealed in the way it is revealed. However, this entails that the distinction between actualist and objectualist perspectives cuts across the distinction between first- and third-person perspectives. The reason is that with *both* first- and third-person perspectives we can apply the distinction between what is revealed from the perspective and the adopting of the perspective that reveals its object in this way. However, when we talk of actualist and objectualist perspectives, the distinction makes no sense. The actualist perspective is precisely the adopting of a perspective which allows an object to be revealed in a certain way; it is not what is revealed from this perspective. This is true whether the perspective adopted is first- or third-person. The actualist conception of consciousness is precisely a conception of consciousness as the adopting of a perspective whereby an object is revealed to be a certain way. It is not, and, if the arguments of the previous chapter are correct, cannot be, what is revealed from the perspective thus adopted.

To return, again, to the concrete. When an object is revealed as red, its being revealed in this way is constituted by an act of consciousness that has a certain phenomenal character; a certain what it is like. And, as I shall argue in the next section, its being revealed in this way is *constituted* by the what it is like of experience. However, and this is the force of the actualist interpretation of phenomenal character, this what it is like is not what is revealed. It is what the revealing of the revealed as being a certain way, as being presented under a certain mode of presentation, consists in. Similarly, when we move to our experience of internal items, the bodily damage is revealed as painful. And this, broadly speaking, is what the experience of pain is: the revealing of bodily damage as painful. However, the what it is like of the experience of pain is not, itself, something revealed in the experience of pain. Rather, the what it is like of being in pain is what *constitutes* the revealing of bodily damage as painful.

3   Phenomenal revealing

A worldly item – object, event, process, fact, property, relation, etc. – can be revealed in several distinct ways. One can perceive the item in a given way; one can also conceive it under a given mode of presentation; one might reveal it to be a certain way through one's intentional activity. Objects are revealed to be certain ways by intentional or representational states – perceptual, conceptual or motor-based; such states do not have to be phenomenal. However, phenomenal states can reveal objects; being in pain, for example, is revealing bodily damage as painful. There is such a thing, that is, as *phenomenal revealing*, and this section examines its general characteristics.

Any phenomenally conscious state is defined by its phenomenal character, by the what it is like to have, or be in, that state. And, according to the actualist account, this character is not an object of consciousness. Moreover, this character is traditionally thought of as being made up of phenomenal constituents: *qualia*. Thus, according to the actualist account, qualia are not objects of conscious awareness. Neither the phenomenal character of an experience, nor its phenomenal constituents, are objects of consciousness, according to actualism. They are not items *of which* we are aware, they are items *in virtue of which* we are aware of the environment (construed broadly enough to include the body). That is, they are items in virtue of which experience reveals an object to be thus-and-so.

I suggest, although defence of this claim will have to be postponed until the next chapter, that we understand the expression 'in virtue of' not causally but *constitutively*. That is, according to the actualist understanding of consciousness, the phenomenal character of an experience does not cause the representational object of that experience to be revealed under a given mode of presentation. Rather, this character constitutes the revealing of the object as being thus-and-so. That is, the phenomenal character of an experience E is what the revealing of E's representational object as being P *consists* in.

Proper defence of this constitutive reading will have to be postponed until after the discussion of phenomenal causation in the next chapter. However, in general outline, the reasons are perhaps already intuitively clear. I have argued that all conscious states are representational states. Indeed, this is one of the consequences of the actualist model. One implication of this is that the representational object of a conscious state is no less intrinsic to the phenomenal content of that state than the object of a cognitive state such as belief is extrinsic to the content of that state. So, consider the relation between the content of a belief and its representational object. It is not as if the content of the belief that Ali G is amusing *causes* Ali G to fall under the mode of presentation denoted by 'amusing'. Rather, Ali G's falling under the mode of presentation denoted by 'amusing' is what the content that Ali G is amusing consists in. Ali G's falling under the relevant mode of presentation, that is, is what constitutes this content. I suggest we understand the phenomenal content of conscious states on analogy with the representational content of cognitive states. Indeed, this, I think, is an entailment of what I called Brentano's thesis: the claim that all conscious states are necessarily representational states. And Brentano's thesis is an entailment of the actualist model of phenomenal character.

The notion of constitution, as employed here, will, in turn, take some unpacking. When a subject, S, undergoes a painful experience of a certain sort then, we can suppose, bodily damage is revealed as painful. And its being revealed as painful consists precisely in S's having an experience with a certain phenomenal character. Thus, S is aware of the bodily damage as painful. But, according to the actualist conception, S is not aware of the phenomenal properties that constitute it as painful. These phenomenal properties are what reveal the bodily damage as painful, and are not themselves revealed. Thus we can say the revealing of the bodily damage as painful consists in the instantiation of certain phenomenal properties in S or, equivalently, the presence of the relevant phenomenal properties in S constitutes the revealing of bodily damage as painful.

Similarly, when I visually experience a red can of Coca-Cola, then the can is revealed (to me) as red. Its being revealed as red to me consists in my instantiating a certain phenomenal property or properties. Equivalently, my instantiating the relevant property constitutes the revealing of the can as red. I am, thus, aware of the can as red. However, according to the actualist interpretation, I am not aware *of* the phenomenal property that constitutes the revealing of the can as red; the property is not something of which I am aware, it is something in virtue of which (constitutively) I am aware. Equivalently, having the property is in what the revelation of the can as red consists, and is not itself something revealed.

If the expression 'in virtue of' should, indeed, be understood constitutively rather than causally, then it is not the case that phenomenal properties cause objects to be revealed in particular ways, or to fall under certain modes of presentation. Nevertheless, there is a causal relation involved here; it is just that it runs in the opposite direction.

To see this, first recall that in any case of revealing, three things should be distinguished: (i) the item that is revealed (the object of consciousness), (ii) the way in which this item (the mode of presentation of the object of consciousness), and (iii) the properties of the act of revealing in which the manner of revealing of the item consists. In the case of pain, say a pain in one's foot, the item revealed might be certain tissue damage. Thus: (i) my foot is damaged, (ii) the damage in my foot is revealed as painful, and (iii) the revealing of the damage to my foot as painful consists in my instantiating the relevant qualia or phenomenal properties. Once we clearly distinguish these three things, then a central role for causation can be found, one which underwrites the claims of constitution.

It is the revealing of the damage to my foot as painful that, on the present account, consists in the instantiation of certain qualia. That is, the qualia *constitute* the revealing of the damage as painful. As such, they do not cause the bodily damage to be revealed as painful. This is not an undischarged constitution claim, however, for the simple reason that there is a relation of causation here, but it runs in the opposite direction. It is the bodily damage itself that causes me to have the relevant qualia, those qualia in which the revealing of the bodily damage as painful consists. More precisely, the bodily damage causes various neural states that *realise* the relevant qualia. Qualia neither cause the bodily damage to be revealed as painful, nor are they caused by the revealing of the bodily damage as painful. Rather, they are caused, via realisation, by the bodily damage. And having been thus caused, they, thereby, constitute the revealing of the damage as painful or, equivalently, they are that in which the revealing of the bodily damage as painful consists. The constitution claim is, thus, grounded, in an inverse causal claim. The revelation of the bodily damage as painful results, causally, from the causation of the relevant qualia by the bodily damage. And, in virtue of this, the revelation of bodily damage as painful consists in the having of certain qualia.

More generally, we can understand the relation between the object of consciousness, the mode of presentation of that object, and the properties of the act of consciousness that constitute that mode of presentation according to the following schema.

(1) Object of consciousness, O

Causes

(2) States (neural) which realise set Q of qualia $= \{q_1 \ldots q_n\}$ in subject S

And so

(3) O is presented to S under mode of presentation M because (causal) O has caused states that realise Q in S

And

(4) Mode of presentation M of O is constituted by P in S, or, equivalently, M of O consists in the instantiation of Q in S.

O causes the instantiation, via realisation, of Q in S. And, then, the fact that O has caused the instantiation, via realisation, of Q in S causes O to be revealed as M to S. And, then, the revealing, to S, of O as M consists in, but is not caused by, the presence of Q in S.

4   Consciousness of and consciousness that

According to the actualist model of what it is like, one is never aware of the what it is like of conscious experience, nor is one aware of the qualia that collectively constitute the phenomenal constituents of this what it is like. Qualia are properties *in virtue of which* objects are revealed to be a certain way; they are not themselves revealed as being a certain way. That is, qualia are conditions of objects being revealed under a phenomenal mode of presentation, they are not themselves revealed under a mode of presentation. Broadly speaking, qualia are properties *with* which (con-stitutively) we are conscious, they are not properties *of* which we are conscious.

However, the fact that we are never aware *of* a given quale, Q, is per-fectly compatible with our being aware *that* we possess or instantiate Q (cf. Dretske 1995; Shoemaker 1994). One is not aware *of* qualia, since these constitute the revealing of the object of consciousness, and are not themselves revealed as objects of consciousness. However, one can be aware that one possesses certain qualia. One is aware *that* one possesses qualia because one is aware *of* an object as revealed in a certain way. Here, awareness *of* is perceptual awareness, and the resulting awareness *that*, introspective awareness, is *displaced* perceptual awareness. One is aware that one instantiates quale Q, because one is aware of the object whose revealing as P is constituted by possession of Q.

More precisely, awareness that one instantiates a given quale Q is a theoretically mediated awareness. If I am not familiar with philosophical accounts of qualia, then no amount of displaced perceptual inference is going to tell me *that* I am instantiating Q. More basic than the awareness that I instantiate Q will be the awareness that I am having an experience that, if veridical, constitutes the perception of an object O under a mode of presentation M. Thus, awareness that I instantiate Q can be explained according to the following three-tiered model.

(1) Aware *of*: object O under mode of presentation M.

(2) Aware *that*: I am having an experience that, if veridical, constitutes a perception of object O under mode of presentation M

where (2) is obtained through displaced perception of (1).

(3) Aware *that*: I instantiate the quale *Mness*

where (3) is a theoretical inference from, or gloss on, (2).

The actualist account, therefore, does not rule out knowledge *pertaining to* one's own qualia, or the what it is like of conscious experience that is constructed out of such qualia. What the actualist account does entail, however, is that such knowledge is knowledge *that*, not knowledge *of*.

5   Representationism

The affinities of the position defended here with representationism are, perhaps, now obvious. To describe conscious acts as ones of revealing is to presuppose that they are essentially directed towards objects. Thus, I have, in effect, conceded that all conscious experiences are representational. To be a conscious experience is, precisely, to reveal (or represent) an object (external or internal) as being a certain way: the conscious act *is* the act of revealing. Nevertheless, as I shall try to show in the remainder of this chapter, the actualist model of phenomenal character as existing in the directing of consciousness is incompatible with representationism about this character.

As we have seen, any act of revealing has a tripartite structure. In any such act, we can distinguish:

(i) That which is revealed: the object of consciousness.
(ii) The way in which it is revealed: the mode of presentation of the object of consciousness.
(iii) The revealing of that which is revealed in the way in which it is revealed: the act of consciousness that represents the object under a particular mode of presentation.

There are, I shall try to show, two distinct ways of developing the thesis of representationism: one which corresponds, in a sense that will be made clear, to (i), the other which corresponds, again in a way that will be made clear, to (ii). However, according to actualism about phenomenal character, such character is constituted by (iii), by the act which reveals objects under a given mode of presentation. And this, in a nutshell, is why representationism must be rejected if actualism is true.

This is all at present, perhaps, intolerably abstract. Let us begin to make the issues a little more concrete by, first, providing a more precise formulation of the thesis of representationism. One common formulation of this thesis is as the claim that with respect to any two conscious experiences e_1 and e_2, the phenomenal differences between these experiences do not outrun their intentional, or representational, differences. Equivalently (roughly) is the claim that for any experience e, the phenomenal character of e does not go beyond its representational content.

The flaw in these characterisations lies in the vagueness of locutions such as 'do not outrun' and 'does not go beyond'. In one clear sense, the actualist account of phenomenal character can agree that such character does not go beyond representational content. As was argued towards the end of the previous chapter, the actualist model is committed to the idea that the what it is like of an experience is not an object of direct linguistic reference. The content of talk of phenomenal character, then, is not to be explained in terms of such talk picking out, or referring to, phenomenal properties. Thus, the actualist account of phenomenal character will agree, with Block and Shoemaker, that the sort of public language terms often thought to specify the phenomenal content of experiences are likely, in fact, to pick out only the representational features of those experiences. Moreover, according to the actualist model, the phenomenal character of experience is not something of which we are aware in the having of that experience; it is not something upon which our conscious awareness can be directed or upon which our conscious gaze can fall. Thus, introspection will not allow us to pick out, or discriminate between, distinct phenomenal properties of an experience. When we focus our attention inwards on our experiences, we find only the public objects and properties which those experiences represent. Thus, the actualist account of phenomenal character is, in fact, committed to the claim that, in terms of what we can focus our conscious awareness on, and meaningfully talk about, the phenomenal features of experiences do not go beyond their representational features; and phenomenal differences between experiences do not outrun representational differences. Thus, on these formulations of representationism, the actualist model of phenomenal character appears committed to a representationist account.

This appearance, however, is misleading, and derives from the inadequacy of the above formulations of representationism. A preferable formulation of representationism is, I think, this: the phenomenal properties of any given experience are *constituted* by the representational properties of that experience. That is, the phenomenal properties of any given experience are one and the same thing as (some, but not necessarily all) representational properties of that experience. Understood in this way, I shall argue, the actualist model of phenomenal character is incompatible with representationism. If actualism about phenomenal character is true, then all experiences that possess phenomenal character are thereby representational; for to possess phenomenal character is precisely to reveal or represent an object phenomenally. However, this does not entail, and actualism is in fact incompatible with, the claim that the phenomenal properties of these essentially representational states are themselves representational properties.

6   Object representationism

There are two logically distinct ways of developing the idea that the phenomenal properties of an experience are constituted by its representational properties. The first, and by far the most common, way is what I shall call *object representationism*. When most people talk of representationism, I think, this is what they have in mind.

Object representationism is the view that the phenomenal properties of any given experience, e, are constituted by the property, possessed by e, of representing a particular object, event, process, situation, state of affairs, etc. The property of phenomenal redness, for example, thought to be possessed by some experience e, is identical with the property, possessed by e, of representing a red object or state of affairs. This is a property which an experience might have even in the absence of an environmental correlate, and so object representationism can account for the existence of illusory and hallucinatory experiences of redness.

Object representationism has been widely criticised, and most of these criticisms conform to a certain type. Essentially, the critical strategy involves trying to show the possibility, with respect to a set of experience tokens, of a variation in the representational properties of those tokens without a corresponding variation in their phenomenal properties. If this type of possibility is genuine, then, it is argued, the phenomenal properties of experiences cannot be constituted by their representational properties.

The most celebrated example of this type of strategy is Ned Block's (1990) *inverted earth* thought experiment, a variation on Putnam's twin earth scenario. On inverted earth, everything has the complementary colour of the colour it has on earth. The sky is yellow, grass is red, the sun is blue, Coca-Cola cans are green, and so on. Thus, if you visited inverted earth, you would see the sky as yellow, the grass as red, and so on. However, the vocabulary of the residents of inverted earth is also inverted. Thus, in talking of the colour of the sky, they use the term 'blue'; and in talking of the colour of grass, they use the term 'green', and so on. Furthermore, because of the differences between earth and inverted earth, the intentional or representational contents of the propositional attitudes and experiences of inverted earthlings are themselves inverted. Thus, when a resident of inverted earth wonders, as he would put it, 'why the sky is blue', he is not wondering why the sky is blue, he is wondering why the sky is yellow.

Suppose, now, you are taken to inverted earth. Then, under normal circumstances, the sky would appear yellow, the sun appear blue. However, suppose that during your transportation, scientists fit you with colour-inverting lenses (fill in the necessary details yourself: you are unconscious during transportation, your body pigments are altered so you don't have a nasty shock when you wake up, and so on). The lenses cancel out the inverted colours on inverted earth; so when you wake up on inverted earth, you notice no difference. The yellow sky looks blue to you, the blue sun looks yellow. And all the inverted earthlings around you describe the yellow sky as 'blue'. So, from the point of view of the phenomenal character of your experiences, nothing is any different from the way it would have been had you stayed on earth.

Initially, the representational contents of your experiences and propositional attitudes would also be the same. The causal rooting of your colour words is grounded, it seems, in your prior use on earth. So, on your first day on inverted earth, when you think that, for example, the sky is as blue as ever, you are expressing the same thought as you would have expressed on earth; it is just that in this case you are wrong. Moreover, your thought is not identical with the one a native of inverted earth would express with the same words. However, it is plausible to suppose that after a suitable period of time, the representational contents of your experiences and attitudes would change. After sufficient time had been spent on inverted earth, your embedding in your new physical and linguistic environment would come to dominate, and your representational contents would, accordingly, shift so as to be the same as those of the natives.

Thus, we seem to have a logically possible situation in which the representational properties of your experiences alter without any corresponding alteration in the phenomenal properties of those experiences. And, if this is correct, the phenomenal properties of experiences cannot be constituted by the representational properties of those experiences.

The inverted earth thought experiment is, perhaps, not decisive. There are various ways of replying to it, or attempting to avoid the conclusions it invites us to draw (see, for example, Tye 1995; Lycan 1996).[2] In my

---

[2] Often, for example, one finds the attempt to deny that the representational properties of experiences do change during the subject's stay on inverted earth. Lycan justifies this counterintuitive claim by an appeal to a teleosemantic account of mental content associated with Millikan. However, this rests on a misunderstanding of the teleosemantic approach. It would be a simplistic form of psychosemantics indeed that entailed that the intentional content of the subject's experiences remained constant following her relocation to inverted earth. Lycan seems to assume that the subject would have various mechanisms whose proper function was to go into state S in the presence of a given colour, but fails to recognise that this simple form of teleosemantics almost certainly applies only to relatively basic perceptual mechanisms that are probably innate, and probably possessed by creatures whose representational capacities are fairly fixed and limited. In order to extend the teleosemantic approach to creatures whose representational capacities are anything like as complicated as those of human beings, we need a different type of mechanism, one whose proper function is precisely to bring the human use of a linguistic item into line with community based norms; i.e. a regularising proper function. This more sophisticated teleosemantic position, then, would support the negation of Lycan's claim.

view, none of these replies work, and the inverted earth scenario does successfully establish that phenomenal properties cannot be constituted by representational ones, at least as the latter are understood by object representationism. To argue here for this claim would take us too far afield. What I do want to argue here, however, is that there is a way of understanding representationism that renders it immune to inverted earth type objections. This latter way of understanding the representationist thesis I call *mode representationism*.

7 Mode representationism

Mode representationism is the view that the phenomenal character of any given experience is constituted by the *mode of presentation* of those objects revealed, or represented, by that experience. More precisely, phenomenal properties are identical with properties of representing objects under particular modes of presentation. The notion of a mode of presentation, of course, is here understood psychologically rather than, as Frege would have it, as an abstract entity.

It is important to realise that this is still a form of representationism. When an object, property, events, process, situation or state of affairs is represented in an experience, or, using my nomenclature, *revealed* in the having of the experience, then it is always so represented under some or other mode of presentation. An object of a certain sort of molecular configuration, thus, might be revealed as a red square. The combination of redness and squareness, thus, provides the mode of presentation of that particular object. However, no one would suppose that the redness and squareness are not represented features of the experience. On the contrary, the object is represented in the experience by way of the representation of redness and squareness. Slightly more precisely (since the expression 'by way of' is likely to suggest the sort of causal construal from which I should like to distance myself), the representation of the object in experience *consists in* the representation of redness and squareness. Thus, to view the phenomenal properties of an experience as identical with properties of representing objects under particular modes of representation is not to abandon representationism.

Mode representationism has notable advantages over its object representationist cousin. Most importantly, it seems immune to the type of inverted earth experiment outlined above. To see this, remember that the inverted earth scenario works by driving a wedge between phenomenal and representational properties of experiences. The moral of the scenario is that the representational properties of an experience type can vary (e.g.

over time) while the phenomenal properties of the same experience type remain constant.

Thus, for example, with respect to the sky of inverted earth, my experience, representationally, is *of*, or about, something yellow; phenomenally, it is *as of* something blue. However, the mode representationist is able to accommodate this intuition. During my arrival on inverted earth, my experience represents the sky under a blue mode of presentation. After a time sufficient for my becoming embedded in the new physical and linguistic environment, however, my experience of the sky still represents the sky under the same mode of presentation. Thus, the mode representationist can deny that the *relevant* representational properties of the experience change. And, if this is correct, the inverted earth scenario does nothing to drive a wedge between phenomenal and representational properties.

This can be supported by the following qualification of the content of the general representationist thesis. It is no logically necessary part of representationism, in either form, that the phenomenal properties of a particular experience be constituted by *all* the representational properties of that experience. Far more plausible is the claim that the former are constituted by, or identical with, *some* of the latter. The mode representationist can allow, then, that during my embedding in a new physical and linguistic environment, some representational shift occurs but, at the same time, deny that this shift involves the representational properties that are constitutive of the phenomenal features of experience. Thus, my experiences, subsequent to my new embedding, are no longer *of* something blue. Nonetheless, they are still of something given under a blue mode of presentation. And it is these latter representational properties, the mode representationist can assert, that are constitutive of the phenomenal character of those experiences.

8   Actualism and representationism

If the above arguments are correct, mode representationism is unaffected by the standard objection to representationism. Nevertheless, in this section, I shall argue that mode representationism is incompatible with the actualist account of phenomenal character. Thus, the arguments for actualism, if successful, give us a reason for rejecting mode representationism. Indeed, they give us a reason for rejecting representationism in either of its forms.

To see the incompatibility between actualism and representationism, recall that the actualist model of phenomenal character entails that any phenomenally conscious experience involves a tripartite structure: (i) that which is revealed: the object of consciousness, (ii) the way in which it is revealed: the mode of presentation of the object of consciousness, and (iii) the revealing of that which is revealed in the way in which it is revealed: the act of consciousness that represents the object under a particular mode of presentation.

If we supposed that the phenomenal features of conscious experience were a part of, or constituted by, what conscious experience reveals (or represents), then we would end up with, in essence, an object representationist account of phenomenal character. If we supposed that the phenomenal features of experience were part of, or constituted by, the way in which what is revealed by conscious experience is revealed, then we would end up with a mode representationist account. However, the actualist account of phenomenal character denies that the phenomenal features of experience are among the objects of consciousness. Since both objects represented in experience, and the modes of presentation of those objects, are clearly among the objects of consciousness (we can focus our conscious gaze on the object and on its redness and its squareness), actualism is committed to denying that the phenomenal features of experience are either objects represented in experience or the ways in which those objects are represented in experience.

Rather, according to the actualist account of phenomenal properties, such properties properly belong to the act that reveals the represented objects of experience in the way they are revealed. That is, the phenomenal features of experience are not what is revealed or represented by experience, neither the object represented nor the mode of presentation under which that object is represented. Rather, such features are what constitute the revealing of the represented object of experience in the way that it is revealed. That is, such properties are what constitute the representing of an object of experience under mode of presentation m_1 rather than mode of presentation m_2.

Representationism is right to the extent that it recognises that the only features of experience upon which we are able to focus our conscious attention are represented objects, and the ways in which these objects are represented. But it is wrong to think that phenomenal properties must, therefore, be one or other of these features. Phenomenal features are what constitute our taking a represented object to be as such-and-such. But they are not the such-and-such that we take such objects to be. The represented objects and properties of experience are indeed the only items of experience upon which we are able to focus our attention, but phenomenal properties of the experience belong to the focusing of attention itself. Thus, despite the similarities between actualism and representationism, phenomenal properties, if the former is true, cannot be accommodated in the representationist account.

10 Consciousness and the natural order

If the arguments of preceding chapters are correct, then there are aspects of consciousness that are not objects of consciousness but, rather, exist in the directing of consciousness towards its objects. And to talk of the directing of consciousness towards its objects is to talk of consciousness revealing, or representing, its objects under one or another mode of presentation. Certain properties of consciousness, and I have argued this includes the phenomenal ones, are not items of which we are aware but those that constitute our being aware of distinct items in certain ways.

There is another way, more Kantian in flavour, of expressing this general idea. There are certain properties of consciousness, the phenomenal properties, that are *transcendental* relative to our experience of consciousness. These are not properties which we experience, but ones *in virtue of* which we experience, properties which constitute our experience as having a certain phenomenal character rather than another. In this chapter, I want to examine the ramifications of the transcendental character of phenomenal properties. In particular, I want to look at what consequences the transcendental status of phenomenal properties has for our understanding of the place of consciousness in the natural order.

1   What it is like and reductive explanation

In this section, I shall argue that the transcendental character of phenomenal properties precludes a reductive explanation of phenomenal consciousness. More precisely, I shall argue that the what it is like of conscious experience will, necessarily, for ever evade reductive explication.

The most immediate problem is that the concept of reduction, on analysis, fragments into a heterogeneous category of logically quite distinct relations. There is, of course, the broad distinction between realist and empiricist models. However, even within a single genre, the variety is notable. Ernest Nagel (1961), for example, the principal progenitor of the contemporary empiricist model, argued that reduction was based on derivation of laws of the reduced domain from those of the reducing domain. Hempel (1969) argued that it required, in addition, derivation of the concepts of the former from those of the latter. Nagel's requirement can be satisfied by the existence of conditional bridge laws linking reducing and reduced domains. Hempel's account, however, requires that such laws be biconditional. Quite a difference. And when we consider the difference between empiricist and realist models, the divergence becomes notably greater.

The result is that to talk of the reduction, and consequently reductive explanation, of consciousness is, potentially, to talk of a number of quite different things. Nor can this problem be satisfactorily resolved by fiat. I propose to circumvent the problem, in so far as this is possible, by employing a very abstract model of reduction. In fact, so abstract is it that it can, with some justification, be regarded not as a model of reduction at all, but, rather, as a pretheoretical picture lurking behind just about anything that *could* count as a model of reduction. It is, in other words, a stereotype of reduction (in roughly Shoemaker's (1994) sense), a stereotype which looks something like this.[1]

Consider a fairly typical example of reductive explanation, say the reduction of heat to molecular motion. Idealising somewhat, we might regard this reduction as beginning with an initial characterisation of heat as that which produces certain feelings in us. To say that something is hot simply means that it produces hot feelings in us, to say that something is cold means that it produces cold feelings in us. However, as was argued in chapter 7, to say that certain things in the world are experienced by us as hot, and certain things as cold, is not to ascribe any *phenomenal* property to those things. Appearing hot is not a genuine property of hot things, any more than appearing to be in a gas station in Nebraska is a genuine property of Elvis. One can allow that hot things possess certain properties (mean molecular kinetic energy) in virtue of which they produce the appropriate feelings in us, but these properties are not themselves phenomenal properties. To say that we experience an object as hot is not to ascribe any phenomenal property to that object; it is to say something about us, not about the object. It is to say that we experience the object as hot. And, at the level of phenomenal properties, this is to say something not about the objects toward which our phenomenal consciousness is directed, it is to say something about the directing of that consciousness. In the directing of consciousness, the world is revealed as hot. And it is revealed as hot in virtue of the phenomenal properties of the act of revealing; its being revealed as hot is constituted by such properties. The

---

[1] The stereotype is actually pretty close to John Searle's account of reduction in *The Rediscovery of the Mind*.

phenomenal properties that we are tempted to associate with the objects of consciousness really belong to consciousness as *act*.

Following the initial characterisation of hot and cold in terms of feelings they produce in us, the next stage is to identify various non-phenomenal properties of the objects that produce these feelings, properties which might explain this capacity of, but that are at least correlated with, the objects in question. Thus, we discover a reliable correlation between molecular motion of a certain kind in these objects and the production of feelings of hot or cold in us. It is important to realise that our attention has now switched from phenomenal properties that, in fact, attach to the act of consciousness to non-phenomenal properties that actually belong to the object of our consciousness.

Finally, heat is redefined simply as those molecular occurrences themselves. The initial characterisation of heat as that which produces certain feelings in us has now given way to a characterisation that does not mention the production of feelings or other subjective states. Heat is, therefore, said to be 'nothing but' molecular motion.

The original phenomenal properties which have been excluded during the process of reduction, as we have seen, belong not to the object, but to the act, of consciousness. Their place has been usurped by properties, such as mean molecular kinetic energy, which belong to the object of consciousness (i.e. various hot objects). Thus, the process of explanatory reduction has, in effect, involved bracketing, or abstracting away from, those properties of the act of consciousness in virtue of which an object is represented, or revealed, in a certain way, for example as hot. The contribution of the act of consciousness is removed, and all that remains are properties that genuinely belong to the object of consciousness. And this is what explanatory reduction, viewed from an extremely abstract vantage point, is: *the removal of the contribution made to the object by the act of consciousness directed towards it.*

Therefore, if we are to provide an explanatory reduction of consciousness, we would have to remove the contribution made to consciousness by its actualist component. We would have to focus on consciousness only as it appears to itself as an object of consciousness. We would, that is, have to adopt an objectualist conception of consciousness. A reductive explanation of consciousness, that is, would necessarily bracket or exclude those properties that belong to consciousness as act, rather than consciousness as object. These are not properties that could be encompassed by the reductive explanation, due, ultimately, to the very nature of reductive explanation. Thus, if, as I have argued, the what it is like of conscious experience, and the phenomenal properties that constitute it, belong to consciousness as act of representing, rather than object represented, then this what it is like, and the properties that constitute it, can never be captured in any attempted reductive explanation of consciousness.

This, then, is ultimately why the what it is like of conscious experience provides a problem, a severe and persistent problem, for attempts to reductively explain consciousness in physical terms. A reductive explanation of conscious experience can, at most, incorporate the *empirical* features of experience. It is, at most, only the experienced features of experiences that can be reductively explained. Reduction necessarily involves a bracketing of the transcendental features of experience, those features that constitute the empirical features of experience, but are not themselves experienced. If such features are, as I have argued, the phenomenal features of experience, then any attempted reductive explanation of consciousness must inevitably exclude the phenomenal.

2 Consciousness and materialism

One way of looking at the argument developed above is as an attempt to demonstrate how a certain form of materialism undermines itself. Constructive materialism is the view that it is possible to reductively explain consciousness in physical terms (Flanagan 1992). It is possible, at least in principle, to provide or identify a physical explanation of how the brain produces consciousness. The argument developed in the previous section, combined with those of the previous chapters, then, is, in effect, that constructive materialism faces a serious dilemma. Constructive materialism is not eliminativist about what it is like. It allows that there is something that it is like to undergo a conscious experience. Then, the constructive materialist is faced with two basic options: what it is like to undergo a conscious experience is either part of the act or one of the objects of consciousness. That is, the constructive materialist can adopt either the actualist or the objectualist interpretation of what it is like. However, if the constructive materialist adopts the latter option, then she is going to be committed either to the existence of phenomenal particulars or to an interpretation of the notion of a phenomenal property that is equally materialistically problematic and arguably entails the existence of phenomenal particulars anyway. And so a consistent objectualist interpretation of what it is like requires the rejection of constructive materialism. On the other hand, if the constructive materialist tries to marry an objectualist interpretation of what it is like with the more plausible interpretation of the notion of a phenomenal property described in chapter 7, then this leads to the collapse of the objectualist position. What it is like cannot now be regarded as belonging to the object of consciousness but, rather, to the act of apprehending or grasping an object of consciousness. And this is a statement of the actualist position. However, if the constructive materialist opts for an actualist interpretation of what it is like, then she is going to be committed to the claim that what it is like can never become an object of consciousness. It is never, that is, an empirical feature of consciousness. And this, at least if the arguments of the previous section are correct, is incompatible with the specifically constructive component of this form of materialism, since what it is like, being transcendental, can never be incorporated into a reductive explanation of consciousness. The objectualist option, then, requires rejection of the materialist component of constructive materialism; the actualist interpretation requires rejection of its constructive component. The position is, in this sense, self-undermining.

This conclusion might be thought to be worrying, given the overall direction of the argument developed in chapters 6 and 7. After all, one of the reasons for rejecting the objectualist interpretation of what it is like was based on the assumption that materialism is true. With the above rejection of constructive materialism, the assumption itself might seem to contradict the central argument of this book. The problem, however, is only apparent. The answer lies in what McGinn has called *transcendental naturalism*, and which is also known as *anticonstructive materialism* (McGinn 1991, 1993). According to anticonstructive materialism, we should in the case of consciousness clearly distinguish ontological and epistemological claims. 'Epistemologically, consciousness outruns what we can comprehend, given the ways our cognitive systems are structured ... Ontologically, however, nothing can be inferred from this about the naturalness or otherwise of the object of our ignorance' (McGinn 1997: 42). According to the anticonstructive position advocated here, consciousness is a natural physical phenomenon. It has, however, no (reductive) physical explanation.

It is worth noting that the form of anticonstructive materialism suggested by the arguments of this chapter differs in two respects from that of McGinn. Firstly, McGinn's anticonstructive position is a form of *noumenal* naturalism: consciousness has a hidden structure that is noumenal relative to our concept-forming capacities. The transcendental nature of McGinn's naturalism derives from the noumenal character of (a part of) consciousness. And, for McGinn, it is the noumenal character of the hidden structure of consciousness that prevents the possibility of a reductive explanation of consciousness in physical terms. The arguments developed in this chapter appeal to no hidden structure of consciousness, noumenal or otherwise. Indeed, the arguments developed here, if correct, work because consciousness, conceived of from the actualist perspective, is simply not the sort of thing that can have structure. Structure, hidden or manifest, belongs to the objectualist conception of consciousness: structure, hidden or manifest, belongs to what appears, not to the appearing of what appears.

Secondly, and relatedly, the anticonstructive position developed here is in at least one respect more radical than that of McGinn. McGinn is willing to allow – indeed insist – that the production of consciousness by the brain is something that can be explained *in principle*. His claim is simply that this explanation may well be, and probably is, beyond the scope of our cognitive capacities, in much the same way that theoretical physics is beyond the intellectual capacities of the chimpanzee. The arguments developed here, however, entail that the what it is like of conscious experience can have no (reductive) explanation: not even God can understand how the what it is like of conscious experience is produced by the brain, produced by the brain though it is. The what it is like of conscious experience is simply not the sort of thing that can be explained, even in principle, even if one's conceptual repertoire is Godlike.

It might be thought that this stretches the concept of naturalism beyond breaking point. A naturalistic view of consciousness, it might be thought, entails, at the very least, that there exist natural explanations *in principle* of consciousness, even if we allow with McGinn that it does not entail the existence of natural explanations *in practice*. This, I think, is largely a matter of stipulation. However, to claim that the absence of naturalistic explanations in principle precludes this being a form of naturalism is, I think, a little sanguine. The fundamental reason why the position developed here is a form of naturalism is that it claims that consciousness – under both objectualist and actualist conceptions – is produced by, and only by, situated physical activity: by an embodied brain situated in a physical environment. Consciousness is not a supernatural substance, nor does it constitute a distinct ontologically primitive category of existent. Individuals are conscious because their brains, bodies and natural environments are a certain way; it is just that neither we nor God can ever see how their brains, bodies and natural environments being this way makes for the what it is like of their conscious experience.

3   Consciousness and causality

According to the position developed here, then, the phenomenal features of conscious experience are transcendental features of that experience. That is, they are not features of which we are aware in the having of experience, they are features with which we are aware. They are features that constitute the representation of an object under a given mode of presentation, but are not themselves represented. This position, I shall try to show, raises genuine and difficult problems about the causal status of phenomenal properties. In the following sections, I shall argue for three claims.

1. The actualist model of phenomenal properties makes it impossible to understand how such properties can fit into the causal order. It makes it impossible to understand, that is, how phenomenal properties can causally produce, or be causally produced by, other properties. The actualist model does not rule out phenomenal properties having causal powers, but it does make it impossible for us to understand how this could be so. The actualist model, that is, goes hand in hand with what we might call an *epiphenomenalist suspicion* about the nature of the phenomenal.
2. This epiphenomenalist suspicion is logically quite distinct from more well-known worries about the causal status of consciousness. These more common worries I shall refer to as the *standard problem of epiphenomenalism*.
3. The epiphenomenalist suspicion that is specific to the actualist model can be explained and, for the most part, allayed. The actualist model of phenomenal properties, that is, raises no new serious problems of epiphenomenalism.

The next section deals with the connection between the actualist account of the phenomenal and worries about epiphenomenalism. The section after that contrasts this with standard epiphenomenalist worries.

4   The epiphenomenalist suspicion

According to the actualist account, the phenomenal properties of experiences are transcendental relative to our consciousness of those experiences. They are, that is, not items of which we are aware but ones which constitute our awareness of distinct items. This, I shall argue, makes it difficult, perhaps impossible, to understand how phenomenal properties can fit into the causal order. The argument runs as follows:

(1) Items understood, or recognised, as causes and effects are essentially empirical items.
(2) Phenomenal properties, according to the actualist account, are essentially transcendental items.
(3) Therefore, we cannot understand how phenomenal properties can be causes or effects.

This, obviously, requires a lot of clarification. Let us consider each premise in turn.

The idea underlying (1) is that for an item to be understood as a cause or effect requires that it be revealed by the adopting of a certain perspective. A cause, or effect, is a portion of the world that is revealed in a certain way. In what way? Roughly speaking, *by categorisation or subsumption under general laws*. Hume, of course, provides the classic illustration of the way in which causes and effects are revealed by a certain type of categorisation. According to Hume, in order for an event to be counted as an item in the causal order, it must be categorised in a certain way. For it to be the cause of a certain event, it must be *contiguous* with that event, it must *precede* it, and there must be a *constant conjunction* of events of similar types. In this way, Hume provides, in essence, an account of what is required for a certain part of the world to be revealed as a causal sequence. It shows how that part of the world must be categorised in order to be revealed as a cause–effect combination.

Not all accounts of causation, of course, are Humean in this simple sense. Even accounts that are broadly labelled 'Humean' typically do not follow Hume in all details; the condition of contiguity, typically, being the most common casualty. Nonetheless, an account that is recognisably Humean is still probably the most widely accepted account of causation. The condition of constant conjunction, in particular, is likely to loom large in any account of causation, receiving expression either in the common view that singular causal relations supervene on general laws, or in the equally popular counterfactual analyses of causation.

Hume, notoriously, claimed that being categorised in this sort of way is *all* there is to being part of a causal sequence. Others have been unwilling to follow Hume on this score, and appeals to natural necessity are, accordingly, quite popular in certain circles. However, even these sorts of accounts typically accept that subsumption under general laws is a necessary condition of an item's being recognised as part of a causal sequence, even if not sufficient for its actually being a cause or effect. And the necessity claim is all that the arguments of this section require.

Therefore, it seems very likely that a necessary condition of understanding an item as part of a causal sequence, as either a cause or effect, is that the item be categorised in a certain way; that it be subsumed under a certain organising scheme, nomic or counterfactual subsumption being the most obvious ones. But this means that for an item to be recognisably a cause or effect, it must be the sort of thing that can be revealed through the adopting of a perspective towards it. Nomic or counterfactual subsumption are the perspectives according to which a certain portion of the world is revealed as a causal sequence. Therefore, causes and effects are items revealed through the adopting of a perspective. They are, thus, in the terminology employed here, *empirical* items. They are items of which we are aware, and which are revealed as such through the adopting of a perspective which constitutes their being represented in this way. And this is what is claimed by premise 1.

Two points should be noted. Firstly, not wishing to adjudicate between broadly Humean and non-Humean accounts of causality, I have assumed nothing more than the claim that for an item to be recognised by us as a cause or effect requires that it be revealed through the adoption of a categorising perspective such as nomic or counterfactual subsumption. I have not assumed the stronger Humean, or allegedly Humean, view that this is all there is to the content of the ideas of cause and effect. If you wish to assume this Humean account, then you may strengthen the conclusion to the following: for an item to be a cause or effect (and not simply recognised as such) is for it to be revealed through the adoption of the appropriate categorising perspective. This will entail an appropriate strengthening of the conclusions of this section, notably that phenomenal properties cannot be causes and effects, and not simply that they cannot be recognised as such. The difference is, of course, extremely important, but one that cannot be adjudicated in the absence of a satisfactory resolution of the debate between Humean and non-Humean accounts of causation; a resolution that I have no idea how to provide.

Secondly, categorisation by nomic or counterfactual subsumption is not the only categorisation required for an item to be recognised as part of a causal sequence. In particular, such categorisation only makes sense given prior categorisation of the world in terms of such quantities as space and time. It is almost certainly true, for example, that the possibility of identification and reidentification of events as causes and effects depends on our being able to pick out those events via their place in a causal network, a causal structure made up of states of affairs, or conglomerations of states of affairs, that is extended in space and persisting through time. This simply reinforces the present point: causal structures are essentially items revealed *from* the adoption of a perspective – nomic, counterfactual and, more basically, spatial and temporal.

Anything that is recognisably a cause or effect, then, is something that is revealed from the adopting of a perspective. It is an essentially *empirical* item, it is something upon which consciousness can be directed. And this is the claim of premise (1). There is nothing in this claim, of course, that rules out the causal role of items revealed from the first-person perspective. The claim is that causes and effects are things that are revealed from a perspective, and not that this perspective must be third-person in character. Thus, the above claim is compatible with the idea that causes can be revealed from both third- *and* first-person perspectives. And, thus, the claim is compatible with the idea that the ordinary denizens of our first-person awareness – pains, tickles, beliefs, desires, and the like – can have causal power, and can figure in causal transactions and causal explanations. This point will prove important later on.

Premise (2) is simply a statement of what the preceding chapters have attempted to establish. The phenomenal properties of conscious experience are not items of which we are conscious in the having of experience. Rather, they are items in virtue of which we are aware of distinct, and non-phenomenal, items, under certain modes of presentation. They are, that is, features of an experience that are transcendental relative to our consciousness of that experience. This is simply the import of the actualist account of phenomenal properties.

Therefore, if understanding an item as a cause or effect requires that this item be something revealed from the adoption of a perspective, and if phenomenal properties are not, and cannot be, items revealed from the adoption of a perspective, then it seems to follow that we cannot understand phenomenal properties as causes and effects. We cannot understand how phenomenal properties can be part of the causal order.

In my view, causal efficacy attaches primarily to event-tokens and their production of other event-tokens. This assumption is by no means accepted by all, but is, in any event, a non-essential part of the present argument. Even if causal efficacy attaches primarily to event-tokens, it makes sense to talk of the causal *productivity* of the properties of which those tokens are tokens, where to say that a property is causally productive is, roughly, to say that instances of that property are causally efficacious vis-à-vis the production of distinct instances of the same property or distinct properties in virtue of the properties which those tokens instance. The claim, then, is that causal productivity, in this sense, belongs only to empirical, and not transcendental, properties. If one believes properties can sustain the attribution of a more robust version of causal productivity, so be it. The claim is that whatever notion of causality is invoked – productivity, efficacy or whatever – this can belong only to items that are revealed through the adopting of the appropriate perspective. That is, causality, in all of its forms, attaches only to empirical items, not to transcendental ones.

The actualist interpretation of what it is like, therefore, seems to rule out the attribution of both causal productivity to phenomenal properties and causal efficacy to instances of those properties. Such properties and their instances are not empirical items, not items revealed from the adopting of a perspective towards them, but transcendental ones: they are items that exist in, and are constitutive of, the particular mode of revealing of distinct, and non-phenomenal, objects. As such, it is impossible for us to understand how they might be causes. Indeed, on some construals of causation, it is impossible for them to be causes.

5   The standard problem of epiphenomenalism

It should, perhaps, be clear how different this epiphenomenalist suspicion is from what we can call the *standard problem of epiphenomenalism*. This latter problem is essentially one of *exclusion*. The standard problem of epiphenomenalism, as applied to consciousness, is in fact simply one version of the wider problem of mental causation.

Suppose I get up from my armchair to go to the refrigerator. I do this, ostensibly, because I am thirsty, and I have decided that the best way to quench my thirst is with a beer. It seems natural to suppose that my desire to quench my thirst is one of the causes of my behaviour, and that this desire is, in part, caused by the fact that my thirst is somewhat unpleasant. The phenomenal properties of my thirst, that is, are ones I would rather do without. Our folk-psychological view of behaviour, thus, seems to assign a causal role to the phenomenal qualities of experience.

The problem with this folk-psychological account, however, is that we know that there is a complete explanation of my behaviour that can be cast at the neurophysiological level. We know, or have every reason to suspect, that my getting up from my armchair, walking to the refrigerator, opening the beer and drinking it can be explained solely by appeal to various neural processes, distribution of electrochemical activity in ensembles of neurons, and the like. So, we have a question. What is the relation between the causes identified by the neurological explanation and those identified by the folk-psychological explanation? This is the general problem of mental causation. The problem of phenomenal causation is a specific version of this. What is the relation between the phenomenal causes identified by the folk-psychological explanation and those identified by the neurological one?

One option, the least satisfactory one, is to claim that the causes identified by the folk-psychological, rather than the neurological, explanation are the genuine causes of behaviour; all other apparent causes are spurious. The implausibility of the denial that neural properties have any causal bearing on how we act is, hopefully, too obvious to require further comment. The second option, almost as unsatisfactory, is to claim that the causes identified by the neurological explanation are the genuine ones, and those identified by the folk-psychological one are spurious. But this leaves us with the highly counterintuitive view that my desire to quench my thirst had no causal bearing on my going to the refrigerator and drinking the beer; and with the equally counterintuitive view that the unpleasant character of my thirst had no causal bearing on my acquiring the desire to be rid of my thirst. A third option is to claim that both the causes identified by the neurological and those identified by the folk-psychological explanation are genuine. However, if we claim that the two sets of causes are distinct, then this would commit us to the almost certainly untenable doctrine of causal overdetermination.

Hence the problem of mental causation. The correctness of the neurological explanation of behaviour seems to logically exclude the correctness of the folk-psychological one. And vice versa. A commitment to materialism, then, seems, at least *prima facie*, to exclude the correctness of the folk-psychological explanation, since to endorse the latter seems to involve either denying that neural properties have any causal bearing on how we behave, or buying into the untenable thesis of causal overdetermination. Therefore, a commitment to materialism seems to doom the items identified in the folk-psychological explanation, including the phenomenal properties of experiences, to the status of epiphenomena. And this is the standard problem of epiphenomenalism.

A common way of developing this problem for the specific case of phenomenal consciousness is in terms of the distinction, encountered in chapter 1, between access-consciousness and phenomenal consciousness (A- and P-consciousness). As Block has argued, assuming functionalism about P-consciousness is false, P-conscious properties are distinct from any cognitive or functional property. A-consciousness, on the other hand, is essentially functional in character. That is, a subject is A-conscious of some information if and only if that information is directly available for the global control of behaviour, where (i) to talk of information being used in the *global* control of behaviour is just to say that this information is available to be brought to bear in a wide range of behavioural processes, and (ii) to talk of information being *directly* available for such control is, roughly, to suppose that it is occurrently rather than dispositionally available (Chalmers 1996: 225).

According to Chalmers, when A-consciousness is defined in this way, then it is plausible to suppose not only that it is always accompanied by P-consciousness, and vice versa, but also that there is a systematic correlation between the structure of A-consciousness and that of P-consciousness. It is this, ultimately, that seems to make the search for the causal role of P-consciousness fruitless. Given the correlation, *any* purported function of P-consciousness can be attributed to A-consciousness instead. Thus, we have a problem of exclusion: any appeal to P-consciousness in an explanation of action seems excluded by the truth of the corresponding explanation couched in terms of A-consciousness. The correlation between access-consciousness and phenomenal consciousness, then, seems to entail the epiphenomenal status of the latter.

However, I am not particularly enamoured with this way of developing the standard problem of epiphenomenalism for phenomenal consciousness. In particular, I think the studies, encountered in chapter 8, on the phenomenon of changeblindness conducted by O'Regan et al. (1996), Blackmore et al. (1995) and Rensink et al. (1996) collectively cast significant doubt on the claims that A-consciousness and P-consciousness are isomorphic in the way asserted by Chalmers. This does not dissolve the problem of exclusion, however. It simply means that we must understand it in the way outlined earlier; in terms of the relation between phenomenal and neural explanans.

A beginning at coming to terms with the problem can be made, I think, by distinguishing two relations, causal *efficacy* and causal *relevance*.

Causal efficacy: An item Q is causally efficacious in the occurrence of event E if and only if Q plays a role in causally bringing about E.

Causal relevance: An item Q is causally relevant to the occurrence of event E only if Q plays a role in causally explaining E.

As Jackson and Pettit have shown, these two relations are clearly not equivalent (Jackson and Pettit 1988; cf. Rowlands 1989a). Given the distinctness of causal efficacy and causal relevance, we face the following question: does the problem of exclusion, as applied to phenomenal items, show that such items are causally inefficacious or causally irrelevant? Does it show, that is, that phenomenal items are epiphenomenal in that they play no role in causally producing behaviour or in that they play no role in causally explaining behaviour?

Actually, if we assume, as I think we should, that causal efficacy attaches primarily to event-tokens and their production of other event-tokens, then the epiphenomenal status of phenomenal event- or state-*tokens* is avoided quite easily. The basis of the defence of the efficacy of phenomenal state-tokens lies in the idea that distinct event types can *share* the same instance (cf. Macdonald 1989; Rowlands 1989b; Heil 1992). Suppose we have an event-token consisting of the exemplification of property P by object x at time t. What is required in order for this event-token to be identical with the token consisting of the exemplification of property Q by object y at time t*? According to Kim's famous criterion of event identity, what is required in fact is the identity of all three items: $x = y$, $t = t^*$, *and* $P = Q$. However, I have argued (1989b) that the third identity is not required. Consider the relation between the property of being red and the property of being coloured. Possession of the former entails possession of the latter but not vice versa, so the properties are plainly distinct. Even so, no one would (or should) want to suppose that an object's exemplification of a colour, say redness, requires first that it contain an instance of the property of being red and then that it contain a distinct instance of the property of being coloured. Despite the distinctness of the properties, the instance of the former is identical with the instance of the latter. Similar remarks surely apply to events. An object's changing from red to blue just is (i.e. identical with) it's changing colour, even though the property of changing from red to blue is not identical with the property of changing colour. Distinct properties can share a common instance.

In this case, the relation between the properties that makes possible their sharing of a common instance seems to be the relation of *entailment*. But similar remarks apply whenever we have a case of the determination of one property by another. And there is no reason to suppose this sort of determination must be logical or conceptual in character.

Is this is correct, then if we assume that (i) neural properties determine phenomenal ones, (ii) neural properties and phenomenal ones can *share* the same instance, and (iii) causal efficacy is a relation between event-tokens, or property-instances, not between event-types or properties, then we can account for the causal efficacy of phenomenal property-instances simply by way of the claim that phenomenal and neural properties share instances. Phenomenal and neural properties, that is, possess *common rather than merely co-occurrent* instances.

The principal source of discontent with this solution is, perhaps, likely to stem from the conjunction of two claims: (i) that the sort of determination necessary for sharing of instances is logical or conceptual in character, and (ii) that the supervenience of phenomenal properties on neural ones is merely natural rather than conceptual. However, in the absence of further argument, there seems little reason for believing (i). Claim (ii) on the other hand, is associated with Chalmers. But, as we have seen in chapter 2, Chalmers is confused on this score. His argument for the merely natural character of conscious supervenience rests on a fallacy of equivocation, a confusion of metaphysical and epistemological concepts of supervenience.[2]

---

[2] If one is tempted to side with Chalmers on this point, however, it is worth noting that Chalmers himself sees the issue of the epiphenomenalism of P-consciousness as, primarily, an issue of *explanatory* rather than causal irrelevance. This is because he sees the concept of causation as itself fraught with metaphysical complexities – perhaps intrinsically connected with those metaphysical complexities surrounding the idea of consciousness – and this makes the issue of the causal efficacy of P-consciousness difficult to adjudicate. In any event, his primary concern is with the idea that P-consciousness has no explanatory role to play vis-à-vis behaviour. And in this, I shall, though for different reasons, follow Chalmers.

If this is correct, then there is, I think, no serious problem in safe-guarding the causal efficacy of phenomenal items understood as state- or event-tokens. The standard problem of epiphenomenalism, however, might be understood as having two further strands. The first of these centres on the notion of causal relevance. It might be thought that even if we can avoid the problem of exclusion for phenomenal state-tokens, the corresponding problem arises for the explanatory relevance of phenomenal items. Here, I shall assume the common view that explanatory power attaches primarily to properties, and derivatively to instances of those properties. If not, then we could presumably account for the causal efficacy of phenomenal tokens by the same route as above. Against this, I shall assume that whether or not a state-token has causal relevance, in the sense defined above, depends, in the first instance, on the identity of the types of which it is a token. This is not, of course, to deny the existence of token-explanatory processes, but rather to point out that when a token functions as the explanans or explanandum in an explanation, it does so in virtue of the types it instances.

The new worry, then, is that the causal relevance of neural properties excludes the causal relevance of phenomenal ones. That is, if a neural-level account provides a true and complete explanation of my drinking the beer, then this precludes the truth of the folk-psychological explanation. However, I think this is far less of a worry than that surrounding the causal efficacy of phenomenal tokens. The possibility of explanatory exclusion has far less bite than the corresponding possibility of causal exclusion. We are, ordinarily, quite willing to accept the possibility of there being two non-equivalent, complete and true explanations of the same event. The truth of the electrochemical explanation of oxidation is not thought to be excluded by the truth of a quantum level explanation of the same thing. So too, I think, there is no reason to suppose that a phenomenal property is excluded from having explanatory value by the truth of a neurological explanation of behaviour. Phenomenal properties can play an explanatory role in a causal explanation of a behavioural to-ken even if there are other properties, neural ones for example, that can play an explanatory role in a distinct causal explanation of that same be-havioural token. Therefore, the problem of exclusion for causal *explanans* (i.e. causally relevant properties, in my terminology) simply does not have the same *prima facie* bite as the problem of exclusion for causal *efficans*. There simply does not seem to be a lot to worry about here.

There is one other way in which the problem of exclusion might be developed. Causal efficacy has so far been understood as a relation hold-ing between event- or state-tokens; between instances of properties rather than properties themselves. Causal relevance, on the other hand, has been understood as a relation holding between properties rather than their instances. It might be thought that this classificatory scheme masks a third possibility. What motivates this thought is the idea that when event- or state-tokens enter into causal relations with each other, they do so *in virtue of* the types or properties of which those tokens are instances. Thus we should expect there to be a type of relation holding between mental properties, rather than their instances, that is not an essentially explanatory one, and so cannot be reduced to the relation of causal relevance as defined above. We can mark this new relation with the label *causal productivity*:

Causal productivity: A property Q is a causally productive one if and only if for any instances q of Q (i) there exists a subset of the total set of causal relations into which q enters, and (ii) q enters into this subset of causal relations *in virtue of* its instantiation of Q.

The core idea here is that event- or state-tokens enter into the causal relations they do in virtue of their instantiation of certain properties. The definition of causal productivity employs the mechanism of a subset of causal relations simply to record the fact that any given event- or state-token may instance many properties, and may enter into distinct types of causal relation in virtue of instancing distinct properties.

If there is a difficult problem of causal exclusion for phenomenal properties, and, indeed, for mental properties in general, then it will, I think, centrally involve the notion of causal productivity in the above sense. For, at least *prima facie*, the relation of causal productivity cannot be assimilated to the relation of causal relevance; and so we cannot avail ourselves of the deflationary solution employed for the exclusion problem formulated in terms of causal relevance. While we are quite willing, it seems, to allow the existence of true, non-equivalent, explanans for the same phenomenon, the existence of distinct causally productive properties seems far more of a problem. It seems that the phenomenon must occur either in virtue of one property or in virtue of the other. But saying that it occurs in virtue of both, it seems, would commit one to the sort of overdetermination thesis that was earlier described as untenable.

So, I think, the difficult problem of exclusion will be framed in terms of the notion of causal productivity as defined above. There are two strategies one might employ for avoiding the problem. The first, which I do not endorse, involves trying to show that, appearances to the contrary, the relation of causal productivity is, in fact, a disguised form of, or essentially derivative upon, the relation of causal relevance. If so, then one can then employ the deflationary strategy outlined above.

The strategy I favour, however, involves trying to show, in effect, that the relation of causal productivity is derivative upon the relation of causal *efficacy* rather than causal relevance. In order to develop the problem of exclusion in terms of the concept of causal productivity, it is necessary to assume that event- or state-tokens enter into causal relations *in virtue of* the types or properties they instance. And, I think, this gets things precisely backwards. The primary locus of causal relations is, I would argue, to be found in concrete, particular, things: in event- and state-tokens, instances of properties rather than properties themselves. When we classify token causal relations, we then bring in types. But it would be a mistake to think that the types thus invoked bring about anything at all. We, of course, talk about particulars interacting because of their properties. But it would, I think, be a serious mistake to regard this 'be-cause' as a causal one. Properties do not bring concrete particular events about; only concrete particular events do that. Properties identified as causally productive, in other words, are not, and never were, the *basis* of causal relations, they are simply reflections of relations fixed by the concrete particulars themselves. That is, they reflect not the causal basis of any relation between concrete particulars but our ways of classifying and systematising relations that obtain between the particulars them-selves.

If this is true, then if there is to be any genuinely worrying problem of exclusion, this problem will have to centre around the relation between phenomenal and neural state-tokens. And, I have tried to show, formu-lated in this way, the problem can be avoided. Thus, I do not think what I have called the *standard problem of epiphenomenalism* is really that much of a problem.

6   The epiphenomenalist suspicion allayed

I am aware that the solution to the standard problem of epiphenome-nalism sketched above will not satisfy everyone. Or perhaps anyone. My real goal here, however, is not to solve the standard problem but to dis-tinguish it from what I have called the *epiphenomenalist suspicion* that is peculiar to the actualist account of phenomenal properties. It should, hopefully, be clear how different the epiphenomenalist suspicion is from the standard problem. The issue of causal/explanatory exclusion that mo-tivates the standard epiphenomenalist problem arises in connection with the relation between (i) what is revealed *by* the third-person perspective and (ii) what is revealed *by* the first-person perspective. Thus, from the third-person perspective, the object of our consciousness is, say, bodily damage; or, as I prefer, a certain item is revealed as bodily damage of a certain sort, possessing certain features, varying degrees of severity, and so on. From the first-person perspective, the object of our consciousness is pain; or, as I prefer, the bodily damage is revealed as painful. We know, or at least strongly suspect, that what is revealed from the third-person perspective can provide a complete causal explanation of our subsequent behaviour, whatever that behaviour might be. Thus, we suspect that what we encounter from the first-person perspective, the pain itself, is epiphenomenal; that is, it has no role to play in the causal explanation of our behaviour.

The epiphenomenalist suspicion underwritten by actualism is quite different. It is not concerned with the relation between, and causal incompatibility of, what is revealed from the third- and first-person perspectives. Rather, it is concerned with the relation between what is revealed *from* any perspective, first- or third-person, and the properties which constitute the revealing of an object as such. Phenomenal properties, according to the actualist interpretation, belong to the latter category. The what it is like of conscious experience belongs to the revealing of objects: it constitutes, and indeed consists in, the revealing of objects to be a certain way. And, as such, it seems to lie outside the causal order.

However, I shall argue that this epiphenomenalist suspicion is unfounded. The standard problem of explanatory epiphenomenalism based on the idea of exclusion may remain, despite the above attempts to undermine it. But the actualist interpretation of the what it is like of conscious experience raises no *new* epiphenomenalist worries. The reason is, in fact, already implicit in the preceding discussion.

In order for something to be understood as a cause, or as providing a causal explanation of an event, it is necessary that it be something capable of being revealed by the adopting of a perspective towards it. The central features of this perspective, I have argued, are likely to be constituted by concepts such as nomic and/or counterfactual subsumption. In any event, the what it is like of conscious experiences, since it is not something revealed by consciousness, can be understood neither as a cause nor as a causal explanans vis-à-vis behaviour. Thus, to take a concrete and, by now, familiar example, the what it is like to be in pain constitutes the revealing of bodily damage as painful, and is not itself something revealed to consciousness. And, therefore, it exists, seemingly, outside the causal order, and is, thus, not the sort of thing that could be understood to be a cause of, or provide a causal explanation of, behaviour (or anything else for that matter).

However, while the phenomenal character, the what it is like, of an experience is not an object of consciousness and is, thus, essentially non-causal, it is also true that this character constitutes the revealing of an object of consciousness as the object it is. The phenomenal character of an experience consists in the revealing of a non-phenomenal object in a certain way (bodily damage, for example, is revealed as painful). The object revealed as being a certain way is an object of consciousness. Therefore, the object revealed as being a certain way can figure in causal transactions and explanations.

Therefore, bodily damage revealed as painful can figure in causal transactions and explanations, even if the phenomenal character of pain, the what it is like to be in pain, cannot. The bodily damage revealed as painful is something revealed *from* the first-person perspective, whereas the what it is like to be in pain is something that exists in, indeed consists in, the revealing of bodily damage as painful. The bodily damage revealed as painful, as something that is revealed *by* or *from* the first-person perspective, can be a cause of, and provide a causal explanation of, our behaviour.

For this reason, I think, the actualist interpretation of what it is like raises no *new* epiphenomenalist worries. The causal relevance of bodily damage *qua* painful has been preserved, even if no role has been found for the phenomenal character of pain as such. It is bodily damage revealed as painful that can play a causal explanatory role vis-à-vis behaviour, since bodily damage revealed as painful is an object of consciousness. And this is true even though the phenomenal character of experience, which constitutes the revealing of bodily damage as painful, is not itself an object of experience.

To summarise. We can understand every act of consciousness as a combination of revealing–revealed. This, in fact, is one way of understanding the idea that consciousness is intentional, is essentially directed towards objects. Then, the idea is that the what it is like of conscious experience belongs to the revealing of objects: it consists in, and constitutes, the revealing of objects to be a certain way. As such, it is not an object revealed, and lies, at least apparently, outside the causal order. Nevertheless, what is revealed – e.g. bodily-damage-as-painful – is an object of consciousness, and, as such, can lie inside the causal order. It can, therefore, play a role in the causal production and/or explanation of behaviour. This, I think, is what (almost) justifies our first-person sense that the phenomenal character of our experience plays a role in causally producing and causally explaining our behaviour. It is not the phenomenal character as such, but the object that, in virtue of that phenomenal character, is revealed as being a certain way that can play a role in causally producing and/or explaining behaviour. It is, perhaps, natural, then, that we should confuse the phenomenal character of an experience with the way in which an object is revealed, and mistake the causal-explanatory role of the latter with that of the former. The causal-explanatory power of phenomenal character is an illusion, admittedly, but it is an understandable illusion.[3]

[3] Perhaps one of the attractions of this account is that it extends quite naturally to other problematic aspects of the mental. In particular, a substantially similar account can be given of our sense of freedom. Anyone who takes the causal closure of the physical realm seriously is going to have a problem explaining how we can ever act freely. The most popular strategy of salvaging our ability to act freely, indeed the only strategy consistent with acceptance of the causal closure of the physical, is *compatibilism*. Freedom is perfectly compatible with causation. Indeed, being the result of a certain type of causal process is just what we mean by saying that an action or decision is free.

The actualist account of the apparent causal potency of the phenomenal character of experience can be readily extended to provide an explanation of the *illusion* of human freedom. It explains why we should believe, perhaps inevitably believe, that we are free even if we are not.

According to the actualist interpretation of what it is like, any creature with a subjective life, any creature for whom there is something that it is like to be the creature, is a creature partly inside and, at least apparently, partly outside the causal order. The what it is like of conscious experience, I have argued, is not the sort of thing that can be understood as being within the causal order, for being so included is a matter of conceptualising – or revealing – an occurrence in the right way. And being conceptualised in the right way involves, at the very least, being capable of being made into an object of consciousness. In order to be conceptualised at all, an occurrence must be focused upon, it must be the sort of thing upon which awareness, in this case with its conceptual capacities, can be directed. (This point emerged in chapter 6, in the attribution to McGinn of an objectualist interpretation of consciousness.) But the what it is like of conscious experience cannot be an object of conscious awareness. Therefore, it is not simply that what it is like cannot be conceptualised – or revealed – in such a way as to be identified as part of the causal order. It cannot be conceptualised, revealed, at all. It is simply not the sort of thing that can be identified as part of the causal order. In this sense, then, the what it is like of conscious experience cannot be identified as a causally determined item.

However, things are very different when we consider the what is revealed by conscious experience. Bodily damage is revealed as painful. And, since this is a genuine object of consciousness, we are quite capable of regarding this as being brought about by certain causes, and as having certain effects. We are quite happy to regard this object of consciousness – bodily damage revealed as painful – as inside the causal scheme of things; as a genuine and legitimate member of the causal order.

However, if, as I have argued we have a tendency to do, we conflate the phenomenal character of experience with the object whose particular mode of revealing to conscious experience is constituted by this phenomenal character, then we would be conflating an item that we are quite happy to regard as a member of the causal order, an item with identifiable or predictable causes and effects, with something that cannot be regarded as part of this order, an item that is simply not the sort of thing that can be identified as causally determined in any way.

In this way, the illusion of freedom, the illusion of our own efficacy and power, might arise from a confusion of, on the one hand, the phenomenal character of experience with, on the other, an object of consciousness whose particular mode of revealing to conscious experience is constituted by this phenomenal character. The idea of freedom has the same origin as the idea of phenomenal potency: the *transcendental* status of the phenomenal character of our experience relative to our experience of it. If we confuse the transcendental with the empirical, then we end up running two very different, but superficially similar, things together. We get the idea of the causal potency or efficacy of our experiences from the empirical object revealed by those experiences and the manner in which it is revealed. Bodily damage revealed as painful is something identifiably inside the causal order. But then we add to this the idea of the transcendental character of the phenomenal, a character that stems from its not being an object of consciousness. Combine those two, and the hybrid that results is the idea of freedom.

Bibliography

Aquila, R. (1988) 'The Cartesian and a certain "poetic" notion of consciousness', *Journal of the History of Ideas* 49, 259–78.

Armstrong, D. (1968) *A Materialist Theory of the Mind*, London, Routledge and Kegan Paul.

Armstrong, D. (1981) *The Nature of Mind*, Ithaca, Cornell University Press.

Aune, B. (1967) *Knowledge, Mind and Nature*, New York, Random House.

Baars, B. (1988) *A Cognitive Theory of Consciousness*, Cambridge, Cambridge University Press.

Bermudez, J. (1998) *The Paradox of Self-Consciousness*, Cambridge, Mass., MIT Press.

Blackburn, S. (1971) 'Moral realism', in J. Casey, ed., *Morality and Moral Reasoning*, London, Routledge and Kegan Paul, 101–24.

Blackburn, S. (1985) 'Supervenience revisited', in I. Hacking, ed., *Exercises in Analysis*, Cambridge, Cambridge University Press, 24–46.

Blackmore, S., Brelstaff, G., Nelson, K., and Troscianko, T. (1995) 'Is the richness of our visual world an illusion? Transasaccadic memory for complex scenes', *Perception* 24, 1075–81.

Block, N. (1983) 'Mental pictures and cognitive science', *Philosophical Review* 92, 499–542.

Block, N. (1990) 'Inverted earth', in J. Tomberlin, ed., *Philosophical Perspectives* 4, Atascadero, Calif., Ridgeview Publishing Co., 53–79.

Block, N. (1995) 'On a confusion about the function of consciousness', *Behavioral and Brain Sciences* 18, 227–47.

Block, N. (1996) 'Mental paint and mental latex', in E. Villanueva, ed., *Philosophical Perspectives* 7, Atascadero, Calif., Ridgeview Publishing Co., 93–121.

Block, N. (1998) 'Is experiencing just representing?' http://www.nyu.edu/gsas/dept/philo ... lty/block/papers/representing/html

Block, N., Flanagan, O., and Guzeldere, G., eds. (1997) *The Nature of Consciousness*, Cambridge, Mass., MIT Press.

Broad, C. C. (1956) 'Some elementary reflexions on sense-perception', in R. Schwartz, ed., *Perceiving, Sensing and Knowing*, Los Angeles, University of California Press, 53–76.

Broad, C. D. (1925) *The Mind and its Place in Nature*, London, Routledge and Kegan Paul.

Carruthers, P. (1996) *Language, Thought and Consciousness*, Cambridge, Cambridge University Press.

Carruthers, P. (1998) 'Natural theories of consciousness', *European Journal of Philosophy* 6, 53–78.

Chalmers, D. (1996) *The Conscious Mind: in Search of a Fundamental Theory*, Oxford, Oxford University Press.

Chisholm, R. (1957) *Perceiving*, Ithaca, Cornell University Press.

Churchland, P. (1989) *A Neurocomputational Perspective*, Cambridge, Mass., MIT Press.

Clark, A. (1993) *Associative Engines*, Cambridge, Mass., MIT Press.

Cornman, J. (1971) *Materialism and Sensations*, New Haven, Yale University Press.

Crane, T. (1991) 'All God has to do', *Analysis* 51, 235–44.

Crick, F. (1994) *The Astonishing Hypothesis*, New York, Scribner's.

Crick, F. and Koch, C. (1990) 'Towards a neurobiological theory of consciousness', *Seminars Neurose* 2, 263–75.

Davies, M. (1992) 'Perceptual content and local supervenience', *Proceedings of the Aristotelian Society* 92, 21–45.

Davies, M. (1996) 'Externalism and experience', in A. Clark, J. Ezquerro, and J. Larrazabal, eds., *Philosophy and Cognitive Science: Categories, Consciousness and Reasoning*, Dordrecht, Kluwer, 1–33.

Dennett, D. (1991) *Consciousness Explained*, Boston, Little Brown.

Dennett, D. (1997) 'An exchange with Daniel Dennett', in John Searle, *The Mystery of Consciousness*, London, Granta Books, 115–19.

Descartes, R. (1984) *The Philosophical Writings of Descartes*, 2 vols., trans. J. Cottingham, R. Stoothoff, and D. Murdoch, Cambridge, Cambridge University Press.

Dretske, F. (1993) 'Conscious experience', *Mind* 102, 263–83.

Dretske, F. (1995) *Naturalizing the Mind*, Cambridge, Mass., MIT Press.

Ducasse, C. (1942) 'Moore's refutation of idealism', in P. Schilpp, ed., *The Philosophy of G.E. Moore*, Chicago, Northwestern University Press, 225–51.

Edelman, G. (1987) *Neural Darwinism*, New York, Basic Books.

Edelman, G. (1989) *The Remembered Present: A Biological Theory of Consciousness*, New York, Basic Books.

Edelman, G. (1992) *Bright Air, Brilliant Fire*, New York, Basic Books.

Evans, G. (1982) *The Varieties of Reference*, Oxford, Oxford University Press.

Flanagan, O. (1992) *Consciousness Reconsidered*, Cambridge, Mass., MIT Press.

Garvey, J. (1998) 'What does McGinn think we cannot know?', *Analysis* 58, 181–4.

Gennaro, R. (1996) *Consciousness and Self-Consciousness*, Amsterdam, John Benjamins Publishing.

Guzeldere, G. (1995) 'Is consciousness the perception of what passes in one's own mind?', in T. Metzinger, ed., *Conscious Experience*, Paderborn, Schieningh-Verlag, 335–7, reprinted in Block, N., Flanagan, O., and Guzeldere, G., eds., *The Nature of Consciousness*, Cambridge, Mass., MIT Press, 789–806. All page references are to the latter.

Harman, G. (1990) 'The intrinsic quality of experience', in J. Tomberlin, ed., *Philosophical Perspectives* 9, Atascadero, Calif., Ridgeview Publishing Co., 52–79.

Heil, J. (1992) *The Nature of True Minds*, Cambridge, Cambridge University Press.

Heinrich, D. (1989) 'The identity of the subject in the transcendental deduction', in E. Schaper and W. Vossenkuhl, eds., *Reading Kant: New Perspectives on Transcendental Arguments and Critical Philosophy*, Oxford, Basil Blackwell, 1989, 121–43.

Hempel, C. (1969) 'Reduction: ontological and linguistic facets', in Morgenbesser, S., Suppes, P., and White, M., eds., *Philosophy, Science, and Method*, New York, St. Martin's Press, 179–99.

Hesse, M. (1966) *Models and Analogies in Science*, Notre Dame, Notre Dame University Press.

Hume, D. (1777/1975) *Enquiries Concerning Human Understanding and Concerning the Principles of Morals*, ed. P. Nidditch, Oxford, Oxford University Press.

Hurley, S. (1998) *Consciousness in Action*, Boston, Harvard University Press.

Jackson, F. (1982) 'Epiphenomenal qualia', *Philosophical Quarterly* 32, 127–32.

Jackson, F. (1986) 'What Mary didn't know', *Journal of Philosophy* 83, 291–5.

Jackson, F. and Pettit, P. (1988) 'Functionalism and broad content', *Mind* 97, 373–89.

Kanizsa, G. and Gerbino, W. (1982) 'Amodal Completion: seeing or thinking', in J. Beck, ed., *Organization and Representation in Perception*, Hillsdale, N.J., Lawrence Erlbaum, 221–47.

Kant, I. (1781, 1787) *Critique of Pure Reason*, trans. Norman Kemp Smith, New York, St. Martin's Press.

Kaplan, D. (1989) 'Demonstratives', in J. Almog, J. Perry, and H. Wettstein, eds., *Themes from Kaplan*, Oxford, Oxford University Press, 1–30.

Kim, J. (1984) 'Concepts of supervenience', *Philosophy and Phenomenological Research* 65, 153–76.

Kim, J. (1993) *Supervenience and Mind: Selected Philosophical Essays*, Cambridge, Cambridge University Press.

Kirk, R. (1974) 'Zombies versus materialists', *Proceedings of the Aristotelian Society*, suppl. vol. 48, 135–52.

Kirk, R. (1992) 'Consciousness and concepts', *Proceedings of the Aristotelian Society*, suppl. vol. 66, 23–40.

Kirk, R. (1994) *Raw Feeling: A Philosophical Account of the Essence of Consciousness*, Oxford, Oxford University Press.

Kripke, S. (1972) 'Naming and necessity', in D. Davidson and G. Harman, eds., *Semantics of Natural Language*, Dordrecht, Reidel, 253–355.

Kuhn, T. (1957) *The Copernican Revolution*, Cambridge, Mass., Harvard University Press.

Kuhn, T. (1962) *The Structure of Scientific Revolutions*, Chicago, University of Chicago Press.

Levine, J. (1983) 'Materialism and qualia: the explanatory gap', *Pacific Philosophical Quarterly* 64, 354–61.

Levine, J. (1993) 'On leaving out what it is like', in M. Davies and G. Humphreys, eds., *Consciousness*, Oxford, Basil Blackwell, 121–36.

Loar, B. (1990) 'Phenomenal states', in J. Tomberlin, ed., *Philosophical Perspectives* 4, Atascadero, Calif., Ridgeview Publishing Co., 81–108.

Locke, J. (1690) *An Essay Concerning Human Understanding*. Reprinted 1959, ed. A. C. Fraser, New York, Dover Publications. All page references are to the latter.

Lycan, W. (1987) *Consciousness*, Cambridge, Mass., MIT Press.

Lycan, W. (1990) 'Consciousness as internal monitoring', in *Philosophical Perspectives*, vol. 9, ed. J. Tomberlin, Atascadero, Ridgeview Publishing Company, 1–14. Reprinted in Block, N., Flanagan, O., and Guzeldere, G., eds., *The Nature of Consciousness*, Cambridge, Mass., MIT Press, 1997, 755–71. All page references are to the latter.

Lycan, W. (1996) *Consciousness and Experience*, Cambridge, Mass., MIT Press.

Macdonald, C. (1989) *Mind–Body Identity Theories*, London, Routledge.

Malcolm, N. and Armstrong, D. (1984) *Consciousness and Causality: A Debate on the Nature of the Mind*, Oxford, Basil Blackwell.

Martin, M. (1995) 'The transparency of experience', unpublished ms.

McCulloch, G. (1992) 'The very idea of the phenomenological', *Proceedings of the Aristotelian Society* 93, 61–78.

McGinn, C. (1982/1997) *The Character of Mind* (2nd edition), Oxford, Oxford University Press.

McGinn, C. (1989) 'Can we solve the mind–body problem?', *Mind* 98, 349–66.

McGinn, C. (1991) *The Problem of Consciousness*, Oxford, Basil Blackwell.

McGinn, C. (1993) *Problems in Philosophy*, Oxford, Basil Blackwell.

McGinn, C. (1995) 'Consciousness and space', in T. Metzinger, ed., *Conscious Experience*, *Journal of Consciousness Studies* 2, 1–22.

McRae, R. (1965) '"Idea" as a philosophical term in the seventeenth century', *Journal of the History of Ideas* 26, 232–53.

Millikan, R. (1984) *Language, Thought and Other Biological Categories*, Cambridge, Mass., MIT Press.

Millikan, R. (1993) *White Queen Psychology*, Cambridge, Mass., MIT Press.

Moore, G. E. (1903) 'The refutation of idealism', *Mind* 12, 433–53.

Moore, G. E. (1922) *Philosophical Studies*, London, Routledge and Kegan Paul.

Nagel, E. (1961) *The Structure of Science*, New York, Harcourt, Brace & World.

Nagel, T. (1974) 'What is it like to be a bat?', *Philosophical Review* 83, 435–50.

Nagel, T. (1986) *The View from Nowhere*, Oxford, Oxford University Press.

Natsoulas, T. (1992) 'What's wrong with the appendage theory of consciousness?', *Philosophical Psychology* 5, 137–54.

Nelkin, N. (1987) 'How sensations get their names', *Philosophical Studies* 51, 325–39.

Nisbett, R. and Wilson, T. (1977) 'On telling more than we can know', *Psychological Review* 84, 231–59.

O'Regan, K. (1992) 'Solving the "real" mysteries of visual perception: the world as an outside memory', *Canadian Journal of Psychology* 46, 461–88.

O'Regan, K., Rensink, R., and Clark J. (1996) '"Mud splashes" render picture changes invisible', ARVO Abstract. *Investigative Opthalmology* & *Visual Science* 37, S213.

Pessoa, L., Thompson, E., and Noe, A. (1998) 'Finding out about filling in: A guide to perceptual completion for visual science and the philosophy of perception', *Behavioral and Brain Sciences* 21, 723–802.

Price, H. (1932) *Perception*, London, Methuen.

Prichard, H. (1950) *Knowledge and Perception*, Oxford, Oxford University Press.

Rensink, R., O'Regan, K., and Clark, J. (1996) 'To see or not to see: the need for attention to perceive changes in scenes', ARVO Abstract. *Investigative Opthalmology & Visual Science* 37, S213.

Rey, G. (1983) 'A reason for doubting the existence of consciousness', in R. Davidson, G. Schwartz, and D. Shapiro, eds., *Consciousness and Self-Regulation*, vol. III, New York, Plenum.

Rosenthal, D. (1986) 'Two concepts of consciousness', *Philosophical Studies* 49, 329–59.

Rosenthal, D. (1990) 'A theory of consciousness', Report 40/1990, Center for Interdisciplinary Research (ZiF), Research Group on Mind and Brain, University of Bielefield.

Rosenthal, D. (1993) 'Thinking that one thinks', in G. Humphreys and M. Davies, eds., *Consciousness*, Oxford, Basil Blackwell.

Rosenthal, D. (1994) 'State consciousness and transitive consciousness', *Consciousness and Cognition* 2, 355–63.

Rowlands, M. (1989a) 'Discussion of Jackson and Pettit: functionalism and broad content', *Mind* 98, 269–75.

Rowlands, M. (1989b) 'Property-exemplification and proliferation', *Analysis* 49, 194–7.

Rowlands, M. (1991) 'A defence of behaviourism', *Behavior and Philosophy* 16, 31–47.

Rowlands, M. (1997) 'Teleological semantics', *Mind* 106, 279–303.

Rowlands, M. (1999) *The Body in Mind: Understanding Cognitive Processes*, Cambridge, Cambridge University Press.

Rowlands, M. (2000) 'Consciousness and higher-order thoughts', *Mind and Language* 16, 290–310.

Ryle, G. (1949) *The Concept of Mind*, London, Hutchinson.

Russell, B. (1905) 'On denoting', *Mind* 14, 479–93.

Russell, B. (1917) 'Knowledge by acquaintance and knowledge by description', in B. Russell, *Mysticism and Logic*, London, Allen and Unwin, 46–79.

Sartre, J.-P. (1936) *The Transcendence of the Ego*, trans. Forrest Williams and Robert Kirkpatrick, New York, Farrar, Strauss and Giroux.

Sartre, J.-P. (1943) *Being and Nothingness*, trans. Hazel Barnes, London, Methuen.

Searle, J. (1983) *Intentionality*, Cambridge, Cambridge University Press.

Searle, J. (1992) *The Rediscovery of the Mind*, Cambridge, Mass., MIT Press.

Searle, J. (1997) *The Mystery of Consciousness*, London, Granta Books.

Sellars, W. (1963) *Science, Perception and Reality*, London, Routledge & Kegan Paul.

Shoemaker, S. (1982) 'The inverted spectrum', *Journal of Philosophy* 79, 357–81.

Shoemaker, S. (1984) *Identity, Cause and Mind*, Cambridge, Cambridge University Press.

Shoemaker, S. (1986) 'Introspection and the self', *Midwest Studies in Philosophy* 10, 71–89.

Shoemaker, S. (1988) 'On knowing one's own mind', *Philosophical Perspectives* 2, 183–209.

Shoemaker, S. (1990) 'Qualities and qualia: what's in the mind?', *Philosophy and Phenomenological Research*, Supplement, 50, 109–31.

Shoemaker, S. (1991) 'Qualia and consciousness', *Mind* 100, 507–24.

Shoemaker, S. (1994) 'Self knowledge and "inner sense"', *Philosophy and Phenomenological Research* 54, 248–314.

Smart, J. (1962) 'Sensations and brain processes', *Philosophical Review* 68, 141–56.

Strawson, G. (1994) *Mental Reality*, Cambridge, Mass., MIT Press.

Tye, M. (1984) 'The adverbial approach to visual experience', *Philosophical Review* 93, 195–225.

Tye, M. (1990) 'A representational theory of pains and their phenomenal character', in J. Tomberlin, ed., *Philosophical Perspectives* 9, Atascadero, Calif., Ridgeview Publishing Co., 223–39.

Tye, M. (1992) 'Visual qualia and visual content', in T. Crane, ed., *The Contents of Experience*, Cambridge, Cambridge University Press, 158–76.

Tye, M. (1995) *Ten Problems of Consciousness: A Representational Theory of the Phenomenal Mind*, Cambridge, Mass., MIT Press.

Tye, M. (1999) 'Phenomenal Consciousness: the explanatory gap as a cognitive illusion', *Mind* 108, 705–25.

Van Gulick, R. (1993) 'Understanding the phenomenal mind: are we all just armadillos?', part 1, in M. Davies and G. Humphreys, eds., *Consciousness*, Oxford, Basil Blackwell.

Wider, K. (1997) *The Bodily Nature of Consciousness: Sartre and Contemporary Philosophy of Mind*, Ithaca, Cornell University Press.

Williams, B. (1978) *Descartes: The Project of Pure Enquiry*, London, Pelican Books.

Wittgenstein, L. (1953) *Philosophical Investigations*, Oxford, Basil Blackwell.

Index